OUTSOURCING SECURITY

OUTSOURCING
SECURITY

Private Military Contractors
and U.S. Foreign Policy

BRUCE E. STANLEY

POTOMAC BOOKS
An imprint of the University of Nebraska Press

Library of Congress
Cataloging-in-Publication Data
Stanley, Bruce E. (Bruce Edwin)
Outsourcing security: private
military contractors and U.S. foreign
policy / Bruce E. Stanley.
pages   cm
Includes bibliographical references and index.
ISBN 978-1-61234-717-2 (pbk.: alk. paper)
ISBN 978-1-61234-760-8 (epub)
ISBN 978-1-61234-761-5 (mobi)
ISBN 978-1-61234-762-2 (pdf)
1. Private military companies—United
States—Case studies.
2. Private security services—United
States—Case studies.
3. United States—Military policy.
4. United States—Foreign relations.
5. United States—History, Military—21st
century—Case studies. I. Title.
UB149.S73 2015
355.3'5—dc23
2015004442

Set in Garamond Premier by M. Scheer.
Designed by N. Putens.

For my parents, Preston and Shirley. Thank you for your unconditional love and support.

CONTENTS

ILLUSTRATIONS

TABLES

ACKNOWLEDGMENTS

This book would not have been possible without the help of my family, friends, and organizations. In particular I would like to thank Jeffery Pickering for his guidance, mentorship, and friendship. I greatly appreciate the professionalism and wise counsel of Emizet Kisangani without which this book would not be where it is today. Kansas State University is lucky to have such great faculty as Dale Herspring, Donald Mrozek, William Blankenau, Dave Stone, and Cheryl Polson, who taught me and many other students how to think.

I would particularly like to think Alicia Christensen, Marguerite Boyles, Tish Fobben, Sara Springsteen, Emily Giller, Andrea Shahan, Judith Hoover, and all the editors and staff at the University of Nebraska Press. Your kindness and professionalism made a seemingly difficult process exceptionally easy for a first-time author.

A special thanks to Kimberley Metcalf and Shelia Lucas for help in editing the early drafts of this book. Your attention to detail and expert suggestions made this book what it is, and I am forever in your debt. I would like to thank Dan Cox, Stephen Melton, and David Isenberg for your feedback and suggestions on the working manuscript. Thanks to William Gregor for your wizard-like ability to produce a key document at a key time that finally tied together the logic of my argument. In addition I would like to thank Kevin Clark, Steven Noel, Meegan Olding, and Ryan Scott for your research on the private security industry, much of which has informed my work.

Gerald Scott Gorman, Richard Dixon, and the current and previous directors of the School of Advanced Military Studies, my deepest appreciation for your support. To my friend Michael Mihalka, thanks for reminding me to think strategically.

I would especially like to thank my parents for their enduring love, support, and encouragement. And I would like to thank my sons, who have grown into fine young men. You make me proud.

OUTSOURCING SECURITY

INTRODUCTION

To date, the scholarly work on the increased use of private security, both domestically and internationally, has failed to produce a working theory of the phenomenon. At best the existing bodies of knowledge describe the private security industry in its contemporary form and provide some understanding of the contextual conditions that allowed for the industry's growth. However, descriptive accounts by scholars have not been tested with empirical evidence to determine which causal explanations are not only necessary but sufficient to explain the growth of the industry. In addition the time horizon must be expanded to include samples prior to the end of the cold war to be considered comprehensive. Most of the scholarly work implies that the privatization of security emerged from the global conditions created at the end of the cold war. While international changes surely played a large role in the increase in the use of private military contractors, it would be unwise to assume that domestic influences had no role in such a large policy shift. This book demonstrates, first, that the use of private security contractors by the United States is not a new condition; second, that the recent increased use of private security as an instrument of military policy or foreign policy may in fact be a consequence of deliberate policy decisions of successive presidential administrations; and third, that the security environment in the target state of an intervention is a factor that produces an increase of private security contractors.

For the purpose of this book, private firms that offer security- and military-related services for the military are considered private military contractors or private security contractors. A private military contractor (PMC) provides services such as technical support, transportation, maintenance, engineering, and logistical support. A PMC can also provide military consulting services and training. A private security contractor (PSC) may provide fixed-base security, convoy security, and individual personnel security to supplement professional military forces during a conflict.

Part of the problem with extant research of the private security industry is that scholars attempt to analyze its use within the paradigm of full militarization of the U.S. military or industrial-age war. Smith (2008, 415) and others assert that the nature of war has transitioned from a massive industrial conflict fought by men and machines to smaller conflicts or "war amongst the people."[1] Smith suggests that nation-states, particularly in the West, retain their industrial armies only because people are willing to pay for a national army and assume they provide a national defense.[2] He argues that this assumption does not match present reality. It is no longer practical for politicians and diplomats to expect our military forces to deter threats to national security or future international problems: "The worlds of security and defense have become closely intertwined — to the point where it is no longer possible to simply divide activities between military and other services" (378).

If Smith is correct that a blending of military and other services have occurred, then something similar to a Kuhnian paradigm shift is needed to break away from the notion that only national armies can provide security. Thus the old paradigm, based on assumptions rooted in the notion of industrial-age warfare (full military mobilization), is no longer sufficient. A new perspective using a supply-demand framework is needed to bring understanding to the growth of the private security industry.

The purpose of this book is to describe the results of a study that examined the causes of the growth of PMCs during the late twentieth- and early twenty-first-century U.S. experience by relying on the demand for and supply of PMCs. It should also provide insight into the use of PMCs by other globally active industrial democracies. In fact if the central tenants of the supply-demand framework advanced here are supported by the empirical evidence, then the results should provide useful information for scholarly studies and policymakers within any modern state that actively uses its military in international affairs. Furthermore, when political leaders choose to reduce their nation's military force structure, they may face conflicts beyond their anticipated scope and duration. As such, decision makers are left with no choice but to legalize and legitimize the use of PMCs, resulting in the increased use of PMCs as a deliberate tool of foreign policy.

This book looks beyond the conventional industrial-age framework of large conscript armies to discern why there has been a rapid growth in the use of private security in U.S. foreign policy over the past two decades. Part of the answer lies in the pull of the seemingly increasing number of postindustrial, asymmetric conflicts across the globe over that period. It may be, as Smith (2008) suggests, that international security threats can no longer be addressed by the military alone, and thus U.S. soldiers dispatched overseas will tend to be accompanied by a growing array of contractors in the years to come. Changes in the external environment probably do not provide a full explanation of the rise of PMCs, however. Beyond the pull of postindustrial conflict, a push has also been provided by domestic changes in the United States and similar advanced industrial democracies. James Carafano (2008, 38) argues that "anxiety is high because many misunderstand both the role contractors have played in combat and the key mechanisms states have used to keep them under control." Furthermore he points out that "much of the current anxiety over contractors in combat comes from the fact that the future arrived so quickly and unexpectedly—almost in the blink of an eye." Overall numbers of soldiers in uniform have declined, and, at least for a short period, there seems to have been a broadening of the types of missions that democratic populations support.

Private military contractors have been alluded to as military firms, military service providers, privatized military firms, transnational security corporations, and security contractors. All of these terms, however, refer to the same concept: firms offering security- and military-related services that until the 1980s used to be considered the preserve of the state ("Private Military Companies" n.d.). Authors have attempted to provide specific definitions that describe the private security industry, although few agree on a common taxonomy of its members or tasks. Shearer (1998, 13) points out that "private military forces cannot be defined in absolute terms: they occupy a grey area that challenges the liberal conscience." O'Brien suggests that "one of the greatest challenges for both policy and law enforcement lies in defining the activities and actors in this area" (cited in Chesterman and Lehnardt 2007, 34). Scahill (2007) consistently uses the term *mercenary* to describe actors in the industry. However, Shearer (1998, 22) argues that "the assumption that military companies merely comprise modern-day mercenaries is simplistic." Therefore a brief discussion of mercenaries is necessary.

While *mercenary* has been used to describe the private security industry and those who work within it, the term conjures up many images, mostly pejorative. Tickler (1987, 15) asserts that "in the public imagination he is a freelance soldier of no fixed abode or loyalty, ruthless, undertaking short contracts for large amounts of money, the sort of men depicted, for instance in the film *The Wild Geese*." Avant (2005, 22) suggests that "the term mercenary has been used to describe everything from individuals killing for hire, to troops raised by one country working for another, to private security companies working for their own country." Kinsey (2006, 19) describes them as freelance operators or "a soldier willing to sell his military skills to the highest bidder."[3]

While some authors continue to use the term *mercenary* when describing the private security industry, Shearer (1998, 13) argues that "using the term mercenary can make it more difficult to understand the strategic implications of private military force." Furthermore, he suggests that "labeling a military company mercenary feeds a set of pre-conceived ideas and obscures the issues at stake" (13). He concludes that "when companies work only for recognized governments, as most argue that they do, then they are exempt from the terms of these conventions" (20). *Mercenary* is but one term used by scholars, pundits, and the media to describe the private security industry, though maybe not correctly in all cases. What follows is an attempt to increase understanding of the industry and reduce some of the conceptual confusion between the terms used to describe it.

Singer (2003) asserts that the private security industry is different from mercenaries or historically similar entities. He uses six criteria to describe the difference:

Organization: Prior corporate structure
Motives: Profit-driven business rather than profit-driven individual
Open Market: Legal, public entities
Services: Wider range, varied clientele
Recruitment: Public, specialized
Linkages: Ties to corporate holdings and financial markets

Singer suggests that "the single unifying factor for the privatized military industry is that all the firms within it offer services that fall within the military domain" (88). Furthermore several authors use the terms *private military firm* and *private security industry* synonymously. Kinsey (2006, 9) asserts that "the categorization of types of companies in any industry, or of the correspondence between them and the realities they typify, is a difficult task, more so in an industry that sees companies able to undertake ranges of activities that cut across different categories of services, as well as moving between vastly different customers." The difficulty of classifying the private security industry in clear terms is challenging because of their corporate nature.

Schaub and Franke (2009–10, 90) point out that "by adopting a corporate business model, these firms are able to recruit and retain former military personnel, develop organizational frameworks within which procedures, doctrine, and innovation can be produced, and, as a result, offer an array of capabilities that cover the gamut of military services beyond mere tactical support." Furthermore "many firms are characterized by a cadre structure with a relatively low number of full-time employees and a reservoir of expertise that can be called upon on a contract basis" (93). The authors conclude that "the fragmented nature of the [PMC] industry, its multitude of firms, heterogeneous labor pool, and difficulties in forging a common corporate identity through coherent and consistent indoctrination, training, and education experiences suggests, however, that armed contractors should at best be considered to be members of a semi-profession" (102). Thus the continuous evolution of the private security industry as it adjusts to the ever changing security environment and demand for its services defies a common definition.

There is little if any consensus on the specific definition or taxonomy of the private security industry after three decades of scholarly work. For example, the activities and services of private security corporations and of private military companies are generally categorized in a similar manner in the literature, though the titles are different. The private security industry trade website PrivateMilitary.org states, "Private Security Companies (contractors, firms) or PSCs are on many occasions contracted to render tasks in conflict and post-conflict environments"; distinguishing between them can become even more difficult when they operate in climates of instability. For this reason several have argued that "in such cases PSCs become localized permutations of the PMC and/or a fast expanding international security industry" ("Private Military Companies" n.d.). The website states that "the offering of security solutions and risk management services is on many occasions intertwined, particularly when firms operate in conflict and post-conflict environments. Hence, it seems prudent to highlight practically this service amalgamation modality inherent in international security provision" ("Private Military Companies" n.d.). Thus many scholars look at which tasks private security companies provide.

Kinsey (2006, 16) points out that "a private security company is generally concerned with crime prevention and public order. The tasks they undertake range from evaluating investment prospects, armed guards to protect government and commercial installations and persons, and finally security advisors for multinational companies." PSCs are also distinguished by their involvement in the international arena (Kinsey 2006); in contrast, commercial security companies focus on their own domestic market and include services such as prison administration, immigration control, and critical infrastructure protection. Two examples of commercial security companies are Brinks Security, which provides armed guards to banks and financial institutions, and Wackenhut Security, which provides critical infrastructure protection for the nation's private nuclear facilities.

Much has been written about regulations and control of the private security industry. Percy (2007, 61) suggests that "PSCs are similar to PMCs but are under a higher level of state control. They offer military advice and training, and guard facilities and individuals, but do not engage in combat. . . . PSCs undertake tasks authorized by the government and so are almost a branch of the national armed services." In general a private security contractor typically is armed, while a private military contractor is unarmed.

However a private military company may offer both armed and unarmed security services: "Private Military Companies or PMCs can be defined as legally established international firms offering services that involve the potential to exercise force in a systematic way and by military or paramilitary means, as well as the enhancement, the transfer, the facilitation, the deterrence, or the defusing of this potential, or the knowledge required to implement it, to clients" (Ortiz 2010, 48). Shearer (1998, 22) asserts that "their essential purpose is to enhance the capability of a client's military force to function better in war, or deter conflict more effectively." While not providing a specific definition of PMCs, Shearer does categorize their activities. Kinsey (2006, 23) describes PMCs as "providing military expertise, including training and equipment, almost exclusively to weak or failing states." He relies on both Shearer's categorization of PMCs and Singer's criteria for the private military industry but adds nothing new to the definition.

Percy (2007, 60) asserts that "PMCs can be defined as 'corporate bodies' specializing in provisions of military skills to governments: training, planning, intelligence, risk assessment, operation support and technical skills." The inclusion of operations support within the taxonomy of allowable PMC activities reflects that PMCs will actually engage in combat. Thus the difference between a PMC and a PSC is the level of state control: PSCs are under tighter control and engage in combat only in a defensive protective role. Percy provides the clearest definition of PMCs in the literature, although it is similar to Singer's definition of a private military firm and Kinsey's definition of a private combat company.

For the purposes of this book, Percy's (2007) definition of PMCs and PSCs is used when describing their general use domestically or as a tool for foreign policy. The term *private military contractor* is used when referring to private firms that offer security- and military-related services. The *term private security industry* is used when referring to all types of private security firms, regardless of the service they provide. The term *private security contractor* or *private contractor* is used when referring to an individual or a group of individuals who work in the private security industry.

The distinction between PMCs and PSCs and their activities is important for several reasons. In their final report to the U.S. Congress, the Commission on Wartime Contracting (U.S. Congress, House, Commission on Wartime Contracting [CWC] 2011) pointed out that as of March 2011 more than 262,000 private contractors were working in Iraq and Afghanistan, and between 2001 and 2011 the United States spent more than $206 billion on contracts and grants that supported contingency operations in those countries. Two-thirds of the money was spent on support services, including logistics, construction, and technical services (see table 1). Moreover there were 2,480 U.S. private contractor fatalities in Iraq and Afghanistan during this time (this number did not include foreign contractor employees; U.S. Congress, House, CWC 2011, 31). Comparatively there were 6,131 U.S. military fatalities in Iraq and Afghanistan during the same period. Contractor fatalities accounted for more than 28 percent of all U.S. fatalities. However, the conflict in Afghanistan is not over. The Commission predicts that a potential contractor surge will occur in Iraq and Afghanistan after the U.S. military withdraws.

On 15 December 2011 the United States pulled its military forces out of Iraq as part of the Iraq Status of Forces Agreement (U.S. Department of State 2008). The Department of State has become the lead agency in Iraq overseeing U.S. foreign policy objectives. In addition to the U.S. embassy in Baghdad, the Department of State plans on establishing five enduring presence posts throughout Iraq (U.S. Congress, House, CWC 2010).[4] Typically the Department of State relies on a host nation to augment the diplomatic security services (DSS) to meet emergency needs for security. However, the conditions in Iraq are neither peaceful nor stable. In the summer of 2010 the undersecretary of state for management, Ambassador Patrick Kennedy, pointed out that the resources of the DSS "are inadequate to the extreme challenges in Iraq" (U.S. Congress, House, CWC 2010, 2). Since 2004 the Department of Defense has provided security and emergency services, such as medical evacuation and armed quick-reaction teams to respond to attacks on U.S. facilities. With the withdrawal of combat troops from Iraq the State Department has identified fourteen security-related tasks, previously performed by the Department of Defense, that must be met to ensure the safety of the remaining U.S. personnel (U.S. Congress, House, CWC 2010).

Table 1. Top Ten Services Performed in Support of
Operations in Iraq and Afghanistan, 2002–11

Service	Total (in billions)
Logistics support services	$46.5
Construction of miscellaneous buildings	10.5
Technical assistance	5.5
Other professional services	5.2
Guard services	3.8
Maintenance and repair, alterations of office buildings	3.5
Construction of office buildings	2.9
Lease-rent or restoration of real property	2.8
Facilities operations support services	2.5
Program management/support services	2.4
Total obligations for top ten services	85.6
Top ten as percentage of total services obligations: 44%	

Source: U.S. Congress, House, CWC 2011, 23.

The Department of State acknowledged that it employed about 2,700 private security contractors in Iraq to augment the DSS as of December 2010. After the departure of combat troops from Iraq, it also estimated that between 6,000 and 7,000 security contractors will be required to provide adequate security for its mission after December 2011 (U.S. Congress, House, CWC 2010). The U.S. military and the Department of State are the two distinct authorities that are responsible for security of U.S. federal civilian employees and contractors abroad (U.S. Congress, House, CWC 2009, 60). Beginning in January 2012 the Department of State assumed responsibility for security for U.S. personnel in Iraq. The CWC is urging Congress to approve resources for the State Department to support the increase in contract costs to "avoid unnecessary and tragic loss of life and avert damage to the U.S. mission in Iraq and to broader policy objectives" (U.S. Congress, House, CWC 2010, 7–8). This means that the State Department fully intends to fill the shortfall in current DSS capacity with private security personnel.

The increased need for private security personnel in Iraq is just one example of the growing relevance of private security for U.S. foreign policy. Because of the rise in the private security industry over the past two decades, the perceived shroud of secrecy in their use by the United States and other Western democracies, and the enormous sums of money spent on their services, the discussion will and should continue into the future about the use of private military contractors. National military budgets, foreign policy decisions on intervention, military force structure, and international legal norms are but a few of the areas that are impacted by the phenomenon of privatized security.

Accurately forecasting the growth of the PMC market requires predicting when and to what extent (e.g., how many military personnel will be needed) the next conflict will occur; this is extremely difficult if not impossible, since the market is frequently changing (Kinsey 2006). There has been a natural transition of the U.S.-based PMC, from providing technical support to operational and training support, enabling U.S. troops to perform more tasks with fewer people (Kinsey 2006). One advantage that U.S.-based PMCs enjoy is a close relationship with the Department of Defense and the Department of State. Kinsey (2006, 101–2) argues that this advantage points toward a continual use of PMCs by U.S. government agencies. Though continued use of PMCs will be based on government requirements, there may be a reduced political risk associated with using PMCs versus national militaries, resulting in the conclusion that politicians will certainly consider their future use in implementing foreign policy (Kinsey 2006). Finally, Kinsey suggests that as nongovernmental organizations (NGOs) increase their involvement in volatile regions around the world, their needs for security will grow, which will be provided by PMCs (107). The private security industry is able to fill this niche market for security since PMCs are likely to be seen as more neutral than a national military force.

It has also been suggested that as long as there continues to be a decrease in qualified and experienced forces to intervene in conflict, PMCs will continue to be used (Rosen 2005). Rosen concludes that the war on terror has redefined the role of and necessity for PMCs and that their use will accelerate. Spearin (2005) concludes that humanitarianism presents a potentially lucrative marketplace for PSCs. Citing the increase in NGO casualties over the past decade, which has curtailed the delivery of assistance due to security concerns, he notes that collaboration with PSCs has become necessary. Spearin also acknowledges that this is a dilemma for NGOs since using PSCs for security may jeopardize the perception of their political neutrality. He asserts that when NGOs and their donors become more educated about PSCs through dialogue, the negative image of PSCs will be replaced with facts. Likewise when PSCs understand NGO concerns they will make adjustments to better handle the needs of humanitarian clients.

There are thus many ideas in the literature concerning the rise of the private security industry, but they have not been subject to systematic empirical scrutiny. To be fair, the goal of the extant literature has been to describe the phenomenon, not to develop a theory that explains the phenomenon. For example, Avant (2005, 30) states that the aim of her well-known book "is to describe the current market and explore its implications rather than explain its rise." Although descriptive accounts are valuable, the subject is significant enough to warrant the development of more systematic knowledge of the phenomenon.

The literature is diverse, but much of it centers on three key influences, emphasized first by Singer (2003) and then by others: the decreasing supply of national troops, decreasing national defense budgets, and the rising demand from global conflicts and humanitarian emergencies. Not only does this study offer the first rigorous quantitative and qualitative test of a supply-demand theory of the rise of PMCs, but it also develops a number of additional influences that have the potential to supplement the supply-demand explanation, such as intensity of the conflict in the target state, key decisions by policymakers to legalize the use of PMCs, and support from the host nation for their use. By rigorously examining these supplemental explanations, this study determines whether the pressures associated with the supply-demand theory truly have driven the rise of PMCs in the late twentieth and early twenty-first century. In sum, this study will add precision to our understanding of the causes of the increased use of PMCs, moving beyond descriptive accounts and laying out a clearly specified theory to explain the phenomenon. And it tests the theory using more rigorous qualitative and quantitative methods than have been used to date.

The qualitative component uses a structured, focused comparison method to examine four historical cases. The use of these cases allows for a greater investigation of the rise of the private security industry in the United States and for tracing interactions among various causal factors. The four cases are the U.S. intervention in Iraq in 1991 (Operation Desert Shield/Desert Storm), the U.S. intervention in Bosnia in 1995 (Operation Joint Endeavor), the U.S. intervention in Afghanistan in 2001 (Operation Enduring Freedom), and the U.S. intervention in Iraq in 2003 (Operation Iraqi Freedom). The justification for the selection is threefold: first, these cases represent American conflicts (supported by its closest Western allies) in the post-Vietnam era; second, the cases occur at a time when the United States had an all-volunteer army (postconscription); third, all the cases involve the use of private contractors. Examination of post-1990 cases provides the unit homogeneity that King et al. (1994) suggest for cross-case qualitative analysis. The use of PMCs also varies across these cases, which should facilitate the development of valid inferences.

The goal of structured, focused comparison is to deal with only certain aspects of the case by employing general questions to guide the data collection and analysis (George 1979). George points out that "a controlled comparison of each case helps identify an outcome of the dependent variable and provides a historical explanation for it and is couched in terms of the independent and intervening variables of theoretical interest" (62). In this instance structured, focused comparison should help to tease out exactly how supply, demand, and other pressures help to stimulate the rise of PMCs.

The second component of the research methodology is a quantitative analysis, which analyzes a larger time period than previous studies and should increase the generalizability of the findings. It also provides insight on the relative explanatory weight of different causal influences. The variables under study are operationalized using historical data from U.S. government sources available from the Department of Defense, the U.S. Census Bureau, and the U.S. Office of Budget and Analysis.

Using a mixed-method approach promises to provide richer complementary results. George (1979, 61) suggests that "controlled comparison of a small N [number of variables] is neither competitive with nor a substitute for quantitative analysis of a large N." King et al. (1994, 3–4) argue that quantitative methods are a systematic generalizing branch while qualitative methods are the humanistic discursive branch; when used together they can reinforce one another and help to provide a systematic analysis. Therefore, "both approaches are of value; in fact, they complement one another" (Mahoney and Goertz 2006, 231).

The use of a mixed-methods approach to examine the rise of the private security industry will help fill a gap in the literature. Carafano (2008, 143) points out that through 2005 most scholars, other than Singer (2003) and Avant (2005), were relatively silent regarding trends concerning the private sector in public wars: "Few pick up the challenges raised by scholars—testing their conclusions, refining theories, adding new evidence; in short, all the effort needed to build and broaden academic studies that provide a robust body of research on a subject. All these things have been missing in the debate over contractors in combat." Utilizing a mixed-methods approach to examine the rise of the private security industry in the United States is an attempt to meet the scholarly challenge proposed by Carafano.

Of course the topic and use of PMCs are more than just an academic endeavor. As the use of PMCs by the United States and other Western democracies has increased over recent decades, questions about their control and status are being raised in the domestic political arena. Their legitimacy is being challenged by sovereign governments where U.S.-based PMCs are deployed. They are also becoming a large market force in the United States and internationally, offering competencies and services not readily available to some nation-states. This book thus provides valuable information to those shaping policy as well.

The book is limited to the availability of data on the private security industry. Public U.S. government records provide data on procurement and contracting, military forces, the U.S. defense budget, and U.S. interventions. Empirical evidence on specific private security firms is limited to public records and secondary sources. Where feasible, attempts were made to obtain primary historical records from private security companies. The study is also limited to an examination of the use of the private security industry by the United States. As the most powerful mature democracy (India is of course much larger by population), it is prudent to begin the debate using the United States as the model. However, limiting the study to the United States exposes a weakness in generalizing the findings across other mature democracies.

The time period examined in the quantitative analysis is limited to 1950–2014 since data are readily available from public records, and the bulk of the data is from U.S. Department of Defense records. This study acknowledges that other branches of the U.S. government also employ private security companies in an international role, yet the Department of Defense spends the largest sum of money on private security, therefore providing a general indicator of the trends. The time period examined in the qualitative analysis is 1991 to 2014.

The book assumes that the United States and other Western democracies will continue to use private security in the future both domestically and internationally. However, the United States is not viewed as a unitary actor but as influenced by multiple private and public actors that impact the use of private security domestically and internationally. Likewise the private security industry is not viewed as a unitary actor but as a complex adaptive system composed of many individuals and companies and their sponsors, each competing in a highly complex business environment. Furthermore, this study acknowledges that the U.S. defense budget fluctuates over time, that Department of Defense personnel are a finite resource, and that the United States is likely to be involved in future conflicts.

This book is organized into eight chapters. Chapter 1 reviews the current state of the literature on private military contracting and develops the theory under review. Chapter 2 introduces the historical case studies and explains the methodological approach used to examine the cases. Chapters 3 through 6 test the theory by using the four historical case studies. Chapter 3 examines Operation Desert Shield and Desert Storm, the 1990 U.S. military intervention to restore the sovereignty of Kuwait. Chapter 4 examines Operation Joint Endeavor, the 1995 U.S. military intervention to implement the Dayton Accords in Bosnia. Chapter 5 examines Operation Enduring Freedom, the 2001 U.S. military intervention to remove the Taliban regime in Afghanistan. Chapter 6 examines Operation Iraqi Freedom, the 2003 U.S. military intervention to overthrow the regime in Iraq. Chapter 7 is a cross-case analysis of the four case studies. Chapter 8 presents the statistical analysis. The conclusion provides a more detailed summary of the main arguments and findings and briefly highlights future research.

CHAPTER ONE

A THEORETICAL FRAMEWORK OF
THE PRIVATE SECURITY INDUSTRY

This chapter presents the rationale for conducting research on the causes of the rise of the private security industry in the United States. Scholars have studied the rise of private security for over a decade, but to date most of the research has been descriptive and has not attempted to systematically discern the causes of this rise. Such descriptive work nonetheless provides implicit arguments about the variables that have created this important rise in the industry. This chapter summarizes the existing literature, most of which assumes that a basic supply-demand process lies behind the increased use of PMCs. As defense budgets and the number of soldiers in uniform have declined (decreased supply) and the external demands, specifically for soldiers, have risen, PMCs have filled the gap.

Thus this study seeks to investigate the relationship between the increase in the private security industry and five potential explanatory variables tied to supply-demand theory: decreased national military capabilities, decreased military outlays, increased conflict, increased duration, and increased bureaucratic controls. It also examines three additional potential explanatory variables: force caps, host nation support, and the permissiveness of the security environment in the target state. What follows is a discussion of the existing literature, the general theory of supply and demand, and the theoretical framework that was used to help bring understanding to the growth of private security.

A decade ago Singer (2003) thrust the topic of the use of private military contractors by mature democracies into the public conscience. He pointed out that "there is no single cause for the rise of private military contractors" and suggested that "the private market filled the security gap as a result of the end of the Cold War" (49). Since his work, scholars, journalists, and lawmakers have attempted to classify privatized security, debated the causes of the rising use of private security, pointed out criminal activity and fraud, and argued for increased regulations and controls on the private security industry. Avant (2005, 3) further describes the private security industry as a provider of a service within the market economy surrounding the defense industry. She brings to light the tension that exists in who controls the force: the state or private actors. While much of the debate has centered on the control of the private security companies, most scholars acknowledge and accept that the private security industry should exist and have legitimate rules.

Indeed the private security industry is not only employed extensively by mature democracies, but it is embedded within them. Mandel (2002) points out that a fundamental tension exists between a public's desire for security and many lawmakers' attempts to provide a public service with limited resources. He highlights the limitations of the existing literature by observing that "many studies focus exclusively on private military activities of a few companies in only limited parts of the world" (2). However, the broader issue is the systemic use of the private security industry by mature democracies. Yet much of the debate on the use of private security highlights the tensions between privatization and statism, civil-private security control, and choices between public homeland security and private critical infrastructure security.

A criticism concerning the literature on the private security industry is that it tends to focus on empirical details and that most writers do not situate their accounts in a theoretical framework (Percy 2007). For example, "a striking feature of the present literature on mercenaries is its lack of theoretical analysis, particularly with respect to international relations" (4). Furthermore scholars "tend to look at how mercenaries behave in a particular state or the nature of their organization and operations, rather than what the behavior or type of organization means for international relations" (4). For example, while Singer (2003) is credited for his analysis on the development and growth of private military and security companies and his consideration of the political implications and morality of using mercenaries, his analysis of the private security industry is done outside of a theoretical framework (Percy 2007, 4). Although Singer (2003, ix) acknowledges that his aim was to organize and integrate what was known about private security firms in a systematic manner in order to allow for the future development of underlying theories, his work is framed by an *implicit* theory. He suggests that "the resultant effect on the supply and demand of military services created a 'security gap' that the private market rushed to fill" (49). He points out that "the end of the Cold War produced a vacuum in the market of security, which manifested itself in numerous ways, feeding both the supply side and the demand side" (49).

Singer's (2003, 50) supply-demand theory asserts that "massive military demobilizations provided a large pool of labor for the private military firm (PMF) industry and cheapening of start-up capital." The massive increase in the global level of conflict since the cold war's end also resulted in a demand for security that most nations were unable to provide (Singer 2003). He concludes that "many states are less willing and less able to guarantee their own sovereign autonomy. Instead, they have increasingly delegated the task of securing life and property of their citizens to other organizations, including PMFs" (56). Thus while it may be true that Singer does not empirically test a well-defined theoretical framework of the rise of the private security industry, his work advances an underlying theory that is worthy of future rigorous analysis.

Avant (2005) too suggests that the increase in private security can be tied to supply and demand. She points out that concomitant with the increase in supply was an increase in the demand for military skills on the private market from Western states that had downsized their militaries, from countries seeking to upgrade and Westernize their militaries as a way of demonstrating credentials for entry into Western institutions, from rulers of weak or failed states no longer propped up by superpower patrons, and from nonstate actors such as private firms, international nongovernmental organizations, and groups of citizens in the territories of weak or failed states.

However, Avant (2005) does not examine the private security industry increases using the theory of supply and demand. Instead she examines how the privatization of security affects state control. Specifically she posits three dimensions of control (functional, political, and social control and their inter-relationships) as the key to controlling violence. In order to assess whether privatization has changed a state's control over force, one can examine whether or not change occurred in a functional sense (Is the use of force more or less effective?), in a political sense (Has there been a shift in the relative power of actors who control force?), and in a social sense (Has there been a change in the way security reflects societal values?).

Furthermore Avant (2005, 6) draws upon "new institutionalism," a diverse set of theories pulling from distinct logics in economics and sociology but united by an interest in institutional mechanisms and how they affect collective outcomes to understand the increase in private security. As a result she attempts to juxtapose economic and sociological institutionalist arguments while arguing that privatization differentially effects force capabilities and the societal values of the armed forces (6). Nonetheless her discussion of private security as a market alternative for military services does relate to a theory of supply and demand since it changes the options available to states for the conduct of foreign policy, for example when the U.S. military chooses to substitute private military contractors for a national military force.

Using market allocation generally advantages executives relative to legislatures, reduces transparency, and reduces the mobilization required to send public forces abroad (Avant 2005). Because of these changes, market allocation makes it easier to undertake adventurous foreign policies — or actions that do not have widespread support of a polity. An additional cost of the use of market alternatives is that the private sector becomes involved in decision making, giving those with commercial interests an influence over policy formation and implementation (Avant 2005).

Since PMCs are relatively new actors in the international security arena, academic research is also needed to help policymakers decide how, or if, they should be used in support of national interests (Kinsey 2006). Part of the concern is that while the market for private security is set to grow, accurately forecasting market growth when the market is frequently changing is extremely difficult if not impossible (3). Indeed the path that a conflict takes is inherently unpredictable once it begins. In comparison, during the cold war geographical conflict was the rationale for the existence of state militaries (Kinsey 2006).

Likewise political factors are still an essential component in the use of state militaries today, but they no longer dominate our thinking as they used to do. For example, sociopolitical and economic pressures have raised questions within modern society as to whether states are the only options available to governments conducting security operations. To a large extent the increasing reliance on PMCs and PSCs reflects concern about monetary efficiency and the application of lethal force to stave off strangers (96).

Kinsey (2006) does not utilize a theoretical framework to examine the rise of the private security industry, but he does provide insights on how choices are made by military leaders for the use of PMCs. He points out that a division of labor is now occurring in the military itself and that "contractors allow the military to concentrate on its core functions, fighting wars, by removing responsibility for the more mundane operations, which are no less important to maintaining operational efficiency, and handing that responsibility to outside agents" (97). Kinsey concludes that within the current international system, the provision of security is closely related to the structure of the security sector as a whole. He suggests that the key factors that define this context in today's international system are military downsizing, technology, monetary efficiency, and political expediency.

Other authors have also examined the inherently political and ideological nature of the decision to contract out military services to private firms (Krahmann 2010). Specifically, Republicanism and Liberalism were used to provide a "fuller understanding of how the growing role of private military forces has become possible" (Krahmann 2010, 4). Although Krahmann uses an ideological framework to help understand the decision to outsource military services to private firms, she does suggest that supply and demand can explain the rise of the private security industry. And she notes that "the changing security environment, budgetary pressures and the market forces of supply and demand result in the rise of the private military industry" (9). In particular, it is argued that the reduction in the number of uniformed soldiers has contributed to the expansion of the private military industry in two ways: large surpluses of ex-military personnel available for recruitment and new demands for military expertise and personnel because of the changing security environment.

Taking a different approach Thomson (1994) examined the decline of mercenaries in the modern state system. She asserts that the contemporary organization of global violence is neither timeless nor natural, that prior to the Peace of Westphalia "people bought and sold military manpower like a commodity on the global market, therefore, the identity of suppliers or purchasers meant almost nothing" (3). Thomson argues further that "the 'disarming' of non-state transnational activities marked the transition from heteronomy to sovereignty and the transformation of states into the national state system" (4). An essential feature of this transformation was a new way of organizing global coercive resources that eventually facilitated the transformation of the institution of sovereignty in the nineteenth century. This transformation resulted in the rise of republican government, the elimination of nonstate violence, and European expansion. Although Thomson focuses on the declining use of mercenaries, her theory that de-legalization followed by de-legitimatization, when reversed (legalization followed by legitimation), may help explain how modern state policymakers enable the increased use of the modern private security industry.

Other literature has examined the norms against mercenary use (Percy 2007). Societal norms against the use of mercenaries has influenced states in their decisions about which type of force to employ and has thus shaped the opportunities available for mercenaries. The norms against their use have two components. First, mercenaries are considered to be immoral because they use force outside legitimate, authoritative control. Second, mercenaries are considered to be morally problematic because they fight wars for selfish, financial reasons rather than for a cause (1). It is likely that the impact of such long-standing and powerful norms against mercenaries has influenced the prospects for private military and private security companies by decreasing the demand (Percy 2007). Percy concludes that "a belief that the use of private force is wrong, whether or not it is grounded in the facts of how these companies have really behaved, provides a significant obstacle to the further development of the private military industry" (13). Percy's work therefore highlights a potential psychological barrier to future PMC use. Although this study does not analyze this norm directly, the dramatic rise of PMC use it documents raises questions about the strength of Percy's argument.

All of the studies mentioned so far use qualitative methods to analyze the private security industry. This is the norm in the literature. Existing research tends to focus on two or three case studies from the past two decades to examine the use of private security in conflicts. While this approach provides specific examples of the use of the private security industry in specific conflicts, it fails to provide trends. Likewise the historical cases are heterogeneous, thus the basic causes may be different.

For example, Shearer (1998) examines the abilities and shortcomings of two military companies, Executive Outcomes and Military Professional Resource Incorporated (MPRI), in providing private-sector military assistance. Shearer concludes that Executive Outcomes played an instrumental role in altering the course of war in Sierra Leone in 1995. Most significant was that its military operations forced the Revolutionary United Front to negotiate with the National Provisional Ruling Council. Likewise the losses suffered by the UNITA rebels in Angola in the late 1990s forced a peace settlement by 2002. Shearer suggests the company's training of the Angolan Army that ultimately led to their success. In the Balkans that the training provided by MPRI to the Croat and Bosnian armies served as part of a program of armed deterrence that has been an effective and convenient instrument of policy for the U.S. administration. Indeed in both cases Shearer concludes that the use of private military companies assisted in ending the violence associated with the conflict; however, there is little discussion of the causal factors in the decisions to use them.

Singer (2003) also examines Executive Outcomes' role in Angola and Sierra Leone and MPRI's role in the Balkans. In addition he examines Kellogg Brown and Root's support to the U.S. military. Singer states that the purpose of the selected cases is to provide highlights of the extent and breadth of the industry, not its entirety. These cases thus conform to Singer's typology of the private security industry, which describes the organizational characteristics, the history of major military operations, and the future of each company. He concludes that providing a heightened appreciation of the private security industry's potential, its underlying dynamics, and its challenges can improve decisions by policymakers.

More generally Avant (2005) examines the practices of contracted private security in Sierra Leone, Croatia, and the United States instead of individual companies. She reviews each country's rate of private security services over several years to illustrate how exports of private security services affect states' ability to control the force that emanates from their territory and to demonstrate how the private financing of security affects the control of force. Avant concludes that individual states can sometimes enhance the capacity of their forces with PMCs and thereby increase functional control. However, she finds that the market undermines the collective monopoly of the state over violence in world politics, and thus is a central feature of the sovereign system.

The literature has also sought to understand the reasons for and implications of the proliferation of private military force in Europe and North America. Krahmann (2010) examines and compares the use of private military contractors in the United Kingdom, the United States, Germany, and international military interventions. In her review of each country, Krahmann assesses the ideological rationale for privatization, analyzes the implementation of privatization, debates how the changes affected the model of professional soldiers, and discusses the consequences of governance. She concludes that the roles of and relations between the state, the citizen, and the soldier in Western democracies have repeatedly been transformed due to changing internal and external circumstances during the past three centuries.

The remaining empirical literature provides descriptive information on various actors in the private security industry. Carafano (2008, 151) states that most commercial writings on PMCs do not add much to understanding the issues surrounding the role of the private sector in public wars. For example, Davis (2000) provides an anecdotal account of the privatization of security from an insiders' perspective. Specifically he describes his experiences in Central America, on the African continent, and in the Balkans working for a variety of security firms. Pelton (2006) invites the reader to travel with him on a journey to experience the characters and scenarios of the private contractor while working in conflict areas. Scahill (2007) focuses on the rise of one private security company, Blackwater, which he refers to them as modern mercenaries for their work for the U.S. government since 9/11. Isenberg (2009) describes the role of multiple private security firms in Iraq since 2003 in an attempt to fill a void in the debate about the use of private contractors. Much of the commercial literature therefore provides either an individual anecdotal perspective on private contractors or focuses on private contracting companies or the industry's involvement in Iraq, Africa, or Afghanistan.

As a result most of the literature focuses on descriptions of the private security industry, analysis of government control, and normative explanations of civil-military relations. Carafano (2008, 143) argues that most scholars have been relatively silent regarding trends concerning the private sector in public wars: "Interdisciplinary studies are often the most difficult to tackle, and as an academic topic, this subject sits at that fault-line of a number of disciplines — military and business history, economics, international relations, law, philosophy, national security, and public policy, to name a few." Carafano observers that "few pick up the challenges raised by scholars — testing their conclusions, refining theories, adding new evidence; in short, all the effort needed to build and broaden academic studies [so] that they provide a robust body of research on a subject" (143). The study described in this book takes on the challenge posed by Carafano.

This study adds to the empirical foundation by providing a new and rigorous test of the supply-demand theory that is implicit in the descriptive and normative literature. Before such tests can be completed, however, the central elements of the supply-demand theory must be outlined. The specific influences (or variables) that supply-demand theory would expect to be important for the rise of PMCs must also be delineated. The next two sections describe the theory in the abstract and its application to the rise of PMCs.

The General Theory of Supply and Demand

Before examining the general theory of supply and demand it is important to begin with a definition of economics and microeconomics. Economics is the study of "how individuals, governments, firms and nations make choices on allocating scarce resources to satisfy their unlimited wants" ("Economics" n.d.). Microeconomics is the study of how individuals and organizations reach decisions about consumption and saving, prices and their output, privatization and efficiency, and market competition, and how labor works ("Definition of 'Microeconomics'" n.d.).

The use of the private security industry by the U.S. government is one example of microeconomics. Mansfield (1985) points out that economics deals with the way resources are allocated among alternative uses to satisfy human wants. He suggests that microeconomics helps to answer many practical problems of businesses and governments and throws important light on many fundamental issues that confront responsible citizens and elected representatives. Mansfield concludes that the market for every good will be determined by its demand from the public and the supply from the industry. Smith (2009) argues that microeconomics and, more specifically, the interaction of supply and demand in markets for particular goods can also illuminate security issues. For example, when governments choose to reduce the size of their national military and then are faced with unanticipated conflicts that exceed their capability, the demand for security increases.

However, in the market supply-demand is a delicate balance. As noted by the philosopher Adam Smith, if there is too little supply for the available demand, then prices rise, producers increase production, and consumers decrease consumption (Beinhocker 2007). If there is too much supply for the available demand, then prices fall, producers decrease production, and consumers increase consumption. This in essence is the theory of supply and demand.

Jacques Turgot's views on the law of diminishing return states that in most production processes (or service businesses), as one inputs more and more of a particular factor (such as labor), at some point one gets progressively less output bang for the input buck (Beinhocker 2007). In essence, given a price in the market, a producer will keep adding more inputs and expanding output until the payoff is no longer worth it. Thus Turgot's law links producer costs to the supply side of the market.

Additionally economic choices are the result of an individual's calculation as to what action maximizes his or her utility. Utility as defined by Jeremy Bentham is a quantity to measure individual pleasure and pain. For example, if you like apples and dislike bananas, and if bananas cost more that apples, when faced with a choice between apples and bananas, you will calculate that consuming the apple will provide you with greater utility and therefore choose it. Bentham's ideas became known as utilitarianism.

Also related to the discussion on supply and demand is Hermann Gossen's idea of the law of diminishing marginal utility. In contrast to utilitarianism, Gossen demonstrated that there was a diminishing benefit to increased consumption. For example, if one is hungry and buys a hamburger, its consumption might provide quite a lot of satisfaction, or utility. However, according to the law of diminishing marginal utility, for each additional hamburger consumed, the level of satisfaction decreases incrementally. At some point purchasing another hamburger is not worth the money, depending on the price. Thus demand falls as price rises and vice versa. Just as diminishing marginal returns keep a producer from producing an infinite quantity of apples, diminishing marginal utility keeps consumers from consuming an infinite quantity of hamburgers.

Most economists agree that the law of supply and demand is one of the fundamental principles governing an economy (Adam 2009). The law of demand states that, if all other factors remain equal, the higher the price of the good, the less people will demand it. The law of supply states that, the higher the price, the higher the quantity of supplies. Producers supply more at a higher price because selling a higher quantity at a higher price increases revenue. Adam points out that supply and demand represent "a symbiotic relationship where each is absolutely dependent on the other. Disruption of one automatically disrupts the other." Accordingly the combination of diminishing marginal returns on production and diminishing marginal utility on consumption means that markets have a natural balancing mechanism: price (Beinhocker 2007). Thus price is the key piece of information shared by producers and consumers.

All microeconomic textbooks indicate that market demand can be represented by a curve that illustrates the quantity of the good that would be purchased at each price (Mankiw 2008). The market demand curve for a good almost always slopes downward to the right; that is, as the quantity demanded increases, the price falls. In other words, the position and shape of the market demand curve for a good depend on consumers' preference, the level of consumer income, the price of other goods, and the length of time to which the demand curve pertains (Mansfield 1985).

Consumer preference therefore is important. If consumers show an increasing preference for a product, the demand curve will shift to the right; for that is, at each price consumers will desire to buy more than previously. In contrast, if consumers show a decreasing preference for a product, the demand curve will shift to the left, since, at each price, consumers will desire to buy less than previously. Thus another factor that influences the position and shape of a good's market demand curve is other prices. Mansfield (1985) points out that increases in the price of a product will shift the market price for a like product to the right (and decreases in the price of the original product will shift to the left).

The market demand curve pertains to a particular period of time, and its shape and position depend on the length and other characteristics of this period (Mansfield 1985). Thus the general theory of supply and demand provides a way to understand the rise of the private security industry as an embedded component of the defense and security market place. For example, in periods of relative peace, a nation may reduce its demand for a large standing military. However, during increased periods of conflict, the demand for a larger standing military or a substitute such as private military contractors increases. Therefore, when examining demand, the context of the period is important. Demand is thus a relationship between the things that determine purchases on the one hand and the amount people buy (or order) on the other hand (Turvey 1971).

Economists are so convinced of the importance of price as one of the factors determining purchases that they often divide these factors into just two groups: price and everything else (Turvey 1971). Mansfield (1985) explains that the competitive market supply can be represented by a curve that shows the quantity of the good that would be supplied at each price. The market supply curve for a good generally slopes upward to the right; that is, the quantity supplied increases as the price rises. The position and shape of the market supply curve for a good depends on the state of technology, input prices, and the length of time to which the supply curve pertains (Mansfield 1985).

A significant factor that influences the position and shape of a product's market supply curve is input price. Mansfield (1985) explains that the supply curve for a commodity is affected by the prices of inputs or resources (e.g., labor, capital, and land) used to produce it. Decreases in the prices of these inputs make it possible to produce commodities more cheaply, so that firms may be willing to supply a given amount at a lower price than they formerly would. Thus decreases in price of inputs may cause the supply curve to shift to the right. On the other hand, increases in the price of inputs may cause it to shift to the left (Mansfield 1985). Similar to the market demand curve, the market supply curve also pertains to a particular period of time (Mansfield 1985). Therefore any examination of the market supply curve requires an understanding of the environment during a particular period.

The closeness of possible substitutes for a market good is a major factor determining the elasticity of demand. Turvey (1971) points out that, other things being equal, when the price of a good falls this will have two effects. One is the substitution effect: a shift in expenditure toward the substitute. The other is the income effect: once the price has fallen and all other prices and income remain unchanged, the total real purchasing power of those who buy the good has necessarily increased. Subsequently the substitution and income effects occur when the price of a good changes or the consumer attains a different level of satisfaction; then he or she is likely to substitute cheaper goods for more expensive goods (Mansfield 1985). Mansfield (1985, 96) explains that the substitution effect is the movement from the original equilibrium point to an imaginary equilibrium point that corresponds to the hypothetical budget line.

One example of supply-demand behavior is when strategic leaders choose to substitute private security contractors for national military force. Carafano (2008, 54) argues that paying for troops has become the most expensive part of running the military; he estimates that the cost for every 100,000 active duty soldiers is approximately $1.2 billion per year. Adequately maintaining a standing armed force simply costs a lot per soldier (54). The upward-spiraling manpower costs and downward-spiraling size of the military have fueled the Pentagon's reliance on contractors (56).

With regard to military economics, there are two dimensions that influence force acquisition. The first is demand: the troops and equipment needed or wanted. The second is supply, which includes the arms industry and the arms trade that provide the weapons (Smith 2009, 118). Smith points out that military expenditures have opportunity costs: the activities that are given up to provide the military resources (159). He argues that "in having opportunity costs, military expenditures are no different from other sorts of government expenditures and one can apply standard public finance theory" to military spending (159).

Smith (2009, 160) observes that governmental budgetary constraints control the flow of money that a government has to balance. The government surplus or deficit, the difference between revenue and expenditure (military and nonmilitary), must match either by changes in the money supply or by changes in government assets and liabilities. Therefore an increase in military expenditure must be financed by some combination of reductions in other government expenditures, increased taxes, printing more money, borrowing by issuing more debt, or selling assets. Smith argues that "nearly all military expenditure is a demand for goods, like weapons, or services, like those provided by the armed forces" (91).

In principle governments should determine how much security is enough by adjusting military expenditure to the point where the marginal security benefit of a little more military expenditure is equal to the opportunity cost (Smith 2009, 88). However, Smith points out that the opportunity cost is what could be gained if the money was used for other government expenditures, like health and education, or used to reduce taxation, which would allow higher private consumption.

The primary factor determining a country's military expenditure is its gross domestic product (GDP), what it can afford. The amount that is "thought appropriate depends on the perceived threat and foreign policy goals. The perceived threat will reflect the danger of armed conflict, enduring hostilities, and domestic political factors which shape perceptions, such as militaristic traditions" (Smith 2009, 94). When the military is given a fixed budget, or a finite amount of spending dollars, then it must choose between quality and quantity (Smith 2009). The balance between quality and quantity will be chosen to maximize force effectiveness, which depends both on the number of units and the capability of each. To maintain this balance, Smith points out that it may be possible to maintain a high-low mix, as the United States did with its modern air force, by combining small numbers of the expensive F15 aircraft with large numbers of the cheaper F16 (133).

If Smith (2009) is correct that the military controls the demand and the arms industry and the arms trade control the supply, then is price the controlling factor, as demand-supply theory suggests? The next section introduces the microeconomic theory of monopsony, which helps explain how demand is the controlling factor for the increased use of PMCs. Following the discussion of monopsony is a review of the variables that influence the political decisions to purchase either troops or PMCs. Variables beyond the supply-demand model that further influence the use of PMCs are also discussed.

Monopsony

As demonstrated earlier, the theory of supply and demand provides the foundation from which the growth of the private security industry can be explained. Furthermore, according to the theory, in a competitive market, price is the factor that determines the amount of purchases. Thus supply controls the behavior of the market. But what happens when the demand controls purchases? Monopsony is a market in which a single buyer completely controls the demand behavior of the market. This section introduces the microeconomic theory of monopsony, examines components of the theory, analyzes how the theory applies to U.S. government procurement, and shows how the theory of monopsony applies to the U.S. military–private security industry relationship.

While the market for any type of good, service, resource, or commodity could, in principle, function as monopsony, this form of market structure tends to be most pronounced in the exchange of services (Boal and Ransom 2010; Parkin 1993; Watkins 2012). Boal and Ransom (2010) observe that a monopsonist has power over price by controlling the quantity demanded. Three characteristics of monopsony are a single firm buying all output in a market, no alternative buyers, and restrictions on entry into the industry. Thus a monopsonized market is characterized by a smaller quantity traded and a lower price than a competitive market with the same demand and other costs of production (Boal and Ransom 2010). A protected monopsony is a firm that has received protection of its monopsonist status from the state (Watkins 2012). A monopsony often acquires, and generally maintains, single-buyer status due to restrictions on the entry of other buyers into the market.

A monopsonist controls the demand side of the market with government license or franchise, resource ownership, patents and copyrights, high start-up cost, and decreasing average total cost (Watkins 2012).

Microeconomic theory states that the protected monopsonist takes into account the effect of additional purchases on the price of the commodity. The marginal cost of a purchase is therefore more than the price of the additional purchases (Watkins 2012). A firm faces a positively sloped supply curve (S), yet higher wages are needed to attract more labor. The positively sloped curve is the marginal factor cost curve (MC), and therefore the value of the extra production generated by each worker is the marginal revenue cost curve (MR; Watkins 2012). In other words, the marginal cost of employing one more worker will be higher than the average cost because to employ one extra worker the firm has to increase the wages of all workers. As a profit-maximizing firm, monopsony hires the quantity of workers that equates marginal factor cost and marginal revenue product found at the intersection of the MC and MR curves. Presuming no externality, S is the MC, so its intersection with the MR corresponds to the level of production and consumption such that marginal benefit is equal to marginal cost and both correspond to the market price. If demand for a product falls, the theory suggest wages are likely to fall (Parkin 1993). While most of the literature on monopsony focuses on the price of labor, Agapos and Dunlap (1970) argue that this explanation is inadequate and severely hinders the understanding of the government-industry relationship.

In general, firms that operate within the government-industry market operate differently from those depicted as profit maximizers in conventional microeconomic theory textbooks (Agapos and Dunlap 1970). Agapos and Dunlap argue that the foundation and operation of government-industry competition does not coincide with private spending, and the operation cannot coincide with conventional economic theory. Specifically the government does not seek to make a profit from the services it provides. Thus the traditional tools of microeconomics are inapplicable because they do not effectively explain the price, output, profits, and cost relationship of a private firm when it deals with the government. The theory, once in practice, is not just about price.

As such the government is not a pure monopsonist (Agapos and Dunlap

1970). Agapos and Dunlap point out that the government does not resell any end product and thus makes no attempt to maximize profits. Its only function is to supply services (e.g., national security or defense) to the general population at a reasonable cost (not necessarily the minimum cost). This difference is reflected in the demand curve. Agapos and Dunlap assert that "instead of demand function (f(d)), a variation, call it a 'need' function, is used" (89). Need here is defined as how critical the items are to the government.

A major difference between this "need" curve and a demand curve f(d) is that the assumption of linearity would probably be in error (Agapos and Dunlap 1970). Agapos and Dunlap illustrate that the government's need curve assumes a constant price; that is, because of budgeting constraints there is a fixed amount of funds that the government can use for procurements, and it tries to maximize its utility by striving for the greatest quantity of end product. The government will accept a lower quantity in end product (x–1) for the predetermined costs as its needs increase. Thus if we assume that the government has budgeted to procure a fixed dollar amount, the less the need, the more quantity of end product it demands to receive; the greater the need, the less quantity it will be willing to accept from its supplier.

To illustrate, Agapos and Dunlap (1970) develop a series of need curves relating price to the quantity of end product for different needs. The combination of three variables — quantity of end product, need, and price — result in a *family of curves*. Agapos and Dunlap's model (figure 1) show a series of curves where price is represented by the Y axis and the quantity of the end product by the X axis. The three curves are functions of need. If there is a high priority for some end product (or service), the cumulative maximum price curve is quadratic. The lower the government's need, the more the curve approaches a straight line; see $G(U_h)$ and $G(U_L)$. A medium or intermediate need is depicted by $G(U_m)$ somewhere between the high and how need curves.

In the model developed by Agapos and Dunlap (1970), it is clear that the market relationship between the U.S. military and the private security industry is more about need than price. Although the U.S. military can be categorized as a protected monopsonist, its goal is not to make a profit. Thus price is less of a factor when examining the supply-demand behavior of the U.S. military and the private security industry. To illustrate this behavior,

Government Maximum Price versus Quantity End Product for Different Needs

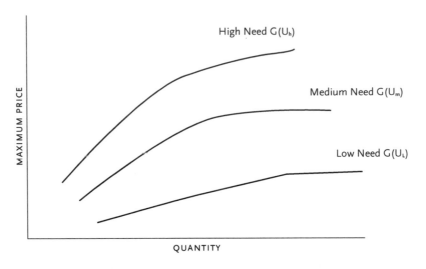

Fig. 1. Family of curves. Source: Agapos and Dunlap 1970.

this study presents a basic model that builds on the microeconomic theory of monopsony and Agapos and Dunlap's theory of need.

The U.S. military requires a certain number of units to meet the national security objectives set out by the president. A unit (x) is the number of soldiers, equipment, services, or organizations required to achieve the objectives. At equilibrium the U.S. military procures one fewer unit to achieve its expected utility $(x-1)$. When the need increases because of conflict, the U.S. military seeks to procure additional units $(x_1, x_2, x_3 \ldots)$ based on the level of need. For example, the U.S. military may choose to activate its reserves (x_1), call National Guard forces (x_2) to active duty, increase the size of the military (x_3), use allied or coalition forces (x_4), hire host-nation contractors (y_1), or hire private military contractors (y_2). Depending on the level of need, the U.S. military may procure the required units using some combination of the following monopsonist model. As such a U.S. military monopsonist model can be illustrated as a simple equation:

$$[(x-1) + x_1 + x_2 + x_3 + x_4 + y_1 + y_2]$$

Although the theory of supply and demand provides the foundation from which the growth of the private security industry can be explained, price is not the determining factor when examining the U.S. military–private security industry relationship. Agapos and Dunlap (1970) argue that the theory of monopsony must be placed in context when examining U.S. government procurement behavior. Therefore the microeconomic theory of monopsony helps explain why demand is the determining factor when examining the increase in PMCs. The theory of monopsony allows a parsimonious model to be developed to help explain the phenomena in this study. In short the U.S. military exhibits monopsonist behavior as its need increases.

The Demand for PMCs

This study asserts that the general theory of supply and demand goes far in explaining the increasing use of PMCs. Singer (2003), Avant (2005) and others (Kidwell 2005; Krahmann 2010) point out that the rise of the private security industry is linked to demand and supply. As the previous section underscores, however, its rise is not driven purely by the market but rather by the needs and constraints of a monopsonist actor: the U.S. military.

BUDGET CONSTRAINTS

Kinsey (2006, 151) points out that "the key factors that define the context of PMCs in the international system are military downsizing, technology, monetary efficiency and political expediency." In particular he asserts that "to a large extent, the increasing reliance on PMCs and PSCs reflects concerns about monitory efficiency and the application of lethal force to save strangers" (96). Carafano (2010, 55) argues that for most of America's history, the federal government's chief budgetary function was funding defense; however, "the two-thirds decline in defense spending since 1962 has substantially altered the makeup and structure of the U.S. national defense." One reason is that mandatory outlays for programs such as Social Security, Medicare, and Medicaid are consuming, and will continue to consume, ever larger percentages of federal spending and the GDP. This increasing pressure on resources available to field more ground troops will likely change how future wars are fought (Carafano 2010).

The U.S. budget for fiscal year 2001 provides a good starting point to demonstrate that military expenditures decreased after the end of the cold war. In 1987 U.S. defense outlays were 28.1 percent of the national budget. By 2001 the U.S. defense outlays were 16.4 percent of the national budget. In 1987 the defense budget represented 6.1 percent of the GDP. By 2001 the defense budget represented only 3.0 percent of GDP. Carafano (2010, 56) concludes that "the upward-spiraling manpower costs and downward-spiraling size of the military have fueled the Pentagon's reliance on contractors." Given the unique market niche they fill, Carafano argues that there are few practical alternatives to PMCs. Thus the extant literature suggests that the decrease in military outlays helps explain the increasing reliance on the private security industry.

DECREASED NATIONAL MILITARIES

Shearer (1998) was the first to suggest that Western military force reductions resulted in an expansion of the private military sector. Furthermore he asserts that "demobilization has released former soldiers on the job market" and "the net result is a sharp increase in expertise in the private sector" (27). The majority of military cutbacks were in support areas, such as logistics (Singer 2003). In addition it is believed that with the end of the cold war, "Americans interpreted a reduced threat to national security that would result in a peace dividend or an accelerated reduction of military size and expenditure" (Kidwell 2005, 27).

Similarly Carafano (2008, 52) explains that "the post–Cold War peace dividend affected all the services. Not only did the numbers drop, but organizations shrank, bases closed, equipment was retired, and civilian employees were let go." Likewise an examination of personnel numbers reveals that "since the end of the Cold War, the U.S. military numbers declined by 780,000 troops in 1991 and 380,000 by 2006, fueling the growth in private contractors" (Kinsey 2006, 95). Ortiz (2010, 52) further suggests that "at least in the United States and the United Kingdom, there appears to be some correlation between the downsizing and the size of their private military industry." In short the literature strongly suggests that the decrease in the size of a nation's military helps explain the increase in the reliance on the private security industry. Concurrent with the reduction in military outlays, the size of the U.S. military decreased as well. In 1987 there were 2,174,217 active duty personnel in the U.S. military. By 2001 that number was 1,376,905 (U.S. Department of Defense, Defense Manpower Data Center, 1954–2012). Additionally the U.S. military reduced the size of its civilian workforce at nearly the same rate: the size of the active U.S. military force decreased by 50 percent. Thus when the size of the U.S. military decreases, it is possible that there is a correlation with the increased use of the private security industry. However, just as the demand market curve pertains to a particular period of time, one must examine the use of PMCs in relation to the environmental conditions. This is particularly evident when increased involvement in conflicts creates a demand for soldiers in uniform.

INCREASED CONFLICT

Some have argued that the driving force behind the privatization of military services has been the increase in global conflict since the end of the cold war (Singer 2003). However, "Western military structures are still largely designed for major total warfare and are often inappropriate for limited interventions" (58). Furthermore as conflicts increase globally, many Western nations "developed a marked intolerance for casualties in conflicts that do not directly threaten the core of the nation" (58). Agreeing with Singer, Kidwell (2005, 27) argues that "the collapse of the Soviet Union spurred the demand for private security and increased military support services."

Ortiz (2010, 7) cautions that "in much of the analysis, PMCs are examined in isolation from the insecure environment encouraging their use." He argues that "the increase in low-intensity conflicts and the perceived lack of effectiveness of United Nations (UN) peacekeepers increases the willingness of some weak states to hire PMCs rather than wait for the UN" (82). Thus the increase in conflict helps explain the increase in the reliance on the private security industry and the increase in demand for the private security industry.

However, according to the Human Security Report Project (2010), the number of conflicts decreased between 1992 and 2006. In 1992 there were fifty-two conflicts. By the time Singer (2003) published his book that number had decreased to twenty-nine. However, by 2006 the number had increased to thirty-four, and between 1989 and 2003 the United States was involved in eight global conflicts. Moreover the United States had much of its military force deployed outside the United States during this time; in 1991 that number was close to 450,000 personnel. In September 2001 there were about 250,000 military personnel deployed overseas. In 2010 the number was over 490,000. It may be that increases in U.S. conflicts and engagements result in the increased use of the private security industry. Thus when a nation's involvement in conflict increases, it is possible that there is a correlation with the increasing use of the private security industry.

As noted earlier, potentially important explanatory variables exist and are not included in supply-demand theory. These variables are examined in the study and may add additional nuance to supply-demand theory, or they may cause us to reconsider the theory and its usefulness for describing the increase in the use of PMCs. One of these variables is bureaucratic controls.

Bureaucratic Controls

A bureaucratic control is defined as the control of an organization and the individuals that make up the organization through standardized rules, policies, written documents, or other formal methods to influence behavior and assess performance. Bureaucratic controls apply corrective measures to ensure that performance achieves the stated objectives. The goal of the control system is to detect and correct discrepancies in execution of the planned activity. According to the philosopher Max Weber (1922), bureaucracies are a rational legal authority whose legitimacy comes from established laws. In the United States the private security industry operates under a set of bureaucratic controls with a standardized set of rules and policies. As such private security companies are not only legal organizations, but they gain legitimacy from the legal authority of the U.S. government.

If Thomson (1994) is correct that de-legitimation and de-legalization led to the end of mercenarism, then it is possible that legalization and legitimation may lead to an increase in private security. Most authors point out that in the United States policy changes enabled a broader use of the private security industry, particularly in the military. In 1996 the U.S. Office of Budget and Management introduced Circular A-76, which laid the foundations for the outsourcing of U.S. military services (Krahmann 2010). However, for much of the nation's history, laws were in place preventing the use of mercenaries.

From the very beginning the United States sought to control the privatization of military force within its borders (Thomson 1994). For example, the Neutrality Act of 1794 (which remains in force with amendments) is the first domestic law in the world to deal specifically with the problem of hostile expedition against foreign countries (such as piracy); it serves as a model for other nations (Thomson 1994). The neutrality laws forbid anyone other than the U.S. central state from raising an army within the territory of the United States to attack a state with which the United States is at peace and prohibits individuals from selling their services as soldiers to another state while within the jurisdiction of the United States. Individuals are also forbidden from hiring others into the service of a state when the transaction is completed within the United States and are prohibited from organizing military expeditions against foreign political entities in their own private interests (Thomson 1994). Shearer (1998) points out that the Neutrality Act of 1795 made it a misdemeanor for an individual to prepare or depart for a conflict abroad.

Likewise in 1798 the U.S. Congress passed legislation to guide the process of military procurement (Kidwell 2005). The U.S. Congress continued its legislative oversight of government contracts through the eighteenth and nineteenth centuries. At the end of World War I the National Defense Act of 1920 returned many contracted military logistics responsibilities to military agencies (Kidwell 2005). Shearer (1998) notes that a new Neutrality Act was introduced in 1937, but it is interpreted as prohibiting the recruitment of mercenaries only within the United States; being a mercenary is not in itself a criminal offense.

Krahmann (2010) asserts that the Clinton administration's expressed objective was to aggressively pursue the outsourcing and privatization of public services and to introduce new management procedures in those public sectors that could not be privatized. In the United States the push for outsourcing of military activities can be traced to the 1996 release of the revised Office of Management and Budget Circular A-76 (Grasso 2013).[1] As a result the first comprehensive multifunctional Logistics Civil Augmentation Program umbrella support contract was awarded in August 1992 to support all U.S. services and United Nations forces in Somalia. In 1998 the Clinton administration introduced the Federal Activities Inventory Reform Act, which succeeded in providing the government with a basis for increasing pressure to expand the use of private suppliers by offering concrete data on the number and types of services that could potentially be outsourced to the private sector (Krahmann 2010, 128).

The U.S. government controls and regulates the international supply of defense articles and services (such as weapons, military supplies, and military advice and training) through the Arms Export Control Act (AECA), first implemented in 1968 (Ortiz 2010). Defense services are defined as furnishing assistance to foreign persons in the development or maintenance of defense articles and military training of foreign units and forces (Ortiz 2010). The AECA confers on the president the authority to control the export and import of defense articles and services (Ortiz 2010). The U.S. Department of State manages the International Traffic in Arms Regulation (ITAR), which controls and regulates defense services outside the United States. The ITAR requires the registration and licensing of U.S. persons willing to export defense articles and services. This means that any U.S. private contractor working overseas must register with the U.S. Department of State and receive a license before services can be provided.

In 1986 the U.S. Congress passed the Diplomatic Security and Anti-Terrorism Act, which authorized the Department of State to use private security contractors to provide for security in support of U.S. missions overseas (U.S. Congress, House, CWC 2009). This legislation followed in the wake of the 1983 attack on the U.S. Embassy in Beirut. Since that time the U.S. Department of State has employed private security contractors in Haiti, Yugoslavia, Palestine, Afghanistan, and Iraq. In 2010 the Department of State requested that Congress approve a request to use between 6,000 and 7,000 private security contractors in Iraq alone to protect U.S. government personnel and facilities (U.S. Congress, House, CWC 2010)

As described earlier, Singer (2003) asserts that massive military demobilizations provided a large pool of labor for the PMF industry and cheapening of start-up capital this was not possible prior to 1995. The Ethics Reform Act of 1989 imposed criminal liability on government employees who engage in prohibited conflicts of interest. Among other things, the act restricted the ability of former government employees to represent contractors before the government and the ability of current government employees to negotiate employment with contractors (Szeliga 2007). However, amendments to the Joint Federal Regulation lifted the five-year restriction on military personnel from obtaining employment by a private contractor. This change essentially allowed a military member to leave military service one day and begin working for a private contractor the next.

Across history bureaucratic controls have allowed policymakers to control the private security industry, particularly its recruitment of a trained labor pool and its ability to provide services outside of the United States. Policymakers can reduce or eliminate the use of private security contractors with the amendments to the existing laws. Therefore if bureaucratic controls on the private security industry decrease, it is possible that there will be a correlation with the increased use of the private security industry.

Of course there may be other variables that impact the use of PSCs and PMCs. While this study focuses on the five highlighted in the existing literature, it also holds out the possibility that in-depth case studies will reveal additional influences on the increasing use of PSCs and PMCs. If additional explanatory variables are found in the case studies, they will be analyzed in the quantitative portion of the study and possibly be added to the explanatory framework. Next is an examination of the rise of the private security industry.

Measuring the Increased Use of the Private Security Industry

Most scholars assert that there has been an increase in the use of private security since the end of the cold war. Various terms such as *expansion* (Shearer 1998), *emerging* (Singer 2003), *tidal wave* (Singer 2003), *proliferation* (Kidwell 2005), and *burgeoning* (Avant 2005) are used to describe the increase in the use of the industry. However, the literature is inconsistent on how to measure the private security industry. Some scholars (Isenberg 2009) use specific numbers of contractors in Iraq as evidence of an increase, while others

(Carafano 2008) use the number of companies to demonstrate the increase. Unfortunately these statistics provide evidence only from a particular period of time and a specific location.

Krahmann (2010) uses U.S. military procurement data to demonstrate an increase in the use of PMCs, which may provide a more accurate measure. For example, contractors are persons or businesses who provide products or services for monetary compensation and furnish supplies or services or perform work for a certain rate of pay based on the terms of the contract (Carafano 2008). Thus a contract for private security most likely does not specify how many contractors to hire, only what service to provide.

Most scholars begin their measurement of the industry with the end of the cold war, 1989. Isenberg (2009) suggests that the private military industry is neither as new nor as big as frequently claimed; he points out that it is evident that civilians have always been instrumental to military operations and have often been in harm's way in support of the military. He concludes that there has been an increased prominence given to the reemergence of an old phenomenon. This study measures the actual number of private contractors used during a U.S. conflict.

Most scholars point out the differences in the use of contractors during conflict based on the ratio of contractor to military. While it may be true that there has been an increase in the use of the private security in the post–cold war era, it is certainly not a new phenomenon, nor are the numbers particularly large in comparison to earlier conflicts. However, "understanding why the private sector has come to play such a prominent role in public wars requires tracing a story as torturous and, at times, as mysterious as the search for the Holy Grail, a tale filled with deceit, greed, courage, selflessness, stupidity, misdirection, and myth" (Carafano 2008, 12).

One of the limitations of the existing literature is the availability of empirical data. Singer (2003) and Avant (2005) provide very little empirical evidence to support their claim that military downsizing and increased conflict result in an increase in the private security industry. Given that the scholarly work does not often rely explicitly on the theory of supply and demand, it is not surprising that the empirical evidence does not exist, even though data are available for examination. However, various U.S. government statistical databases and reports provide some initial evidence to support the claims in the literature.

Another challenge with the literature is the identification of multiple causes for the increased use of private contractors. Multiple causation results in overdetermination, which occurs when several causes are present, any one of which could have produced the observed outcome (Thompson 2003). Failure to rank-order these causes and explore the relationship between or among them can make such explanations difficult to refute and easy to confirm tautologically (Lebow 2001). It may be that some scholars are looking for a parsimonious explanation for a seemingly complex event, yet whether their explanations are applicable in a wide range of situations requires further testing.

This study will add precision to our understanding of the causes of the increased use of the private security industry. It moves beyond descriptive accounts and advances a parsimonious theory to explain the phenomenon. This study thus advances our knowledge through the application of the theory of supply and demand to the investigation of the increasing use of PMCs.

Of course the growing acceptance of PMCs in foreign policy decisions is of more than academic interest. As their use has grown over recent decades, questions about their control and status are being raised in the domestic political arena. Their legitimacy is being challenged by sovereign governments where U.S.-based PMCs are deployed. PMCs are also becoming a large market force in the United States and internationally, offering competencies and services not readily available to some nation-states. This study should thus not only fill a gap in the existing academic literature on private security industry; it should provide valuable information to those shaping policy as well.

This study maintains that the private security industry fills vacuums created when the U.S. government does not have the means or the will to provide domestic and international security. It will also examine the impact that other variables (not examined in the literature) have on the U.S. military's use of private security forces, including bureaucratic controls, force caps, and host-nation permissiveness. Understanding the broader context of the private security industry's relationship to mature democracies enables the current debate to be expanded to reflect how domestic choices impact foreign policy choices. Based on a review of the literature, this study focuses on five hypotheses:

> *Hypothesis 1*: The theory of supply and demand posits that when military outlays decrease there should be an increase in the use of the private security industry.
>
> *Hypothesis 2*: The theory of supply and demand asserts that when the size of a national military decreases there should be an increase in the use of the private security industry.
>
> *Hypothesis 3*: The theory of supply and demand states that when the number of military disputes, engagements, and conflicts increases there should be an increase in the use of the private security industry.
>
> *Hypothesis 4*: The theory of supply and demand posits that when the duration of a military conflict increases there is a likely increase in the use of the private security industry.
>
> *Hypothesis 5*: According to the theory of supply and demand, when there is a decrease in bureaucratic controls and regulations there should be an increase in the utilization of the private security industry.

Kidwell (2005, 65), Avant (2005, 253), and Singer (2003, 230) hypothesize that the use of the private security industry will continue to increase not only in the United States but throughout the international community. That increased use will impact foreign policy decisions, domestic decisions on force structure, and international regulatory regimes. The goal of this research is to test the hypotheses and to determine the validity of a supply-demand theory of the private security industry. If the parsimonious theory is correct, it will provide scholars and policymakers with relatively easy, traceable indicators that may help predict whether the United States or other advanced democracies might experience rising or decreasing levels of private security industry. Additionally the results may inform policymakers involved in developing solutions to foreign policy problems requiring military intervention in areas not directly related to immediate or evident national security concerns. State policymakers may be able to use the results of the study to inform decisions on military budgeting, structure, or civil-military relations.

CHAPTER TWO

A QUALITATIVE EXAMINATION OF
THE PRIVATE SECURITY INDUSTRY

This chapter introduces the qualitative approach to test the explanatory power of private security supply-demand theory. The theory predicts that if the size of the national military decreases one should find an increased demand for the private security industry. Likewise as U.S. involvement in conflict increases there should be an increased demand for the private security industry. Moreover the theory predicts that decision makers will choose between not becoming involved in conflict or choosing to use private security to fill gaps in security gaps left by diminishing military forces, depending on which has the lower cost. By analyzing the historical record of specific U.S. conflicts, this study can track distinct policies, events, and decisions that led to the increased use of the private security industry by the United States. This research also creates approximate measures of supply-demand choices in a much wider array of cases to cross-validate whether the case study findings are specific to just a few conflicts. Therefore the following case studies and statistical analysis serve to reinforce one another. The case studies include the U.S. involvement in the first Gulf War (1991), Bosnia (1995), Afghanistan (2001), and Iraq (2003). Each case allows the reader to directly compare the supply-demand choices with historical events.

The case study approach is a detailed examination of an aspect of a historical episode to develop or test historical explanations that may be generalizable to other events (George and Bennett 2005). The approach has a number of strengths: it allows a researcher to achieve high levels of conceptual validity; it can help identify new variables and hypotheses; it can examine the operations of causal mechanisms in individual cases in detail; and it has the ability to accommodate complex causal relations such as equifinality, complex interactions effects, and path dependency (George and Bennett 2005). The strongest means of drawing inferences from case studies is the use of a combination of within-case analysis and cross-case comparisons with a single study or research program (George and Bennett 2005). This study relies on the strength of this combined approach to examine the increased use of the private security industry.

The case study approach does involve a trade-off among the goals of attaining theoretical parsimony, establishing explanatory richness, and keeping the number of cases to be studied manageable (George and Bennett 2005). Case study researchers are more interested in finding the conditions under which specific outcomes occur and the mechanisms through which they occur rather than uncovering the frequency with which those conditions and their outcomes arise (George and Bennett 2005, 31; Flyvbjerg 2006, 223). Some have argued that case studies produce context-dependent knowledge and that in the study of human affairs, there appears to exist only context-dependent knowledge (Flyvbjerg 2006).

This study relies on the method and logic of structured, focused cross-comparison to examine the four cases under review. This cross-comparison method is structured in such a way that the researcher writes general questions that reflect the research objective and that these questions are asked of each case under study to guide and standardize data collection, thereby making possible systematic comparison and accumulation of the findings of the cases (George and Bennett 2005). The method is a within-case analysis since it deals only with specific aspects within the historical cases examined. The method was devised to study historical experience in ways that would yield useful generic knowledge of important foreign policy problems (George and Bennett 2005). The method of structured, focused comparison asks the same questions to different problems representing different foreign policy situations to identify similarities in factors and conditions across the situations. The method also requires that the study be focused; that is, it should be undertaken with a specific research objective in mind and a theoretical focus appropriate for that objective (George and Bennett 2005).

Following King et al. (1994), this study includes significant variation on the independent (or causal) variables of interest. In the context of testing the private security choices of the United States and other Western democracies, this method suggests finding cases with differing expectations of the utility of using the private security industry to supplement the national military. The four cases include both longitudinal and cross-sectional variance on key concepts such as bureaucratic controls, intensity of violence in the target state, the duration of the intervention, the size of the military, the military budget outlays, and the number of conflicts of the participants during a given year. For example, the U.S. intervention in Iraq (1991) happened shortly after the end of the cold war and just prior to the decrease in the size of the U.S. military. Decision makers were in the early stages of using the private security industry to support military operations. The U.S. intervention in Iraq (2003) occurred at a time when privatization was at its peak, the size of the U.S. military was half the size of the 1991 military, and decision makers were fully committed to using the private security industry to support military operations. In addition each conflict reviewed was a conflict of choice. Although political leaders asserted that each was vital to the national security, the United States was threatened neither directly nor indirectly by the target nations involved. Thus decision makers made choices prior to the intervention to rely on the private security industry to supplement military operations or not become involved in the conflict because of insufficient availability of troops.

Similarly there is considerable variation in the type of U.S. intervention reflected in the reviewed cases, particularly their scope and duration. The size of the U.S. intervention in Iraq (1991) was significantly larger than in Bosnia or Iraq (2003), but the duration was considerably shorter. In contrast, the size of the U.S. intervention in Bosnia was much smaller compared to the other cases; however, the duration of the Bosnia intervention lasted significantly longer than political or military planners anticipated. The size of the intervention in Iraq (2003) was much smaller than actions in Iraq in 1991, yet the Iraq intervention was far longer in duration than military planners had predicted. Furthermore the commitment of U.S. forces around the world in places such as Europe and Korea limits their use to military planners. Exogenous factors play a role in the decisions made as well as add uncertainty to outcomes once there is an onset of conflict.

Several questions guide the cross-comparison case study analysis. The important device of formulating a set of standardized, general question to ask of each case will be of value only if those questions are grounded in and adequately reflect the theoretical perspective and research objectives of the study (George and Bennett 2005). This research will use the following questions to focus the comparison both across and within cases:

1. What is the rate of involvement of the private security industry in each intervention? This question attempts to determine how many private military contractors and private security contractors participated in the intervention. Two factors are examined: actual numbers of private security contractors (where data are available) and the amount of military procurement funds spent on contracts during the intervention (following Krahmann 2010).

2. What role did the private security industry play during each intervention? The roles that the private security industry played (support or security) should provide insights into how much support a host nation provides and the permissiveness of the security situation in the target country.

3. What laws, regulation, and controls were in place during the intervention? This question specifies the limitations or constraints of U.S. bureaucratic controls on the private security industry. It is possible that the more limitations and constraints, the less the private security industry is used, and when limitations and constraints are removed, the more private security is used. Legalization of the private security industry is assumed to be necessary (see Thomson 1994).

4. What was the duration of the conflict? Examining the duration of the conflict, specifically from the beginning of the deployment of forces until a drawdown in the conflict area, is important since military forces require logistics support, technical advice, and security even when not directly involved in combat. The expected duration of the intervention is contrasted with the actual duration to analyze decision makers' planning assumptions. The duration of the intervention should reveal whether decision makers' choices in

utilizing private security forces changed during the conflict based on expected price or a change in price.

5. What was the scope of the conflict? Specifically how many troops were used during the intervention? This question attempts to determine if the scale of the intervention results in an increased use of the private security industry. There should be an increase in private military support in relation to the number of troops used during a conflict. Additionally how the military forces were staged for the intervention, employed during the conflict, and arrayed at the end of hostilities should reveal the scope of the conflict. For example, if the military force deployed from one main base, limited its intervention to a small portion of the rival's country, and redeployed through one main base, we should see a smaller use of the private security industry in support.

6. What other conflicts or deployments were ongoing during the same time period? Due to the finite amount of the total forces available to commit to a conflict, it is necessary to determine how many other military commitments exist that potentially reduce the availability of the total military force.

7. How many troops participated in other conflicts or deployments during the same time period? This question examines the larger role of the military in international affairs. The commitment of military forces to areas other than the intervention limits their availability to participate in any given conflict. The result should be an increased demand for the private security industry to fill the gap in available military assets.

8. What was the size of the military during the conflict? The number of military forces available during the time of the intervention includes all branches of the U.S. military, reserve, and National Guard forces. Although the active military force is immediately available, policymakers must choose to activate reserve and National Guard forces. It is possible that as the overall size of the military decreases one should expect to see an increase in reliance on the private security industry (Avant 2005; Singer 2003). Additionally this question should highlight the opportunity costs or shifts in supply that policymakers face when choosing between the private security industry and national armies.

9. What percentage of the national budget did military outlays represent during the conflict? This question looks at the U.S. military defense budget

at the time of the intervention from the standpoint of total dollars spent on defense as a percentage of gross domestic product and a percentage of the U.S. budget outlays dedicated to defense. As the size of the defense budget decreases over time, there should be an increased reliance on the private security industry due to decreased spending on national armies. This should illustrate a shift in the supply curve away from higher costs of personnel for national armies.

10. Did policymakers or military leaders have choices other than using the private security industry? If so, did they use them? These questions look beyond the availability of national armies and military budgets to determine if policymakers had choices available other than the private security industry. For example, increased participation of allies, coalition partners, and host nations should provide an alternative to the private security industry.

The case studies rely on information from diplomatic, military, and personal histories, as well as original government documents. In all cases there are sufficient primary and secondary sources to reconstruct the cases. As Gaddis (2002) notes, many times historians themselves disagree over the interpretation of past events and the interpretation of choice may be incorrect. In each case, where contradictions are found, the historical interpretations are explained in relation to their bearing on the argument, where applicable.

CHAPTER THREE

OPERATIONS DESERT SHIELD AND DESERT STORM

This chapter provides the first cross-comparison case test using Operations Desert Shield and Desert Storm, the Coalition offensive in the Persian Gulf War from 17 January to 28 February 1991. The argument is that the details of Desert Shield and Desert Storm contradict assertions in the literature on private security; however, the results tend to corroborate the theory as an early post–cold war example of private security supply-demand behavior. The war's main lesson for most observers — that few contractors were used — is inconsistent with the conflict's actual conduct. The Coalition's low contractor count cannot be explained without considering the nature of the intervention, the decisions by senior Coalition leaders on force deployment, and the support provided by the Saudi government.

The cross-comparison method requires each of the historical cases to be reviewed in a similar manner; therefore for each case, including those in upcoming chapters, the following structure will be applied. The motivation and rationale for selecting the case will be reviewed, then a description is provided of the main events of the conflict. Next is a discussion of key independent variables for the conflict. The role of private military contractors and the supply-demand theory and other considerations will be assessed in regard to the conflict's outcomes. A summary assessment concludes the section.

Operations Desert Shield and Desert Storm are considered a least likely case (George and Bennett 2005), in which extreme values make the theory unusually unlikely to succeed; even if the theory were generally valid, under such unfavorable conditions it might well fail anyway (Biddle 2004). Theories that survive the difficult test of a least likely case may prove to be generally applicable to many types of cases, as they have already proven their robustness in the presence of countervailing mechanisms (George and Bennett 2005). King et al. (1994) suggest that if the investigator chooses a case study that seems on a priori grounds unlikely to accord with the theoretical predictions—a least likely observation—but the theory turns out to be correct regardless, the theory will have passed a difficult test, and we will have reason to support it with greater confidence. Eckstein (1975) argues that in a least likely case the independent variable is at a level that supports only a weak prediction; however, because it nonetheless produces an outcome it is strong supporting evidence for the theory. Therefore, the strongest affirming evidence for a theory is a case wherein the theory makes only a weak prediction: a least likely case.[1]

There are many reasons private security contractors should not have been used in Desert Storm; however, they were used anyway. When the war began the size of the U.S. military and its budget were essentially at their peak cold war levels. Although the scope of the intervention was significant, it lasted less than a year. Aside from the military commitments to NATO and Korea, the United States faced very few competing conflicts around the world during the time of the intervention. More important, the ratio of private military contractors to military forces was smaller than in interventions of subsequent decades. Even so, U.S. military leaders required close to 10,000 private contractors to support operations in Saudi Arabia (Isenberg 2009).

Although the operations in Kuwait and Iraq occur in the post–cold war era, scholars such as Singer (2003), Avant (2005), tend to overlook this case when studying the rise of the private security industry. At first glance the case does not possess the causal factors forwarded in the supply-demand theory. However, the key lies not in the theory's gross predictions for the use of the private security industry but in the underlying conditions in which the United States found itself after the cold war.

The lower ratio of private contractors used in Desert Shield and Desert Storm obscures the fact that the United States was able to achieve its goals because of their use. The question is why private contractors were needed and why the ratio was lower relative to other interventions. What initial conditions existed that resulted in the use of private contractors? The outcome is important in its own right, and it also provides critical methodological leverage in distinguishing the relative validity of the theory. As such the case offers a challenging test as a least likely case because of benefits to the overall analysis.

Overview of Events

In the months preceding the Iraqi invasion of Kuwait, Iraq was nearly $90 billion in debt after its war with Iran in 1980–88 (Powell 1995). President Saddam Hussein blamed Kuwait and the United Arab Emirates for preventing Iraq from working its way out of this massive debt. He charged that "they had thrust a poisoned dagger into Iraq's back" (Powell 1995, 459; Herspring 2005) by busting the oil quotas set by the Organization of Petroleum Exporting Countries, thus driving the price down and reducing Iraq's income. Furthermore Saddam claimed that Kuwait had siphoned off $2.5 billion in oil from the Rumaila field, which the two countries shared (Powell 1995, 460). He covetously eyed two Kuwaiti-held islands, Warba and Bubiyan, which blocked his access to the Gulf and asserted that the Kuwaitis were not Arab brothers, but "greedy lapdogs" of the West (460). In mid-July 1990 the Iraqis deployed three armored divisions along the Kuwaiti border to intimidate the Kuwaiti leadership (Woodward 1991); by the end of July all indications were that the Iraqis would attack (Powell 1995; Woodward 1991).

At 0200 hours on 2 August 1990 the Hammurabi Armored Division and the Tawakalna Mechanized Division of the Iraqi Republican Guard crossed the Kuwait border and quickly overran the single Kuwaiti brigade deployed along the frontier. The Kuwaiti brigade had little hope of checking the onslaught of nearly one thousand T-72 tanks. By evening the Iraqi Army had secured Kuwait City and begun establishing defensive positions along the Kuwait-Saudi border (Scales 1994; Sultan 1995). It took less than a day for Iraq to overcome organized Kuwaiti resistance (Pagonis and Cruikshank 1992). Iraq's violation of the sovereignty of a weak Arab state was the sufficient cause of the Gulf War of 1990–91. Swain (1994) observes that this action alone—which threatened Saudi Arabia, the minor Gulf States, and the regional and global economic balance of power—called the anti-Iraq Coalition into existence.

Pagonis and Cruikshank (1992, 6) assert, "To this day it remains a mystery why Saddam Hussein didn't continue his advance through Kuwait and on into Saudi Arabia." On the day of the invasion, the United Nations Security Council passed Resolution 660, condemning the invasion and calling for the immediate and unconditional withdrawal of Iraqi forces from Kuwait (Swain 1994). Swain points out that "with the collapse of the old world order, a clear precedent was called for in the form of united military action that would punish this wanton act by a mighty nation against a weak one and place it beyond the pale of legitimate international behavior" (1). In addition to the UN resolution, the United States imposed an embargo on Iraq, and President George H. W. Bush ordered the U.S. Joint Chiefs of Staff to begin deployment of air force tanker squadrons and the movement of the USS *Independence* Carrier Battle Group into the North Arabian Sea (Swain 1994).

On 6 August 1990 King Fahd of Saudi Arabia requested U.S. assistance in the defense of his country (Woodward 1991). That same day the UN Security Council passed Resolution 661, calling for an international embargo on Iraq and occupied Kuwait, and on the following day President Bush directed the commitment of U.S. military forces to the defense of Saudi Arabia (Swain 1994). U.S. Secretary of Defense Dick Cheney called Gen. Colin Powell, the chairman of the U.S. Joint Chiefs, from Jidda, Saudi Arabia, and issued the order to start moving troops to Saudi Arabia (Powell 1995, 467; Herspring 2005). Pagonis and Cruikshank (1992, 67) explain, "The mission was to deploy American troops and weaponry into Saudi Arabia to establish a defensive position and deter an invasion of the Kingdom (of Saudi Arabia) by the Iraqi forces occupying Kuwait." Thus began the military actions of August 1990 to January 1991 (Operation Desert Shield) and those of January 1991 and February 1991 (Operation Desert Storm).

Swain (1994, 1) writes, "The war occurred in a 'new world' context. . . . The old post–World War II framework of Soviet-American confrontation had been supplanted by a new multipolar global community." Operations Desert Shield and Desert Storm were part of the strategic response by the United States, Saudi Arabia, and their Coalition partners to the Iraqi aggression. The

Gulf War was thus a coalition war, and it remained a war of limited objectives. At no time was the destruction of Iraq a serious consideration (Swain 1994).

Beginning on 10 August 1990 the first U.S. ground combat soldiers departed for Saudi Arabia. By the end of the month more than 12,000 soldiers from the 82nd Airborne Division were on the ground (Scales 1994). President Bush announced in the same month that his stated goal was "the immediate, complete, and unconditional withdrawal of all Iraqi forces from Kuwait; and the restoration of Kuwait's legitimate government"(Powell 1995, 470).

Powell (1995) writes that the first offensive planning discussion occurred in Washington on 6 October. Just after the midterm elections on 8 November, President Bush announced that another 200,000 U.S. troops were on their way to the Gulf (Herspring 2005). Bush stated that their mission was "to insure that the coalition has an adequate offensive military option" (Powell 1995, 489). This action signaled a transition from Operation Desert Shield, the defensive phase, to planning for Operation Desert Storm, the offensive phase. On 29 November the UN passed Resolution 678 authorizing *all necessary means* to remove Iraq from Kuwait, making it clear that the mission was only to free Kuwait (Powell 1995).

Operation Desert Storm began on 17 January just after midnight Saudi Arabia time, when Coalition air forces launched an assault on strategic and military targets in Iraq and Kuwait (Pagonis and Cruikshank 1992). After thirty-eight days of continuous air attacks on targets in Iraq and Kuwait, Bush directed the U.S. Central Command to proceed with the ground offensive; in just under one hundred hours the United States and its Coalition partners destroyed or forced the withdrawal of the forty-three Iraqi army divisions defending Kuwait (Stewart 2010). The objectives of Operation Desert Shield and Operation Desert Storm were achieved. At midnight on 27 February 1991 the United States suspended military operations in Iraq. The Iraqi Army had withdrawn from Kuwait (Powell 1995).

Private Contractors in Operations Desert Shield and Desert Storm

U.S. forces rapidly deployed to Saudi Arabia with very little warning to fight on a distant and unexpected battleground; thus establishing the basis for an indigenous assistance and contracting program became a critical component of the overall logistical effort (Stewart 2010). With over 60 percent of the army's logistics support personnel in the reserves, the United States would be dependent on supplies and fuel from Saudi Arabia (Woodward 1991). An agreement for peacetime and wartime help had long been in force between the United States and the Federal Republic of Germany, where the United States had thousands of soldiers, but none covered the American presence in Saudi Arabia until 1990 (Stewart 2010; Herspring 2005).

Swain (1994) and Sultan (1995) suggest that because of the heavy investment of oil revenues in modernization and the need to accommodate the annual influx of pilgrims to the Islamic holy sites, the Saudi commercial structure was already heavily dependent on contracting as a way of doing business. This structure facilitated the acquisition of large-scale support to sustain U.S. and Coalition forces. Gen. Gus Pagonis, the senior logistics officer to U.S. Central Command, responsible for all logistics support in Saudi Arabia, including all contracting, points out that the early goal of logistics in Saudi Arabia was to establish civilian infrastructure to support a now definite U.S. intervention. He explains that the United States had to deploy combat forces as rapidly as possible; therefore logistics forces had to wait, and to fill the logistical void the United States had to use host-nation assets (Pagonis and Cruikshank 1992). Saudi general Khaled Bin Sultan (1995, 284) asserts that "the Gulf War was a quartermaster's heaven because supplies were abundant and support was lavish."

Pagonis describes his work to fill the logistical void: "In effect, I would be doing a market survey, much as a corporation does when it contemplates opening a new facility. In many cases, subcontracting for facilities, personnel, and other resources is much more cost-effective than shipping all needed assets to the new site" since there was such an urgent need to get fighters on the ground (Pagonis and Cruikshank 1992, 76). Whenever a military unit needed supplies or equipment, a contracting officer would simply pay cash on the spot and send the bill to the Saudis (Pagonis and Cruikshank 1992). In the first months of the buildup, the U.S. Support Command had to go to extraordinary lengths to purchase goods and services fast enough to keep up with the accelerating arrival of troops. Housing, transportation, and food were contracted locally from the Saudis (Scales 1994; Sultan 1995).

In the early days of Desert Shield, Pagonis and Cruikshank (1992) asserts, many of his questions had to do with contracting, which he took to be the key sustainment issue. Satisfying as many supply requirements as possible from local sources allowed for a reduction in the number of American support units ultimately deployed to the theater of operation (Stewart 2010). Fortunately for the United States and its Coalition partners, the Saudi Arabian government made it clear from the start that it would shoulder many of the expenses of the deployment (Stewart 2010; Sultan 1995). As Herspring (2005) suggests, the cooperation of the Saudis was the key to the success of Desert Shield and Desert Storm.

In response to support requests, the Saudis reacted energetically and cooperatively, providing 4,800 tents, 1,073,500 gallons of packaged petroleum products, 333 heavy-equipment trailers (HETs), 20 million meals, and 20.5 million gallons of fuel per day, as well as bottled water for the entire theater and supplies for Iraqi prisoners of war, transportation within Saudi Arabia, real estate and facilities construction, and civilian labor support (Scales 1994; Stewart 2010; Bourque 2002). By December that assistance was valued at $2.5 billion over one year (Stewart 2010). Over 600 Saudi contractors and subcontractors supported the Coalition logistic requirements (Sultan 1995).

Pagonis asserts that during Desert Shield and Desert Storm, his support command drew up, executed, and monitored over 70,000 contracts (Pagonis and Cruikshank 1992). Sultan (1995) writes that over 592 Saudi companies' secured war contracts, in addition to the thousands of individuals who rented their houses, vehicles, and other items of equipment. However, not all items were contracted through the Saudis. Powell (1995, 496) points out that when there was a shortage of shelter, the West Germans provided the huge tents they used for festivals. In addition to the 333 HETs provided by Saudi Arabia, 270 HETs were leased from Czechoslovakia, East Germany, and Poland (Scales 1994).

The system of Saudi support and contracting matured with time and helped sustain American forces in theater (Stewart 2010); for example, army logistics officers contracted for buses and materials-handling equipment to move soldiers and their baggage through the airport at Dhahran (Scales 1994; Bourque 2002). Because the heat in Saudi Arabia hovered somewhere in the range of 120 degrees in the afternoon, Pagonis sent his logistics officers into the local community in search of bottled water and refrigerated vans: "We needed to secure permission from the king to procure fresh food and fruit, along with other critical goods and services, from the local economy" (Pagonis and Cruikshank 1992, 72). He points out that locally procured food was both better and cheaper than meals ready to eat, which cost about $4 apiece and for which soldiers developed a number of colorful nicknames.

A Saudi, Zahir Masri, had been ordered by the king to feed the American troops (Sultan 1995). Pagonis and Cruikshank (1992) describe him as a highly successful food producer and distributor in Saudi Arabia. Masri contracted for Saudi and Filipino cooks and set up mess halls throughout the theater. He served produce from Astra Foods, the largest covered farm operation in the world, which was already on contract by King Fahd to feed the Saudi military. In all, Astra Foods subcontracted with over 125 Saudi companies to supply food to the Coalition, serving over 300,000 troops per day with these contract meals, paid for by King Fahd (Sultan 1995). Pagonis and Cruikshank suggest that the generosity of the king, as well as the entrepreneurial spirit, greatly improved the quality of life for the U.S. and Coalition soldiers and insist that the food supplied by Masri had a direct impact on the success of the war.

When it came time to move the two U.S. Army corps into attack position in western Saudi Arabia, Pagonis turned to contractors for support; for the logisticians in theater and their colleagues back in the United States, the flanking movement represented an enormous challenge (Pagonis and Cruikshank 1992). VII Corps was trucked 330 miles across the desert, and XVIII Corps was trucked 500 miles west and north (Bourque 2002). This required Pagonis to assemble nearly 4,000 heavy vehicles of all types, many of which had to be contracted for and for which drivers had to be hired. He determined that by using rented buses it was a fairly simple task to relocate the forward divisions in the desert and to set them up with temporary Bedouin-tent quarters (Pagonis and Cruikshank 1992). Additionally he needed large numbers of HETs, big flatbed trucks with a huge carrying capacity (Clancy and Franks 1997). The army had only 112 HETs in theater, but Coalition allies had additional HETs, and the Saudi private sector was willing to rent more, with which Pagonis was able to assemble a fleet of nearly 1,300 HETs and tractor trailers, most of which came equipped with experienced third-country national drivers to move the two U.S. Army corps west (Pagonis and Cruikshank 1992; Sultan 1995).

Pagonis and Cruikshank (1992) suggest that contracted support was the key to survival in the desert. Likewise Scales (1994) concludes that Saudi contributions substantially shortened the time needed to prepare for combat and undoubtedly shortened the length of the conflict once hostilities commenced. Thus although the number of recorded contractors supporting the United States during Operations Desert Shield and Desert Storm were relatively low compared to subsequent decades, this obscures the fact that the Saudi Arabian government provided substantial support to the United States and its Coalition partners.

The Number of Private Contractors Used

What was the number of PMCs used during the intervention? To answer this question two factors are examined: actual numbers of private security contractors (where available) and the Department of Defense procurement funds spent on contracts during the intervention (measures utilized by Krahmann 2010). This question also explores what role the private security industry played in the intervention: support (PMC) or security (PSC).

Approximately 10,000 contractors supported military operations in Saudi Arabia, almost a 1:58 ratio of military troops to private contractors (Isenberg 2009). The United States relied on private contractors to provide logistic support and transportation to combat troops. The majority of the private contractors were third-country nationals working in Saudi Arabia. There is insufficient data on how many private contractors were U.S. citizens.

In 1990 the Department of Defense spent over $157 billion a year on procurement contracts. Of this total Defense spent an average of $47 billion a year on service contracts, about 31 percent of the total procurement purchases. The estimated cost for Operations Desert Shield and Desert Storm was $61 billion. The United States contributed $7.4 billion, while Saudi Arabia contributed over $16 billion (Sultan 1995).

Examining the laws, regulations, and controls in place during Operations Desert Shield and Desert Storms aids in specifying the limitations and constraints of U.S. bureaucratic controls in place for the use of the private security industry. According to the theory of supply and demand, the more limitations and constraints, the less likely the private security industry will be used; conversely the fewer bureaucratic limitations and controls, the easier it is to employ the private security industry and therefore the greater the likelihood of their increased use.

At the beginning of Desert Shield and Desert Storm there were few legal constraints barring the use of the private military industry. Controls on civilian contracting in support of military operations were governed by Department of the Army pamphlet 690-80, *Use and Administration of Locals in Foreign Areas during Hostilities*, dated 12 February 1971, and U.S. Army Regulation 700-137, Logistics Civil Augmentation Program (LOGCAP) dated 16 December 1985. The U.S. Department of the Army (1971, 2) pamphlet states, "In order to conserve military manpower and reduce logistical support requirements, maximum use will be made of the services of available local national civilian personnel, consistent with operational requirements and the essential manpower needs of the local economy." Regulation 700-137 (U.S. Department of the Army 1985, 1) states, "The objective of LOGCAP is to preplan for the use of civilian contractors to perform selected services in wartime to augment Army forces." Civilian contractors in a theater of operation can fill shortfalls in the military forces available or release military units for other missions and provide the army with an additional means to adequately support the current and programmed forces in theater.

In general Regulation 700-137 (U.S. Department of the Army 1985, 2) asserts, "The Army continually seeks to increase its combat potential within peacetime resource allocations. To achieve the maximum combat potential, maximum support from as many sources as possible is necessary. This requires pursuit of support from external resources." One method of external support suggested by the regulation is host-nation support, typically negotiated through government-to-government agreements. The aim of LOGCAP is to provide another support alternative by capitalizing on the civilian sector in the continental United States and overseas locations; it is designed to be used primarily in areas where no multilateral or bilateral agreements or treaties exist.

Regulation 700-137 acknowledges the risk associated with using contractors in a wartime situation (U.S. Department of the Army 1985, 3): "The use of civilian contractors versus U.S. military personnel involves a higher degree of risk. Contractor employees have supported the Army in overseas locations during previous crises and can provide continued support in the future. However, their performance cannot be accurately predicted." Although the regulation primarily focuses on peacetime contracting, it acknowledges that a crisis situation may occur that is not covered by preplanned contracts: "To provide rapid support in such cases, deviations or waivers from regular procedures should be sought to the maximum extent possible" (4).

Pagonis observes that in the mid-1980s the U.S. military relied on contractor support in Germany, particularly during the yearly military exercise Return of Forces to Germany (REFORGER). He points out, "In Europe, the basic infrastructure within which REFORGER participants were transported, processed, fed, and housed was well established. Lines of supply, including host-nation support, were defined by dormant contracts, which automatically kicked in at the beginning of the maneuver. . . . Huge stockpiles of supplies and equipment were already in the theater, available to be drawn upon by incoming soldiers" (Pagonis and Cruikshank 1992, 66). Pagonis relied on his experience in Europe and the existing army regulations to guide his contracting effort in Saudi Arabia. He acknowledges, "My subordinates and I were expected to observe the rules, fill out the forms, and adhere to doctrine—whenever possible" (111).

The U.S. military followed the guidance provided by Department of the Army regulations during Operation Desert Storm. Stewart (2010) points out that because of the fluid situation in August 1991, contracting for host-nation support was conducted in a decentralized and informal manner. Initially there were no controls, and people at all levels did their own contracting. However, "on 10 September 1990, King Fahd verbally committed his nation to provide comprehensive support, although the details remained unclear until mid-October, when the Department of Defense sent a negotiating team to Saudi Arabia. Instead of concluding a contract or international agreement with the Saudis, the team reached an understanding that became a de facto agreement" (12). Thus after a month of negotiations the *Implementation Plan for Logistics Support of the United States Forces in Defense of the Kingdom of Saudi Arabia* was signed by the United States and Saudi Arabia (Sultan 1995). "That was done to prevent bureaucratic delays and to make *gifts* from Saudi Arabia to the United States as easy as possible while accommodating the kingdom's continuing desire to avoid formal ties" (Stewart 2010, 12).

During Operation Desert Storm it appears that no private military company or private security company provided support to the U.S. military. However, support did come from private individuals and small Saudi companies paid for primarily by the Saudi king. The U.S. military and General Pagonis in particular relied on the preexisting army regulations to guide their contracting activities during the first Gulf War. In fact the Department of Defense entered Saudi Arabia with an established procedure for contracting: the Department of the Army (1971) pamphlet *Use and Administration of Locals in Foreign Areas during Hostilities*, which encouraged the U.S. Army to contract for host-nation support as a substitute for military forces. Although the U.S. military did not hire private military companies, the laws, regulations, and control measures in force enabled the use of private contractors from the host nation, Saudi Arabia.

Duration of the Intervention

From the beginning of the deployment of forces until a drawdown in the conflict area military forces require logistics support, technical advice, and security even when not directly involved in combat. The expected duration of the intervention is contrasted with the actual duration to analyze decision makers' planning assumptions based on the theory of supply and demand. The duration of the intervention should reveal if decision makers' choices to use the private security industry changed during the conflict based on expected price or a change in price.

The Gulf War can be divided into three distinct phases: deployment (Desert Shield), combat (Desert Storm), and redeployment (Desert Farewell; Pagonis and Cruikshank 1992). Operation Desert Shield, which lasted from 7 August

1990 until 16 January 1991, consisted of three waves that included the deployment of a joint military force to defend American and allied interests against Iraqi aggression (i.e., a force of sufficient strength to enforce UN sanctions while defending the Arabian base; Swain 1994). Swain asserts that the first wave of Desert Shield was intended to provide an immediate deterrent force and consisted of the concentrated naval forces organized around two carrier battle groups and air force units to provide air cover for the light ground troops. The second wave of Desert Shield brought in ground-attack aircraft, additional air fighters, and U.S. Marine Corps forces (Swain 1994, 37). The third wave completed the deployment of the heavy ground, air, maritime, and sustainment forces required to ensure a successful defense of Saudi Arabia (37). Desert Shield lasted just over 150 days.

Operation Desert Storm began on 17 January 1991, when U.S. and Coalition planes bombed targets in Kuwait and Iraq (Pagonis and Cruikshank 1992). The air campaign against Iraq, the Iraqi Air Force in theater, and Iraqi ground forces in Kuwait lasted six weeks, until 24 February (Leyden 1997). The Desert Storm ground campaign to force the withdrawal of Iraq from Kuwait began on 25 February and lasted just under one hundred hours. Hostilities ended on 27 February (Leyden 1997). On 3 March Iraqi and Coalition forces met at Safwan, Iraq, and signed a cease-fire. President Bush announced on 6 March that the war had ended (Pagonis and Cruikshank 1992). The United States turned over the mission in the demilitarized zone to the United Nations Command on 6 May and removed the last U.S. soldiers from southeastern Iraq on 9 May (Swain 1994). Thus Desert Storm lasted just under 120 days.

Desert Farewell began almost immediately after hostilities ended (Pagonis and Cruikshank 1992). The redeployment took place in two stages, first personnel then equipment. The first stage required the redeployment of two army corps to Europe and the United States (Bourque and Burdan 2007). This involved the movement of over 365,000 troops and their equipment within 90 days. The second stage took more than a year to accomplish; it involved the movement of the food, ammunition, fuel equipment, and supplies (Pagonis and Cruikshank 1992). By January 1992 U.S. logisticians had cleaned and shipped more than 117,000 wheeled and 12,000 tracked vehicles, 2,000 helicopters, and 41,000 containers of supplies from Saudi Arabia.

With the help of civilian contractors the remaining 30,000 short tons of supplies were shipped back to the United States (Pagonis and Cruikshank 1992). Thus Desert Farewell lasted about 240 days.

Although combat operations lasted just under six weeks, the duration of Operations Desert Shield, Desert Storm, and Desert Farwell lasted much longer. In a period of seventeen months the United States and its Coalition partners deployed to Saudi Arabia, conducted offensive combat operations to remove Iraqi forces from Kuwait, and redeployed their troops and equipment. Stewart (2010) asserts that the expectation of rapid deployment and redeployment would become a way of life for thousands of servicemen and women in the United States and overseas, and the material means to support that way of life became increasingly available as the decade progressed.

Military forces began deploying to Saudi Arabia in August 1990, but the duration of the military intervention was relatively short, approximately 510 days. The military phase of Operations Desert Shield and Desert Storm lasted seven weeks, from 17 January to 27 February 1991. The air phase took 38 days, and the ground war took 4 days (Woodward 1991, 365). The majority of the combat forces had departed the Gulf theater of operations by 6 May 1991, within nine months of the initial deployment of forces, and the redeployment of equipment and supplies continued through January 1992. Therefore the total duration of Operations Desert Shield and Desert Storm was seventeen months.

There is no evidence to suggest that the Bush administration placed a time constraint on Desert Shield and Desert Storm; therefore it is difficult to contrast the expected duration with the actual duration of the operation. However, the surprisingly short duration of the operations reduced the U.S. military's requirement to rotate troops in and out of theater, which reduced the operational tempo on the forces deployed. As a result the Department of Defense did not have to substitute its existing force with private military contractors.

Scope of the Operations

The theory of supply and demand would predict that an increase in the scope of the intervention would result in the increased use of the private security industry. Specifically as military logistics support become privatized, there should be an increase in private military support in relation to the number of troops used during a conflict. Additionally how the military forces are staged and employed during the conflict and arrayed at the end of hostilities should reveal the scope of the conflict. For example, if the military force deployed from one main base, limited its intervention to a small portion of the rival's country, and redeployed through one main base, we should see less use of the private security industry in support.

Scales (1994) asserts that prior to Operation Desert Shield the U.S. Army had never projected such a large force so quickly over so great a distance. The United States sent over 560,000 troops to the theater of operation and deployed some 1,200 tanks, 1,800 warplanes, and 100 warships (Pagonis and Cruikshank 1992). An additional 35 nations provided manpower, armaments, or money (Powell 1995); 28 nations committed forces, including the Gulf States, France, Canada, Italy, Egypt, and Syria (Sultan 1995). Countries unable to contribute troops helped finance the buildup (Powell 1995).

Swain (1994) points out that conducting military operations in Saudi Arabia was no simple task. The Arabian Peninsula is approximately the size of the United States east of the Mississippi. The distances are great between major cities; for example it is 334 miles from Dhahran to the theater logistics base at King Khalid Military City near Hafar al Batin, and it is 528 miles from Dhahran to Riyadh, along the northern main supply route. However, the country's few urban areas possess a modern commercial infrastructure from which U.S. forces could draw support, and food, fuel, water, a modern phone system, and shelter were all available if they could be tapped. Notwithstanding the absence of a developed road network, buses and trucks — particularly line-haul trucks — were present in abundance (Swain 1994).

Based on the size of the Arabian Peninsula and other logistic challenges the United States and its Coalition partners faced a daunting task. They had to deploy combat forces to Saudi Arabia and establish a defense with sufficient combat power to prevent Iraqi forces from invading that country (Herspring 2005). Despite this, three months after being alerted for deployment, the XVIII Corps had in place almost 800 tanks, 525 artillery pieces, and 227 attack helicopters, manned, maintained, and supported by 107,300 soldiers

(Scales 1994). And the operation could not progress without capitalizing efficiently on indigenous Saudi support (Scales 1994).

Due to the enormous logistical support needed, Pagonis asserts, "we were in desperate need of soldiers to run logistics operations, especially in light of the enormous numbers of combat personnel arriving in the theater each day. In the two-week period between 10 August and 25 August, we received more than 40,000 troops in Saudi Arabia, essentially without benefit of a prepositioned or predefined logistical structure" (Pagonis and Cruikshank 1992, 100). In spite of some unforeseen problems and occasional delays, the U.S. Army succeeded in establishing a logistics infrastructure capable of supporting half a million troops from all services, the same number sustained in Vietnam at the peak of deployment (Scales 1994).

In the year between August 1990 and August 1991, over 122 million meals were planned, moved, and served. According to Pagonis and Cruikshank (1992), that is comparable to feeding all the residents of Wyoming and Vermont three meals a day for forty days. During the same time over 1.3 billion gallons of fuel were used, seven times the consumption of Washington DC in the same period (Pagonis and Cruikshank 1992). The fuel supplied by Saudi Arabia was worth $1.9 billion (Sultan 1995). One day's worth of ammunition for the VII Corps weighed 9,000 tons carried in 450 truckloads; the XVIII Airborne Corps required slightly less ammunition resupply: about 5,000 tons per day (Pagonis and Cruikshank 1992).

By the time Desert Storm commenced, over 3,500 vehicles moved across a road network of over 2,746 miles to provide logistics support to the combat forces (Scales 1994). Across a one-year span, the supply units and their contracted drivers drove almost 52 million miles in the war theater (Pagonis and Cruikshank 1992); that is the equivalent of more than 10,000 round-trips from Los Angeles to New York. For half a year, from November 1990 through April 1991, the suppliers and transporters of the Gulf War moved 500 short tons of mail per day; all told, they handled over 31,800 tons of mail—an amount that would cover twenty-eight football fields in mail six feet deep (Pagonis and Cruikshank 1992).

Once President Bush authorized the deployment of an additional 200,000 troops in November 1990, the scope of the deployment doubled. VII Corps included several mechanized and heavy divisions, comprising more than 6,000 tracked combat vehicles and 59,000 wheeled vehicles and 220,000 troops requiring 769,000 short tons of equipment (Clancy and Franks 1997; Pagonis and Cruikshank 1992). However, getting the combat units into theater was only part of the problem. Clancy and Franks point out that when VII Corps arrived in Saudi Arabia, everything became a struggle as basic survival needs had to be met in the desert.

The Coalition plan to liberate Kuwait called for two U.S. Army corps to move from eastern Saudi Arabia almost 500 miles west into the Arabian Desert. When the air campaign of Desert Storm commenced in mid-January 1991, the corps began their movement west. VII Corps had to travel more than 330 miles and XVIII Corps had to move some 500 miles just to get into position for future offensive operations (Pagonis and Cruikshank 1992; Sultan 1995). By 3 February both corps had closed in their attack position with no significant glitches (Bourque 2002). Pagonis and Cruikshank (1992, 146) praise the private contractors who drove many of the heavy equipment trucks during that timeframe: "We owe special thanks to those contracted civilians from Saudi Arabia, South Korea, Pakistan, Egypt, the Philippines, India, Bangladesh, and a dozen other countries who drove up and down our main supply routes (MSRs), in many cases entering enemy territory to supply Logbase Charlie and Echo."

Based on these accounts, Operations Desert Shield and Desert Storm were enormous in scope. The military operations covered over 500 square miles in Saudi Arabia alone. With the exception of the Gulf State Coalition partners, most of the military formations deployed from either the United States or Europe with all of their equipment (Bourque 2002); for the United States alone that means close to 7,500 air miles. To transport, house, feed, and maintain the equipment of the Coalition forces exceeded the U.S. military force structure, even though the size of the U.S. military was at its cold war peak. In comparison, there were 500,000 U.S. military personnel at any one time during the peak years of the Vietnam War (1965–68), which took over two years to build up to that strength (Scales 1994).

The size of the Coalition force assembled in Saudi Arabia exceeded 750,000 men and women. The United States and its Coalition partners deployed close to 750,000 troops for Operations Desert Shield and Desert Storm. The U.S. military force accounted for 500,000 of that total number. The United States deployed 250,000 troops to defend Saudi Arabia as part of Operation Desert Shield. When Bush decided to restore Kuwait's sovereignty, an additional 250,000 troops deployed to Saudi Arabia to participate in Operation Desert Storm.

All of the U.S. and Coalition forces deployed to Saudi Arabia to stage for operations in Iraq and Kuwait. (All Coalition forces went through one of a few points of entry in Saudi Arabia.) Furthermore the U.S military and its Coalition partners staged forces throughout Saudi Arabia, extending in some cases up to 500 miles into the western desert. Due to the amount of equipment and the extended supply routes, the U.S. military relied on individual private contractors to transport much of its heavy equipment and supplies to the western staging areas.

Other Conflicts or Deployments during Operations Desert Shield and Desert Storm

The theory of supply and demand would posit that the commitment of military forces to other areas would limit their ability to participate in the intervention; consequently there should be an increased demand for the private security industry to fill the gap in available military assets.

It is important to note that even though the U.S. military deployed over half a million troops in support of Operations Desert Shield and Desert Storm, another half-million troops were forward deployed supporting ongoing treaty commitments in Europe and Asia (U.S. Department of Defense, , Defense Manpower Data Center 1954–2012). Thus 25 percent of the active U.S. military was not available to support operations in the Gulf.

Scales (1995) asserts that Gen. Carl E. Vuono, U.S. Army chief of staff, would not let the Gulf crisis drain the army dry and prevent a response to another crisis that might arise in some other part of the world. Although stability in Europe was promising, other hot spots were always ready to demand army intervention. Vuono relied on a base of active forces and trained reserves to meet these contingencies. For example, during Desert Shield there was an ongoing crisis in Liberia and Somalia that eventually led to evacuation operations. The United States also had troops in the Philippines, Korea, and Latin America, and these areas might require rapid response by forces not involved in the Gulf. In addition the army mission at home, ranging from firefighting to emergency relief, was always a concern (Scales 1994).

In 1990 the U.S. military had troops committed to NATO and Korea. Of the total force, 609,422 troops were stationed outside of the continental United States; over 291,000 were supporting NATO, and over 87,000 were stationed in Korea. This represents 30 percent of the total force deployed and over 42 percent of the available ground force in the Department of Defense. By November 1990 the U.S. military had deployed 500,000 soldiers and marines to Saudi Arabia from the continental United States and Europe. Yet the U.S. military still required private contractors to augment its military capability.

The Size of the U.S. Military during Operations Desert Shield and Desert Storm

Based on the theory of supply and demand, fluctuations in the total number of military forces available during the intervention would influence the supply and demand of the private security industry. All the military forces available would include all branches of the U.S. military and reserve and National Guard forces. Although the active component is immediately available, policymakers can also choose to activate the reserve and National Guard forces. Supply and demand theory would posit that as the overall size of the military decreases, there should be an increase in the reliance on the private security industry. Additionally the theory should highlight the opportunity costs or shifts in supply that policymakers face when choosing between military forces and the private security industry.

Globally in the fall of 1989 the postwar power structure had broken down (Swain 1994). The Soviet Union was undergoing dramatic internal stresses, while its European empire was falling away rapidly. As Soviet interest turned inward, military planners everywhere considered the emerging multipolar world as the strategic environment of the 1990s. U.S. estimates examined the restructuring of the military in light of new threat assessments (Swain 1994).

At the end of September 1989 the total U.S. active military was slightly more than 2,130,000. This all-volunteer force included ground combat forces from the U.S. Army and U.S. Marine Corps, totaling 769,741 and 196,956, respectively (U.S. Department of Defense,, Defense Manpower Data Center 1954–2012). Additionally the U.S. Department of Defense employed 1,075,437 government civilians, who supported a wide range of functions for the active military. In essence the U.S. military was at its peak troop size by the time of Operation Desert Shield.

In August 1990 President Bush delivered a speech to the Aspen Institute in Colorado concerning the need to restructure U.S. military forces in response to changes in the global environment, specifically the rapid decline of Soviet power (Herspring 2005; Swain 1994). The president's proposal called for an orderly reduction of U.S. military forces over five years. Many scholars point out that during the period of Desert Shield and Desert Storm the army was well down the road of restructuring into a smaller force (Scales 1994). Responding to budget pressures and the negotiation of the Conventional Forces in Europe Treaty, then in progress, army planners anticipated removing one U.S. corps from Europe (Scales 1994). When Saddam invaded Iraq, the U.S. military had already shed close to 100,000 from its active duty roles. However, as Swain points out, the plan to reduce the size of the military was about to suffer a temporary interruption due to Operation Desert Shield and Desert Storm.

If one determines the total size of the military — including all branches, reserve forces, and National Guard forces — then one can examine the relationship of a decreasing military and the private security industry. According to the theory of supply and demand, if the overall size of the military decreases there should be an increase in the reliance on private security services. However, in 1990 the total active military strength was 2,046,144 personnel. Of this number, 929,055 were U.S. Army and U.S. Marine Corps ground troops. This represents the height of the cold war U.S. military strength. As such the theory of supply and demand suggests that there should not have been a need for private contractors. Yet the U.S. military still required about 10,000 private contractors to augment its forces during Desert Shield and Desert Storm. This highlights the opportunity costs or shifts in supply that policymakers face when choosing between private contracting and military force.

Military Outlays during Operations
Desert Shield and Desert Storm

The theory of supply and demand would hypothesize that as the size of the defense budget decreases over time there should be an increased reliance on the private security industry due to decreased spending on military forces. This is represented as a shift in the supply curve away from higher costs of personnel in the military forces to those in the private security industry. I will now examine the U.S. military defense budget during Operations Enduring Desert Shield and Desert Storm from the standpoint of total dollars spent on defense, percentage of GDP, and the percentage of U.S. budget outlays dedicated to defense.

At the end of the cold war the U.S. government allocated over $303 billion for defense spending. This amounted to 5.6 percent of the GDP and 26.5 percent of total U.S. budget outlays. In comparison, the U.S. government allocated over $568 billion for human resource spending (Social Security, education, health, and veterans' entitlements). These programs amounted to 10.5 percent of the GDP and 49.7 percent of the total budget outlays (U.S. Office of Management and Budget 1950–2012, for 1989).

In 1990, and the beginning of Operation Desert Shield, the defense budget began to decrease. The U.S. government allocated over $299 billion for defense spending; that amounted to 5.2 percent of the U.S. GDP and 23.9 percent of budget outlays, or a decline of 0.4 percent of GDP. In comparison, the U.S. government allocated over $619 billion for human resource spending: 10.8 percent of GDP and 49.4 percent of total budget outlays (U.S. Office of Management and Budget 1950–2012, for 1990).

Although a slight decrease from the 1989 high, defense outlays in 1990 represented a cold war high in defense spending and represented about 30 percent of total budget outlays and 5.6 percent of GDP. During this same period the Department of Defense spent over $157 billion on contracts, 54.3 percent of total Defense outlays. The spending on service contracts amounted to over $49 billion, or 31.2 percent of Defense contracts. Service contracts differ from product contracts or research and development contracts (U.S. Department of Defense, Defense Manpower Data Center 1954–2012).

Thus even though U.S. defense spending represented a cold war high, the U.S. military still required private contractors to support Operations Desert Shield and Desert Storm.

Choices Other Than Private Military Contractors

The theory of supply and demand posits that other conditions and situations influence the use of the private security market. Beyond the availability of military forces and defense spending, were choices available during Operations Desert Shield and Desert Storm other than the private security industry, for example, increased participation by allies, Coalition partners, or the host nation?

Although the United States and its coalition partners relied on host-nation contractors to augment shortfalls in logistics support, there is no evidence of a demand for the private security industry. The Saudi government, which maintained a significant security force, invited and hosted the United States and its Coalition partners during Operations Desert Shield and Desert Storm. In essence Saudi Arabia provided a broad range of security tasks so the Coalition could focus on the defense of Saudi Arabia and eventually the liberation of Kuwait.

Saudi Arabia provided over 45,000 troops, 200 tanks, 250 aircraft, and 8 frigates in support of Operations Desert Shield and Desert Storm (Leyden 1997; Herspring 2005) and had several paramilitary forces, totaling 100,000 men (Woodward 1991). Cordesman (1997) points out that this reflects a system of layered forces designed to protect the regime. Specifically there is a regular army that provides external security but is kept away from urban areas; the National Guard provides internal security using loyal tribes and groups under a different chain of command; there is a separate Frontier Force; and the Ministry of Interior — under the direction of a prince — and other groups provide internal security at the political and intelligence levels.

The 10,500-man Frontier Force covers Saudi Arabia's land and sea borders; about 4,500 of these men are assigned to the Coast Guard. The Ministry of Interior maintains a security service called the General Directorate of Investigation and a Special Security Force of about 500 men. Saudi Arabia also has a large gendarmerie or national police force with more than 15,000 men

(Cordesman 1997). There are approximately 35,000 paramilitary policemen in the Public Security Police equipped with small arms and some automatic weapons; they are assigned to provincial governors and are under the aegis of the interior minister (Cordesman 2003).

The public security forces are recruited from all areas of the country and maintain police directorates at provincial and local levels. Cordesman (2003) asserts that these forces, particularly the centralized Public Security Police, can be reinforced by the National Guard in an emergency or can get support from the regular armed forces. These formal state institutions carry out most internal security and criminal justice activity in urban areas (Cordesman 2003). This means that critical infrastructure, such as supply routes, ports, airfields, and supply depots, are protected by the Saudi security forces. The United States and its Coalition partners could thus focus on the defense of Saudi Arabia and not on force protection.

The United States also relied on its Coalition partners to provide forces for Operations Desert Shield and Desert Storm. In fact the Coalition partners provided one third of the total ground forces during the operations. The United States activated substantial reserve and National Guard forces to supplement its active duty force in Saudi Arabia. However, the speed at which active duty forces deployed to the Gulf surpassed the logistics capability of the U.S. military. A short-term logistic crisis resulted in the U.S. military substituting host-nation contractors while awaiting the arrival of its reserve logistics capability to deploy to the Gulf region.

Private Security Supply-Demand Behavior: An Assessment

The theory of supply and demand predicts that given a situation where the demand for a service increases, in this case support services, the military will contract for host-nation support service to fill shortfalls in capability. In the case of Operations Desert Shield and Desert Storm, private security supply-demand behavior is evident for support services but not security services.

An analysis of supply-demand behavior must start with an examination of the initial conditions prior to Operation Desert Shield. Gordon and Trainor (1995, 475) write, "Benefiting from the Reagan military buildup, the military used the most advanced high technology against the Iraqis. But, the weak side of the Reagan military buildup was exposed. In a single-minded pursuit of high-tech weaponry, the military ignored some unglamorous but essential areas." Pagonis and Cruikshank (1992, 100) argue, "Beginning in 1971, *The Total Force Concept* stipulated that the majority of slots in the Army's combat and infantry units would be filled by regular, active-duty soldiers; while slots for logistics personnel, whose many civilian skills such as forklift operation, truck driving, and so forth are directly related to the military support role, would be filled by reservists." Therefore even though the size of the U.S. military was at its peak in 1991, the active duty force structure was weighted heavily toward combat formations.

During the cold war the U.S. military was built to defend Western Europe against a Soviet ground attack. Swain (1994, 3) points out that "the armed forces committed to the Arabian Peninsula had been designed and structured originally for a very different war — a forward defense of NATO on the Central Front in Europe." He argues that this accounts for such anomalies as the army's shortage of line-haul trucks, particularly HETs, the large flatbed trucks used to transport heavy armored vehicles to the front. Swain observes, "A force built for attack has different communications, logistics, intelligence, and force structure requirements than one created for deterrence and defense and under political guidance to deploy only minimum essential force" (3). The relatively predictable strategic environment of the cold war was gone (Clancy and Franks 1997).

When Iraq invaded Kuwait, there was no significant U.S. military presence in Saudi Arabia (Herspring 2005). Fearful that Saddam would continue his attack south into Saudi Arabia, military planners urgently needed to get combat forces into that country. However, "the decision to bring in combat forces first was not without cost. It meant that forces in theater would have to maintain themselves under austere conditions for some time and that host-nation support, both donated and contracted, was a sine qua non to sustain the force for the immediate future" (Swain 1994, 35). Assistance from Saudi Arabia was therefore imperative (Sultan 1995, 289).

At the outset of Desert Shield "the lack of U.S. troops in the theater would necessitate the creation of a military presence, including infrastructure, from scratch, although the (potential) host nation's excellent ports and airbases would offset some of these challenges" (Pagonis and Cruikshank 1992, 68). During an early planning session with the Saudis, Gen. John J. Yeosock, the Third U.S. Army commander, required a list from General Pagonis of the requirements and assistance needed from Saudi Arabia. Yeosock needed to tell the king what was needed logistically—in other words, a shopping list fit for a king (67). Fortunately the military planners were familiar with the usable and contactable resources of the various Middle Eastern nations (Pagonis and Cruikshank 1992).

Military leaders made certain decisions regarding the phasing of the operation knowing that they could count on the support of the host nation. As Swain (1994, 45) observes, "It was known at the outset that much of the absent support structure could be compensated for by host-nation support, but the ability of the host nation to supply support, or perhaps more important, the limits on this ability, was by no means immediately apparent to either Third Army planners or the host-nations government." Thus military planners chose to send combat troops to Saudi Arabia first, before the logistics troops (Woodward 1991). "The combat troops moved up the list, and the logisticians—even logisticians who made up the combat units—moved down" (Pagonis and Cruikshank 1992, 89). Swain (1994, 35) asserts, "This decision was only possible because of the availability of supplies—particularly tentage, food, and ammunition—prepositioned on ships in the Indian Ocean." Sultan (1995) observes that the situation would have been different if the host nation was poor, hostile, or both. His point correctly foreshadowed the U.S. military's 2001 experience in Afghanistan and 2003 experience in Iraq.

Based on previous army war games, the logistics overhead for Operations Desert Shield and Desert Storm eventually should have grown to 120,000 personnel (Scales 1994). Moreover most of the structure would have to come from activated National Guard and reserve units; military planners estimated a requirement for 33,772 reservists, assuming combat operations had not begun, and 88,000 if they had (Swain 1994). Thus on 15 August 1990 the secretary of defense requested that the president employ his authority to call up the selected reserves (Swain 1994; Herspring 2005). However, on 22 August President Bush signed an Executive Order that called only 48,000 reserves to active duty by 1 September (Pagonis and Cruikshank 1992; Woodward

1991). To complicate matters, it has been argued that the army did not activate many well-trained, well-prepared units that could have provided substantial logistical support (Scales 1994).

In October decision makers determined that the minimum essential force level deployed into theater did not exceed 250,000 (Swain 1994; Herspring 2005). This resulted in a modification of the force deployment. Swain (1994, 40) writes, "Third Army had long based its war plans on the assumption that Reserve Component forces would be available immediately for any large-scale deployment." However, the flaw in the concept was that events might not wait upon the convenience of defense decision makers. As a result of the decision to limit the number of troops in theater, the initial army logistics support element reduced its force size from 20,000 to 12,500 and the theater logistics support command from 25,000 to 10,400 (43).

Swain (1994, 43) explains the difference in personnel numbers "was to be made up by host-nation support, the remainder by risk and a less than desirable sustainment and transportation capability." Ultimately the combat troops would bear part of the cost involved in an austere desert environment. Fortunately host-nation support was available to support the deploying troops, and King Fahd agreed to feed and house the Coalition forces in Saudi Arabia for the duration of the operation (Swain 1994; Sultan 1995). Additionally he reimbursed the United States for the cost of contracts between August and September 1991 and assumed responsibility for paying for all Coalition forces contracts after 1 October 1991 through the end of Operation Desert Farewell, a hefty sum of over $16 billion. Sultan (1995) concludes that no host country has ever given such vast and unstinting support to allied troops fighting on its soil.

Summary and Analysis

Supply-demand behavior is evident during Operations Desert Shield and Desert Storm. Military planners and decision makers entered Operation Desert Shield with a force optimized for the defense of Western Europe. The demand for an expeditionary logistics force capability was low, and most of the U.S. logistics force structure resided in the reserve force. Military planners substituted existing logistics support for host-nation support from Saudi

Arabia. As Clancy and Franks (1997) point out, the new security stance for the United States required a distinctly different posture for the U.S. Army.

An early decision to deploy combat forces to Saudi Arabia first resulted in an immediate shortage of U.S. logistics support. Thus the demand for capabilities such as transportation, housing, and food increased dramatically, and military planners immediately turned to host-nation contractors as a substitute. Decisions to impose a ceiling on forces deployed into theater and the ability of the Saudi government filled the void in logistical support. U.S. military planners consequently reduced their requirement for additional homogeneous logistics capabilities. These events represented shifts in the U.S. demand curve.

The theory of supply and demand predicts that if the size of the national military decreases, one should find an increased demand for the private security industry; likewise as involvement in conflict increases, there should be an increased demand for the private security industry. The theory further predicts that decision makers will choose between not becoming involved in conflict or using private security to fill gaps in security left by diminishing military forces, depending on which has the lower cost. The evidence from Operations Desert Shield and Desert Storm suggests that most of the assertions in the literature are supported. There was no decrease in military outlays; however, in 1990, 30 percent of the total U.S. military force was deployed outside the continental United States; Operations Desert Shield and Desert Storm lasted one year and five months (17 months); U.S. Army regulations encouraged contracting for host-nation support as a substitute for military forces. Therefore the U.S. military hired 10,000 private contractors.

The examination into the events of Desert Shield and Desert Storm provides an alternative explanation for the use of private military contractors. First, the initial force cap of 250,000 U.S. soldiers required military leaders to choose between deploying combat forces or logistics forces into theater. When they chose to deploy combat soldiers first, they substituted military logistics support for host-nation private contractors. Second, King Fahd provided significant financial support, transportation, food, housing, equipment, and labor (Sultan 1995). As a result, the U.S. military relied on private military companies for support. Third, U.S. and Coalition forces operated in a permissive security environment while preparing for combat operations. As a result they did not have to allocate troops for force protection; the 110,000-man Saudi security forces provided the security.

According to Swain (1994), Operation Desert Storm was a transitional war in which forces raised and trained to fight on the central front in Europe against a great power were instead deployed to the open desert to fight a local tyrant and the willing participation of Saudi Arabia was absolutely essential to the achievement of U.S. goals. Additionally Operation Desert Storm had two important, even decisive conditions that may not occur in future contingencies: "Saudi Arabia was well endowed with exactly the sort of infrastructure that could compensate for the allies' own shortcomings in the strategic projection of heavy forces" (343), and "the global balance was such that there were no other strategic distractions; the theater of operations could enjoy the full support of the entire American military" (343).

Even though the size of the U.S. military and its budget were essentially at their cold war height, the U.S. military was structured and resourced for a defensive war in Germany, not an offensive war in the desert. The capabilities necessary to conduct expeditionary operations in an austere environment are significantly different from those for defending in an established theater of war. The shortfalls experienced in Operations Desert Shield and Desert Storm would be magnified as the United States conducted expeditionary operations through the remainder of the twentieth century and into the early twenty-first century.

CHAPTER FOUR

OPERATION JOINT ENDEAVOR

This chapter provides a cross-comparison case study test utilizing the events of Operation Joint Endeavor, the NATO peacekeeping operation in Bosnia from December 1995 to December 1999. The details of Joint Endeavor support some of the assertions in the literature on the use of the private security industry after the cold war. The peacekeeping operation in Bosnia has proven influential for examining the role of the private security industry in operations as well as the theory of supply and demand to understand their increased use. The most descriptive fact concerning the operation is that the number of contractors on the battlefield equaled the number of U.S. forces. The contractor count cannot be explained without considering the nature of the intervention, the decisions by senior U.S. leaders to limit the size of U.S. forces in Bosnia, and the scope and duration of the operation.

Operation Joint Endeavor is a most likely case as defined by George and Bennett (2005), with very strong evidence of contractor presence. In a most likely case, because the independent variable strongly predicts a particular outcome, the outcome must occur or the theory is suspect (George and Bennett 2005, 121). Biddle (2004) explains that a most likely case is one where extreme values put a theory on its strongest possible ground of occurring. If the theory is going to be supported (i.e., shown to be true) it should be supported in a most likely case. Biddle argues that for such cases, a valid theory should fail very rarely; if we nevertheless observe failure, this surprising result warrants a greater loss of confidence in the theory than would a single dis-confirmatory observation under less ideal conditions. However, most cases usually fall somewhere between being most and least likely for particular theories (George and Bennett 2005). Therefore the strength of a theory depends to a considerable extent on the difficulty of the test (King et al. 1994; Gerring 2001).

As this chapter demonstrates, the size of the U.S. military and its budget in Bosnia were significantly less than the peak cold war levels. The scope of the intervention is also significant: the operation lasted for over six years, and the United States faced competing conflicts around the world during the time of the intervention in addition to its military commitments to NATO and Korea. For all of these reasons, the likelihood that the United States would have to utilize significant support from the private security industry was high, therefore increasing the demand.

The use of contractors was so essential to the mission that numerous schol-ars focus on this case when studying the rise of the private security industry. U.S. reliance on PMCs was due mainly to the political imposition of various force caps on troop size throughout the mission. Operation Joint Endeavor thus demonstrates both the utility of supply-demand theory as well as some of its limitations. As such it offers a challenging test of theory in the form of a most likely case (George and Bennett 2005).

Overview of Events

Many scholars assert that the Balkan conflict was multicausal, multidi-mensional, and complex (Metz 2001). Herspring (2005) argues that ethnic cleansing occurred in Bosnia prior to Operation Joint Endeavor. Prior to the breakup of Yugoslavia in the early 1990s it was a complex state formed after World War I from a diverse patchwork of cultures, ethnic groups, religions, traditions, and histories (Metz 2001). The polyglot combination made Yugoslavia a fragile state from its inception, with many fissures that could be manipulated by ambitious or unscrupulous political leaders. How-ever, following World War II, Josip Broz Tito, Yugoslavia's leader, held his fractious state together with a complex system of rights and overlapping sovereignties.

Tito died on 4 May 1980, and for much of the remaining decade Yugoslavia's economy began to falter. In the years immediately following his death the Yugoslav federation started to fall apart (Albright 2003). Between 1990 and 1992 Slovenia, Croatia, Bosnia, and Macedonia seceded from Yugoslavia, leaving Serbia and Montenegro as the constituent parts of the Federal Republic of Yugoslavia (Metz 2001, 4). Three waves of conflict and war followed. The first involved Yugoslavia's northern tier states, Slovenia and Croatia. Metz observes that when Slovenia opted for independence in 1990, Yugoslav military forces initially attempted to stop the secession, but after a short and nearly bloodless war they withdrew, leaving Slovenia to seek its economic and political future with Western Europe. However, the divide between Croatia and Yugoslavia was more difficult.

Soon after Croatia declared its independence in June 1991, a civil war, fueled by a Serbian invasion, broke out in Krajina, the former Austro-Hungarian military border area settled by ethnic Croatians, Germans, Hungarians, Serbs, and other Slavs (Metz 2001).[1] In January 1992 the United Nations sponsored a cease-fire and established the United Nations Protection Force to monitor it. The U.S. Army in Europe supported this UN mission with medical and logistics support (Kirkpatrick 2006, 389). However, a cycle of conflict and cease-fire continued until August 1994, when Croatian forces recaptured Krajina with a major offensive and some 150,000 Serbs fled the region, many to Serb-held areas in Bosnia (Metz 2001, 4). The conflict in Bosnia proved even bloodier and more complex: between 1991 and 1995 over 300,000 were killed in the former Yugoslavia (Holbrooke 1999).

In contrast to other Balkan states, which tended to have a dominant ethnic group, Bosnia was more evenly split among ethnic Serbs (40 percent), Bosnian Muslims known as Bosniaks (38 percent), and ethnic Croats (22 percent; Metz 2001). Cigar (1995) asserts that the avowed aim of the Bosnian Serb leadership, backed and originally incited by Belgrade, was the achievement of an *ethnically pure* state, even at the cost of using brutal force and the violation of internationally recognized borders; the Bosnian government pursued an inclusive, plural, and tolerant social and political environment, although imperfectly implemented. However, it appears that all sides in the conflict may have committed some form of war crime (Klajn 2007).

In February 1992 the Bosnian government held a referendum on independence, and Bosnian Serbs, supported by neighboring Serbia, responded with armed resistance in an effort to partition the republic along ethnic lines and drive other ethnic groups from the territory they controlled. In March 1994 the Bosniaks and ethnic Croats created the Federation of Bosnia-Herzegovina, leaving two warring parties: the Muslim-Croat Federation and the Serb-dominated Republika Srpska. War between them continued through most of 1995. It was ended by extensive outside pressure and the sheer exhaustion of the combatants (Metz 2001).

Croatia, Bosnia-Herzegovina, and the Federal Republic of Yugoslavia reached an agreement that they initialed on 21 November 1995 and formally signed in Paris on 14 December 1995 (Kirkpatrick 2006, 406; Herspring 2005). The formal conclusion came with the General Framework Agreement for Peace (usually known as the Dayton Accord) in December 1995 (Holbrooke 1999). Herspring observes that the resulting agreement gave 49 percent of Bosnia to the Serbs and the rest to the Muslim-Croat Federation.[2] Madeline Albright (2003) argues that three factors ended the Bosnian war: overreaching on the part of the Bosnian Serbs, the changing military situation, and President Bill Clinton's willingness to lead.

The United Nations Security Council Resolution 1031 gave the North Atlantic Treaty Organization (NATO) the mandate to implement the military aspects of the Dayton Accords (Metz 2001). An Implementation Force (IFOR) was created to maintain the cessation of hostilities, separate the armed forces of the Federation and Republika Srpska, transfer territory between the two entities, and move military forces and heavy weapons into approved sites (5). At the time of the cease-fire the three militaries in Bosnia had over 400,000 men under arms, including civilian militias and an estimated 45,000 police that fought in conjunction with the three armies (U.S. Government Accountability Office 1998c).

The NATO mission in Bosnia was to establish an environment adequately secure for the continued consolidation of peace without further need for NATO-led military forces (U.S. Government Accountability Office 1998c). The following conditions had to be met for this objective to be realized:

The political leaders of Bosnia's three ethnic groups must demonstrate a
commitment to continue negotiations as the means to resolve political
and military differences.

Bosnia's established civil structures must be sufficiently mature to assume
responsibility for ensuring compliance with the Dayton Agreement.

The political leaders of Bosnia's three ethnic groups must adhere on a
sustained basis to the military requirements of the Dayton Agreement,
including the virtual absence of violations or unauthorized military
activities.

Conditions must be established for the safe continuation of ongoing, nation
building activities. (U.S. Government Accountability Office 1998c)

During this time the U.S. objectives in the Balkans were to maximize the
chances that the region would become stable, prosperous, and integrated
into Europe and to sustain NATO's leading role in European security in
such a way that the U.S. military remained able to implement the national
military strategy, in particular to fight and win two nearly simultaneous
major theater wars (Metz 2001). Operation Joint Endeavor began with the
NATO IFOR crossing the Sava River at the end of December 1995, and the
U.S. military began operations in eastern Bosnia around Tuzla (Herspring
2005; Holbrooke 1999).

In December 1996 NATO activated the Stabilization Force (SFOR) to
implement the military aspects of the Dayton Accord as the legal successor
to IFOR (Swain 2003). Like IFOR, SFOR operated under Chapter 7 of the
UN Charter (peace enforcement; Metz 2001, 6). According to NATO (Metz
2001), its specific tasks were to deter or prevent a resumption of hostilities
or new threats to peace, promote a climate in which the peace process could
continue to move forward, and provide selective support to civilian organizations within its capabilities. This phase of NATO involvement was named
Operation Joint Guard.

In November 1997 President Clinton announced U.S. support for extending the NATO Bosnia operations to June 1998 (Holbrooke 1999). Clinton
presented this as a new mission because progress in Bosnia had not been as
rapid as anticipated (Swain 2003). In late January 1998 he decided that the

United States would prefer to contribute about 6,900 troops to the SFOR follow-on force in Bosnia rather than continue to provide about 8,900 troops. As a result NATO lowered its operational requirements for the follow-on force after the United States decided to draw down forces, which began in mid-July 1998 (U.S. Government Accountability Office 1998c). Operation Joint Forge became the official designation for NATO-led forces in Bosnia after 20 June 1998 (Munden 1999).

Swain (2003) believes that the most notable change in the circumstances in Bosnia in 1998 was the empowerment of the United Nations High Representative, which shifted SFOR's priorities even more from the mandated military provisions to the civil implementation authorities. However, as Swain points out, SFOR remained the essential default force for preservation of civil order absent the full acceptance of the rule of law. Further a gradual but substantial force reduction of NATO troops from 32,000 to 20,000 was announced in September 1999 (Swain 2003). By 1999 the threat of military violence was well under control, though it still represented a potential threat as opposed to an immediate challenge. Because of the potential for renewed armed conflict, SFOR remained in place, but due to NATO's military intervention in Kosovo the commitment to SFOR became smaller and less central to international efforts (Swain 2003).

Private Contractors in Operation Joint Endeavor

From the beginning of the planning process, U.S. military planners had been constrained by the imposition of the 25,000-man force cap on Task Force Eagle, the name assigned to the U.S. military task force employed in Bosnia (Kirkpatrick 2006). Kirkpatrick explains that army planners were heavily biased toward combat forces because of uncertainty about the situation that Task Force Eagle would confront. Thus the composition of the task force necessarily skimped on such things as construction engineers and the use of the Logistics Civil Augmentation Program, or LOGCAP, to build camps became an essential part of the plan (Kirkpatrick 2006). LOGCAP is a U.S. Army initiative for peacetime planning that allows for the use of civilian contractors in wartime and other contingencies. These contractors perform selected services to support U.S. forces on Defense Department missions.

Use of contractors in a theater of operations allows the release of military units to perform other missions or to fill contingency shortfalls (Clements and Young 2005).

The principal LOGCAP contractor, Brown and Root Services Corporation of Houston, Texas, began providing support of Operation Joint Endeavor in Hungary, Bosnia, and Croatia on 27 November 1995 and continued to provide support for the successive increments of U.S. Army Europe troops deployed to Bosnia (Shrader 1999). Services included base camp construction, transportation, the distribution of ice and water, petroleum support at selected locations, food service, laundry and tailoring, showers, latrines, garbage removal, contingency equipment, the maintenance of organizational clothing and equipment, and supplying an unskilled labor pool (Shrader 1999).

The original plan for Bosnia was to build eight base camps, each with a population of around 3,000 soldiers (Kirkpatrick 2006). However, once in Bosnia, U.S. Army engineers discovered that the compartmentalization of terrain in the area of operations, combined with the presence of far more land mines than anticipated, meant that Task Force Eagle instead needed more than twenty smaller base camps to facilitate efficient peace enforcement operations. This decision produced a major change in infrastructure planning, which created further delays because the efficiencies the logistical planners meant to gain by having large bases were lost (Kirkpatrick 2006).

The changes in infrastructure plans also impacted contractor support. Brown and Root had agreed to deliver sufficient housing units within a specified amount of time (Kirkpatrick 2006). However, the investments in site clearance — meticulous removal of mines — and living facilities, power generation, water supply, and waste management were constants, whether a base camp held 3,000 soldiers or 200; therefore construction requirements mushroomed accordingly. By the time the construction was under way, some areas were experiencing repeated snow falls with up to fourteen inches of snow a day (Kirkpatrick 2006).

It became apparent that Brown and Root had not contracted for engineering support on the scale required. Furthermore availability of tentage proved to be a problem. Contractors on 10 December estimated that they could emplace tents for about 3,000 soldiers within five days; in fact they were unable to do so until 18 December, a three-day extension that seemed short to planners but long to soldiers living in the cold (Kirkpatrick 2006, 412).

As a consequence of contractor limitations, the task force made use of navy Seabee construction units and air force Red Horse construction and Prime Beef power teams to get the work under way (Kirkpatrick 2006). Brown and Root, aided by these military engineers, eventually built some twenty-five camps to accommodate 20,400 U.S. troops in Bosnia and Hungary (Shrader 1999). Those troops had to be inserted into the personnel force flow into Bosnia, at a cost of some further disruption of the plan, and allowances had to be made to deliver their heavy equipment, for which transportation likewise had to be arranged. By that time the multiple base camps also required much more construction material and gravel fill than had been allowed for in the original planning (Kirkpatrick 2006).

Although the main LOGCAP contract in support of Operation Joint Endeavor cost $480.41 million (up to 27 December 1996), U.S. Army authorities claim that the use of Brown and Root and other contractors resulted in significant cost savings (Shrader 1999).[3] The participation of Brown and Root in Operation Joint Endeavor was typical of its activities as the principal LOGCAP contractor (Shrader 1999). Operation Joint Endeavor was the largest and most complex logistical effort undertaking by the U.S. Army Europe since World War II. Munden (1999) suggests that most military commanders recognize the availability and contribution of the Department of Defense civilians and contractors as part of the total force. Civilians often provide expertise not readily available, thereby allowing commanders to more effectively use assigned resources. Munden observes that since civilians are not counted against a force cap in the area of operation, military commanders can maximize their manpower by using contractors when feasible.

During Operation Joint Endeavor the logistics services provided by contractors included force provider, setup and maintenance, base camp operations and maintenance, facilities management, theater transportation and distribution support, fuel distribution, prime power, water and ice production, laundry and bath, airfield operations, supply operations, firefighting, security assistance, and mortuary affairs (Clements and Young 2005). The effort was facilitated, indeed made possible by the participation of a number of contractors, including Lockheed, Raytheon, Martin Marietta, Serv-Air, Esko, Ogden, and various Hungarian, Bosnian, and Croatian firms (Shrader 1999). However, logistics support was only one component contracted out by the military.

One form of U.S. military activity in the Balkans was military-to-military activities designed to help with the development and professionalization of local security forces; this included the provision of professional military education using International Military Education and Training and Extended International Military Education and Training programs, security assistance, mobile training teams, and combined exercises (Metz 2001). However, there were insufficient military forces available to conduct this training, so the Bosnian Federation hired the U.S. firm Military Professional Resource Incorporated (MPRI) to train and integrate the Bosniak and Bosnian Croat militaries. The two-year contract was valued at $80 million (U.S. Government Accountability Office 1998b).

Beginning in 1996 MPRI helped establish and train the Federations Ministry of Defense, the Joint Military Command, and the Joint Logistics and Training Command and conducted trainer courses in small unit tactics for nine of the fifteen Bosniak and Bosnian Croatian brigades. In October 1996 MPRI established the Federation Army School, which trained about 1,900 Bosniak and Bosnian Croat officers and noncommissioned officers. The school's leadership and technical training ranged from basic noncommissioned officers classes up to brigade and battalion commander and staff courses (U.S. Government Accountability Office 1998b).

In January 1997 MPRI opened the Federation Army combat simulation center near Hadzici, which trained Bosniak and Bosnian Croat commanders and staff on defensive strategy and defensive warfare. By 1998 the company had trained an additional 1,500 officers and noncommissioned officers at the Federation Army School, and 1,823 Federation Army personnel completed training on the operation and maintenance of the U.S.-provided tanks and armored personnel carriers (U.S. Government Accountability Office 1998b). Over $250 million in international cash donations were committed to funding the Federation training program (U.S. Government Accountability Office 1998b).

In addition to military training, the United States provided about $8.4 million to assist in training and equipping the local police forces in Bosnia and the U.S. Justice Department committed $9.97 million for the International Criminal Investigative Training Assistance Program for police training and other assistance in Bosnia, such as human dignity and basic skills training, the establishment of model police stations, the purchase of forensics equipment and training, executive development, and development of the Federation Police Academy (U.S. Government Accountability Office 1998b). It is unclear if contractors were hired to implement these programs.

As a result of the extensive mine clearance necessary between July and December 1997, three regionally based teams formed joint ventures with international demining companies and conducted demining operations funded by the World Bank. In March 1998 the regional teams (and their international partners) commenced work on another series of demining contracts financed by a U.S. grant to the World Bank Demining Trust Fund (U.S. Government Accountability Office 1998b, 188). The European Union, Bosnian government, nongovernmental organizations, and private contractors contributed to the effort to rid Bosnia of landmines in 1997. The European Union hired a contractor that trained, equipped, and supervised eighteen demining teams of twelve people each; six teams conducted demining operations in Republika Srpska, and twelve teams operated in the Federation (U.S. Government Accountability Office 1998b). Nine explosive ordnance disposal teams of four people each were trained, equipped, and supervised under another contract; funded by the European Union, they were the only dedicated teams of this type operating in Bosnia in 1997 and were responsible for clearing approximately 66 percent (13,000 pieces) of the total unexploded ordnance (U.S. Government Accountability Office 1998b).

From 1997 to 2000 approximately 14,000 contractors provided logistics support to combat troops, trained the Federation military forces, conducted demining, and participated in demining operations in Bosnia (Isenberg 2009). As a result the United States was able to reduce its military presence in Bosnia, which never exceeded 15,000 ground troops, who were able to focus on peacekeeping operations, the military portion of the Dayton Agreement.

Size of the Private Security Industry Used in Operation Joint Endeavor

To determine how many private security contractors participated in the intervention two factors are examined: actual numbers of private security contractors (where available) and the amount of Defense Department procurement funds spent on contracts (measures utilized by Krahmann 2010). Additionally this question explores what role, support (PMC) or security (PSC), the private security industry played in the intervention.

Approximately 14,000 contractors supported military operations in Bosnia, almost a 1:1 ratio of military troops to private military contractors. The United States relied on private contractors to provide logistics support to combat troops, train the Bosnia Federation military forces, and conduct demining operations throughout Bosnia. There are insufficient data on how many private contractors were U.S. citizens, third-country nationals, or Bosnian, Croat, or Serb nationals.

Between 1995 and 2000 the Defense Department spent an average of $150 billion a year on procurement contracts. Of this total, an average of $40 billion a year, about 40 percent, went to service contracts. The U.S. Government Accountability Office (1998b) estimates that the military and civilian costs for Operation Joint Endeavor exceeded $10 billion. Although there are insufficient data on the total cost for private contractors in Operation Joint Endeavor, $1 billion is a fair estimate.

Bureaucratic Controls on the Private Security Industry in Operation Joint Endeavor

Examining the laws, regulations, and controls in place during Operation Joint Endeavor aids in specifying the limitations and constraints of U.S. bureaucratic controls in place for the use of the private security industry. According to the theory of supply and demand, the more limitations and constraints, the less likely the private security industry is to be used; conversely the fewer bureaucratic limitations and controls, the easier it is to employ the private security industry. At the beginning of Operation Joint Endeavor there were few legal constraints barring the use of the private military industry.

The U.S. military entered Bosnia with an established procedure for contracting, the LOGCAP, a U.S. Army initiative for peacetime planning that allows for the use of civilian contractors in wartime and other contingencies. The first utilization of the LOGCAP program was in 1985, when the Third U.S. Army requested that the U.S. Army Corps of Engineers contract out a management plan to construct and maintain two petroleum pipeline systems in Southwest Asia in support of contingency operations (Clements and Young 2005).

The first LOGCAP contract for contingency operations in Bosnia was awarded to Brown and Root on 3 August 1992 as a cost-plus-fee contract with a one-year base period and a four-year option (Clements and Young 2005). The contract required services such as food preparation and services, laundry, logistics support such as local transportation, building large portions of the base camps, and performing other construction as directed by the army. In 1995 the U.S. Navy awarded the Construction Capabilities Contract, and the U.S. Air Force followed suit with the Air Force Contractor Augmentation Program contract in 1997 (Whitson 2001).

The contract for contingency operations expanded on the guidance from U.S. Army Regulation 700-137 (LOGCAP) dated 16 December 1985. Instead of relying on the services of available local national civilian personnel, as the U.S. military did in Desert Storm, the new contract relied on a U.S. company for logistics support. Whitson (2001) points out that by the conclusion of Vietnam, civilian contractors had established an acceptable means of augmenting logistical capabilities, especially during contingency operations conducted on short notice and usually in the rear area of operations.

The U.S. government controls and regulates the international supply of defense articles and services through the Arms Export Control Act, first implemented in 1968 (Ortiz 2010). Defense services are defined as furnishing assistance to foreign persons in the development or maintenance of defense articles and military training of foreign units and forces (Ortiz 2010). The U.S. Department of State manages the International Traffic in Arms Regulation that controls and regulates defense services outside the United States and requires the registration and licensing of U.S. persons willing to export defense articles and services. This means that any U.S. private contractor working overseas must register with the U.S. Department of State and receive a license before services can be provided. In the case of Bosnia approval from the State Department was necessary before Brown and Root was allowed work outside the United States.

Thus the Department of Defense entered Bosnia with an established procedure for contracting (LOGCAP); private contracting firms received approval from the Department of State to work in a foreign country; and the AECA and ITAR served as the control measures for the U.S. government to monitor the activities of private military companies in Bosnia. Therefore the laws, regulations, and control measures enabled the use of private military contractor use in Operation Joint Endeavor.

Duration of Operation Joint Endeavor

Beginning in December 1995 the United States and its allies deployed military forces to Bosnia-Herzegovina to implement the military elements of the Dayton Peace Accords. Operation Joint Endeavor marked the first time that NATO committed forces. The military component was designated IFOR. On 20 December 1996 IFOR came to a successful conclusion and the SFOR began Operation Joint Guard. On 20 June 1998 the NATO-led SFOR in Bosnia-Herzegovina transitioned to a slightly smaller follow-on force. Simultaneously Operation Joint Guard ended and Operation Joint Forge began ("Operation Joint Endeavor" n.d.).

On 2 December 2003 SFOR confirmed that due to the improved security situation in Bosnia and Herzegovina it would reduce to a deterrent force of approximately 7,000 multinational soldiers by June 2004. At the Istanbul Summit in June 2004, NATO heads of state and government agreed that in light of the improved security situation in the country SFOR could be concluded at the end of the year. A ceremony in Sarajevo on 2 December 2004 marked the conclusion of the NATO-led SFOR mission in Bosnia and Herzegovina and the beginning of the European Union's follow-on mission. The NATO-led SFOR was brought to a successful conclusion almost exactly nine years after NATO deployed forces in Bosnia and Herzegovina in what was the Alliance's first peacekeeping operation ("Operation Joint Forge" n.d.).

However, the successful termination of SFOR did not spell the end of

NATO's engagement in Bosnia and Herzegovina. The Alliance retained a military headquarters in Bosnia and Herzegovina, but the nature of NATO's engagement was very different. NATO Headquarters, which is headed by a one-star U.S. general with a staff of around 150, focused on security sector reform in the country, as well as counter terrorism, apprehending war crimes suspects, and intelligence gathering ("Operation Joint Forge" n.d.).

The military phase of Operation Joint Endeavor lasted nine years, although the Clinton administration had expected it to last only one year. However, the fragile security situation in Bosnia required the United States and its NATO partners to maintain a military presence to ensure security while the civilian component of the Dayton Peace Accords were implemented. This meant the private military industry had to provide logistics over a much longer period than expected. Establishing, training, and equipping the Bosnian Army also required more time than expected. As a result, there was a significant increase in the use of private military contractors in Operation Joint Endeavor.

Scope of Operation Joint Endeavor

Operation Joint Endeavor marked the first time that NATO committed forces in Europe. The United States and its NATO partners deployed into Bosnia a military force of 54,000 as part of the initial implementation force. The U.S. military force accounted for 16,200 of that total, plus 6,000 troops in Croatia and Hungary to support IFOR operations in Bosnia (U.S. Government Accountability Office 1998a). Most of the U.S. troops deployed to Bosnia came from military formations stationed in Germany. In all, thirty-six countries provided military forces to support both the IFOR and SFOR operations in Bosnia (U.S. Government Accountability Office 1998c).

In December 1996, when the IFOR operation transitioned to the SFOR mission, Operation Joint Guard, both the United States and its NATO partners reduced the size of this military force. From the initial 54,000 that supported IFOR, a total of 31,000 NATO troops remained to support the SFOR operation. The United States provided 8,300 troops to this NATO force, with an additional 3,400 support troops in Croatia and Hungary (U.S. Government Accountability Office 1998a, 2). In June 1998 NATO once again reduced its military presence, this time to 27,588. The United States provided 6,900 soldiers as part of Operation Joint Forge, with an additional 2,600 support troops in Hungary and Italy (U.S. Government Accountability Office 1998c). Even at these reduced numbers, the United States provided the largest military contingent to IFOR and SFOR.

Most of the U.S. troops participating in Bosnia were active duty forces; however, almost 16,000 army reservists and about 10,000 Air Force Air Reserve Component members participated in the Bosnia mission between its inception in December 1995 and January 1998 (U.S. Government Accountability Office 1998a). This required that the president invoke the Presidential Selected Reserve Call-up (PSRC), which can call military reservists to active duty for a maximum of 270 days. Yet the duration of the Bosnia mission led to a situation where, in some instances, all of the reservists with needed capabilities had been ordered to duty and served the maximum time allowed for a single call-up (U.S. Government Accountability Office 1998a). Requirements for these personnel totaled several hundred persons per rotation.

Between 1995 and 1998 the United States provided about $10.6 billion for military and civilian support to the Bosnia peace operation. From this total about $8.6 billion was spent on military-related operations and about $2 billion for civilian-related operations (U.S. Government Accountability Office 1998b). The U.S. civilian-related operations focused on programs designed to assist in the economic, political, and social transition taking place in Bosnia. Most of this assistance, almost $250 million, was funded by the U.S. Agency for International Development (USAID). The State Department provided about $190 million; the remainder was obligated by other civilian agencies, including USAID and the Departments of Justice, Commerce, and the Treasury (U.S. Government Accountability Office 1998b).

The type of peacekeeping operation and the terrain encountered by the troops further expanded the scope of the U.S. operation. Initially the United States planned to occupy and operate out of eight base camps in Bosnia. However, the limited availability of suitable terrain and the extensive minefields caused the United States to increase the number of base camps (Johnson 1999). Instead of eight base camps occupied by about 3,000 soldiers, the United States built over twenty base camps throughout Bosnia. Additionally the nature of the mission and the size of the zones of separation spread the U.S. military forces over an area the size of Connecticut (Johnson 1999).

In order to get troops into Bosnia, the United States deployed forces from Germany that traveled about nine hundred miles through Austria, the Czech Republic, Hungary, and Croatia into Bosnia. It typically took three to four days to reach Hungary by rail from Frankfurt am Main, Germany. Once the military units got to the Sava River, they had another thirty miles, or two hours by road march, to reach Tuzla. Between December 1995 and February 1996 the United States deployed more than 16,000 personnel, 1,000 vehicles and pieces of equipment, and 145 helicopters into the U.S. sector of operations in Bosnia and Herzegovina. The force deployed into twenty-four base camps in and around the zone of separation, from where it could best monitor the terms of the Dayton Accord. Sustaining the deployed forces required a daily flow of three convoys and twelve air sorties carrying 75,000 meals, 192,000 gallons of water, 130,000 gallons of fuel, and 133 short tons of supplies (*The U.S. Army in Bosnia and Herzegovina* 2003).

The scope of Operation Joint Endeavor resulted in an increased use of the private security industry. The size of the U.S. military force committed to IFOR, although substantial, lacked the logistical support necessary for sustained operations over a vast area. As noted previously, the U.S. military planned to conduct operations from eight base camps in Bosnia. However, the availability of suitable terrain and the extensive minefields forced the U.S. military to build a total of twenty-four base camps in Bosnia. With a self-imposed force cap the U.S. military turned to the private security industry to fill the gap in base support and logistics.

Other Conflicts or Deployments during Operation Joint Endeavor

Besides over 16,000 troops in support of operations in Bosnia, in 1995 the U.S. military had troops committed to NATO, Korea, and Haiti. Of the total force, 238,064 troops were stationed outside of the continental United States: over 109,000 troops were supporting NATO, over 75,000 were stationed in Korea, and 1,600 troops were still in Haiti supporting Operation Uphold Democracy. This represents 15 percent of the total force deployed and over 19 percent of the available ground force in the Defense

Department (U.S. Department of Defense, Defense Manpower Data Center 1954–2012).

Due to ongoing military commitments to NATO exercises most units were away from their home stations in Germany between 40 and 50 percent of the time (Swain 2003). These figures make it clear how little room for maneuver the commander of U.S. forces in Europe actually had to mitigate the intense personnel tempo for his units, even before he had to send a third of his command to conduct operations in Bosnia (Swain 2003). Moreover, Secretary of Defense William Perry had adopted as one of his personal priorities the initiation of frequent professional contacts with former Warsaw Pact defense establishments to encourage and facilitate their progressive democratization. Swain points out that in January 1994, NATO undertook a program of exchanges called Partnership for Peace, for which the U.S. Army in Europe supported nineteen of the fifty-one teams. As a result the United States increased its use of private military contractors to fill the shortfalls in logistics in Operation Joint Endeavor.

The Size of the U.S. Military during Operation Joint Endeavor

At the end of September 1995 the number of active U.S. military troops was slightly more than 1,513,000. This all-volunteer force included ground combat forces from the U.S. Army and U.S. Marine Corps, totaling 508,559 and 174,639, respectively (U.S. Department of Defense, Defense Manpower Data Center 1954–2012). Additionally, the U.S. Defense Department employed 820,189 government civilians, who supported a wide range of functions for the active military. This was a 30 percent decrease from its peak size during Operations Desert Shield and Desert Storm.

The size of the U.S. military in 1995 represented the base force envisioned by General Powell and President Bush. The outcome of the Gulf War influenced executive decision making on the size of the military (Snider 1993). Specifically the Gulf War validated the strategy of crisis response and supported the assumption that U.S. high-technology capabilities could decisively defeat the other forces; therefore troop strength could be reduced while funding for high-tech capabilities increased. However, the military restructuring was also a result of the collapse of the Soviet Union, which eliminated the immediate threat to the United States (Herspring 2005). And increasing national fiscal problems left the Pentagon deeply in debt, which resulted in significant cuts in the force structure. However, there may have been a mismatch between national-level strategic objectives and the force end strength that affected the role of the army in the Balkans: the high operational tempo in the 1990s, particularly in the Balkans, forced the U.S. military to postpone many procurement programs and stretch out maintenance and replacement activities (Metz 2001). Due to the decrease in the size of the military force the United States increased its use of private military contractors during Operation Joint Endeavor to fill shortfalls in logistics and training.

Military Outlays during Operation Joint Endeavor

By 1995 and the beginning of Operation Joint Endeavor, the U.S. defense budget was over $272 billion (U.S. Office of Management and Budget 1995). This amounted to 3.7 percent of the U.S. GDP or 17.9 percent of budget outlays. In a matter of five years since the end of the cold war, U.S. military spending decreased over $32 billion, a 2 percent reduction in GDP allocation or a 9 percent reduction of the total U.S. budget outlays. Herspring (2005) asserts that the Bush I administration significantly changed the face of the U.S. military.

In comparison the U.S. government allocated over $923 billion for human resource spending, 12.6 percent of GDP or 60.9 percent of total budget outlays. U.S. spending on domestic programs increased by almost $400 billion over a five-year period, which amounted to a 2 percent increase in GDP or 11 percent increase of budget outlays.

The U.S. Department of Defense (Defense Manpower Data Center 1954–2012) spent over $157 billion on contracts: 54.3 percent of the total Defense outlays. The spending on service contracts amounted to over $49 billion or 31.2 percent of Defense contracts. Service contracts differ from product contracts or research and development contracts.

Thus between 1991 and 1995 the United States decreased its defense spending by 9 percent of the total budget outlays. However, the use of private contractors in Operation Joint Endeavor increased as the U.S. defense budget decreased. Herspring (2005, 325) points out that a number of members of Congress argued that these defense cuts provided a peace dividend.

Choices Other Than the Private Security Industry

Although the United States and its NATO partners relied on private military contractors to augment shortfalls in logistics support and conduct the train-and-equip mission, there is no evidence of a demand for private security companies. The Dayton Agreement resulted in an end to hostilities in Bosnia prior to Operation Joint Endeavor. Therefore the NATO forces operated in an environment that was semipermissive. In essence IFOR and SFOR provided their own security tasks along with the military tasks outlined in the Dayton Accords.

Moreover Bosnia-Herzegovina did not provide host-nation security; each party maintained local security within their zones of occupation in an environment with over 400,000 men under arms (Bosnian Serbs, Croats, and Bosniaks), including civilian militias with an estimated strength of 45,000. In spite of this, there were only a few U.S. casualties due to hostile action. The U.S. and NATO forces were able to maintain security for themselves and their civilian counterparts working throughout Bosnia. Therefore there was not a demand for additional private security forces.

The United States relied on its NATO partners to provide forces for Operation Joint Endeavor; in fact NATO provided the bulk of the ground forces during the operation. Furthermore the United States activated a substantial amount of its reserve and National Guard force to supplement its active duty force in Bosnia. However, congressional restrictions on the time that reservists could remain on active duty limited their use as the operation in Bosnia extended beyond its first year. Additionally the nature of the mission in Bosnia, peace enforcement, prevented the United States and NATO from using host-nation security forces. Therefore the United States turned to private military contractors as a substitute.

Private Security Supply-Demand Behavior: An Assessment

In the case of Operation Joint Endeavor, private security supply-demand behavior is evident for support services but not necessarily for security services.

Kaufman (2002) points out that domestic political considerations and economic realities directly affected NATO's decisions. Additionally, by 1991 most Western countries were facing economic recessions that caused them to focus inward rather than outward (4). As Yugoslavia was beginning to disintegrate, the governments of Western Europe and the United States had other concerns of higher priority than the Yugoslavia crisis (Woodward 1995). They had just fought the Persian Gulf War and were not eager to engage in another conflict, preferring to pay attention to domestic concerns (Kaufman 2002).

Snider (1993) asserts that when the Bush administration came to office in early 1989, the government was financially broke and priority had to be placed on reducing the twin deficits of budget and trade. Thus the decision of ramping down America's defenses was very strongly—perhaps most strongly—influenced by domestic economic problems. As a result General Powell, the chairman of the Joint Chiefs, began to develop his ideas for an altered force structure that would respond to the changes in both the strategic and the fiscal environments in a way that would make it possible for the United States not only to maintain a strong defense but also to retain its superpower status (Jaffe 1993).

Powell believed that major force realignments were necessary because if funding continued to decline while the size of the armed forces and their missions remained unchanged, the number of commitments around the world would stretch the U.S. military beyond its capability (Jaffe 1993). Jaffe observes that Powell regarded his principal challenge as chairman to be reshaping defense policies and the armed forces to deal with the changing world and the declining defense budget. His proposed solution was a new military force structure: the base force (Herspring 2005).

The base force would have a total active strength of 1.6 million instead of the current 2.1 million and a reserve component strength of 898,000 instead of the current 1.56 million. The conventional component would be composed of 12 active and 8 reserve army divisions, 16 active and 12 reserve air force tactical fighter wings, 150,000 personnel in the 3 active Marine Corps divisions and 38,000 in the Marine Corps reserve divisions, and 450 ships, including 12 carriers in the navy (Jaffe 1993, 21). Since the late 1940s the United States had based its national military strategy on the necessity of deterring and, if deterrence failed, successfully fighting a global war against the Soviet Union (Jaffe 1993). However, Powell argued that with the prospect of an accelerated decline in defense funding, together with the sweeping changes taking place with the former Warsaw Pact, the base force would not only meet U.S. defense needs in the new era but would provide an expandable base on which a larger force could be reconstituted should the need arise (Jaffe 1993). Interestingly Cheney allowed Powell and the service chiefs to decide which forces they should cut (Herspring 2005).

By the summer of 1995 there were slightly more than 62,500 army troops stationed in Europe, in contrast to more than 216,000 in 1989. This represented a 66 percent reduction as a result of the base force strategy and policy (Swain 2003). Furthermore the army's budget in Europe decreased from $6 billion to $2.5 billion (59 percent), and only two combat divisions remained in Germany (Swain 2003). Metz (2001) asserts that the U.S. defense budget and force size affected the role of the army in the Balkans. He also states that nearly every analyst of U.S. defense strategy admits that there was a mismatch between national-level strategic objectives and the force end strength. Yet the army planners were delighted to find that, for the first time, they were not constrained on the number of soldiers that could be used in Bosnia (Kirkpatrick 2006).

U.S. planners developed a force structure for Operation Joint Endeavor based on the assumptions that the units would operate in northern Bosnia and that they would have to monitor a zone of separation between warring parties (Kirkpatrick 2006). The plans provided a range of options that called for 31,000 to 38,000 ground troops; however, a force cap of 25,000 was eventually imposed on the total U.S. strength in Bosnia (Kirkpatrick 2006). Faced with this limitation, the military planners concluded that American troops could be augmented by some three brigades of multinational forces, each of which would bring its own logistical support. However, as Kirkpatrick points out, the U.S. division assigned the Bosnia mission would also need augmentation.

The force cap was reduced again, to 20,000, in August 1995, and the train-and-equip mission for the Bosnian Army was deleted, later to be given to private contractors (Kirkpatrick 2006). A few days later the force cap was reduced again, this time to 14,900 (Swain 2003). Military planners responded to the force limitations by asking V Corps which parts of the force could satisfactorily be replaced by multinational units. The corps staff concluded that foreign construction engineers, combat engineers, and bridging units would present no interoperability problems (Kirkpatrick 2006). Similarly transportation units for line haul could be from other armies, as could the chemical units, heavy rotary-wing aircraft, and some signal units. Medical support, however, should remain based on American units. Much of the logistics support would be located outside of Bosnia, in Kaposvar-Taszar, Hungary. Military personnel assigned to the U.S. national support element would not count against the 15,000 force cap (Swain 2003).

The U.S. Army has always found itself short of skilled logistical support personnel, particularly during periods of relative peace (Shrader 1999). The rationale has been that combat service support personnel are in the "nice to have" rather than the "essential" category, and when economic and political pressures for reductions in defense spending and the size of the standing army have risen, logistical personnel and capabilities have often been the first to be sacrificed (Shrader 1999). Thus since the late 1950s no major operation undertaken by the army—including Vietnam and Gulf wars as well as a host of large and small contingency operations—could have been successfully completed without the assistance of civilian contractors (Shrader 1999).

By mid-1998 the extended mission in Bosnia caused the military services to seek alternative ways to provide some needed capabilities. One U.S. government report pointed out that although the vast majority of the ground-based combat support and aviation-related requirements were filled, about a dozen unit capabilities required special attention because the capabilities were primarily in the reserves and many of these capabilities had been mobilized and deployed in support of the operation (U.S. Government Accountability Office 1998a). The report suggested that if U.S. Atlantic Command was unable to find other services to meet these requirements, other solutions were possible, including using more ad hoc units, contracting civilians to perform the function, and seeking to have other NATO partners assume some of these responsibilities. For example, firefighting functions normally performed by military engineers would be contracted out to private firms.

In October 1998 U.S.-trained Hungarian air traffic controllers replaced U.S. controllers, further reducing operator requirements, and in November the U.S. Air Force planned to hire contractors for the maintenance portion of the mission. Thus in the case of Operation Joint Endeavor some specialty capabilities were transferred to other countries after the United States trained their personnel (U.S. Government Accountability Office 1998a).

The president initiated a PSRC, ordering units and members of the selected reserve to active duty for 270 days without their consent. That allowed time for mobilization, training, six months to execute the mission in Bosnia, and demobilization (Munden 1999). By 1998 most reserve units with the skills required for Bosnia had already served their 270 days on active duty, and the president chose not to initiate a second PSRC. Prior to 1995 PSRC authority had been used twice: for the Gulf War and the operation in Haiti (U.S. Government Accountability Office 1998a). However, the statute also caps at 200,000 the total number of reservists who may be serving on active duty under PSRC at any one time.

Summary and Analysis

Supply-demand behavior is evident during Operation Joint Endeavor. Military planners and decision makers entered the operation with a force significantly reduced from its cold war peak. The demand for an expeditionary logistics force capability was high, yet most of the U.S. logistics force structure resided in the reserve force. Military planners substituted its homogeneous logistics support for contractors hired through the LOGCAP program. An early decision to deploy combat forces first into Bosnia resulted in a requirement for logistics support as the demand for transportation, housing, and food increased dramatically; in response military planners immediately turned to private contractors as a substitute. Decisions to impose a ceiling on forces deployed into theater and the ability of private contractors to fill the void in logistics support reduced the need for additional homogeneous logistics capabilities. These events represented shifts in the U.S. demand curve.

The case study provides an alternative explanation for the use of the private security industry. In 1995 a force cap of 15,000 U.S. soldiers required military leaders to choose between deploying combat or logistics forces into theater. They chose to deploy combat soldiers and hired logistics support from private military companies.

Second, the U.S. military did not have host-nation support from the Bosnian Serbs, the Bosnian Croats, or the Bosniaks. Instead it relied on private military companies for essential services like base support, transportation, and maintenance.

Third, the U.S. and NATO forces operated in a semipermissive security environment while conducting peace enforcement operations. Moreover the U.S. and Coalition forces allocated a portion of their troops for force protection. As a result the U.S. military relied on private military companies for support, not security.

U.S. participation in Bosnia involved a major commitment of national resources and prestige to an alliance effort for a prolonged period of time in a dangerous undertaking of doubtful positive political value and during a period of radical political division at home (Swain 2003). Swain suggests that because of the unique nature of the mission and the force cap limits, creativity was required in designing the mission. That creativity resulted in the use of private military contractors to supplement U.S. military forces in Bosnia.

In particular the U.S. Army corps assigned to the Bosnia mission had little influence on the force structure decisions, particularly in light of the centrally directed drawdown of forces that was even then gradually coming to an end in Germany (Kirkpatrick 2006). Thus the corps was obliged to accept shortages in deploying units and borrowed soldiers and equipment from units that would remain in Germany. For other essential services, private contracting filled the void. The widespread use of civilian contractors enabled military units not committed to Bosnia to be available for other major regional conflicts and solved the problem of troop ceilings (Reeve 2001). Political constraints limited the number of troops in Bosnia, so the United States gave most support functions to contractors because they were not included in the total force figures (Reeve 2001).

The overall performance of Brown and Root and other civilian contractors in Bosnia was excellent (Shrader 1999). Although some difficulties were encountered, on the whole the logistical contractors worked diligently and effectively to support U.S. troops. Whitson (2001, 12) points out another advantage of using contractors that is not quite so evident: when contractors hire local civilians, contractor support becomes a political tool for putting hard-pressed local nationals back to work in what is frequently a depressed economy. The use of contract labor in support of the mission in Bosnia produced a definite economic impact on the region secured by U.S. forces and supported a basic pillar in the operational commander's strategic campaign plan (Whitson 2001).

Operation Joint Endeavor is a most likely case for examining private security supply-demand behavior. Although the number of employed contractors used by the United States did not exceed 14,000, the high ratio of contractors to troops (1:1) fits the demands of a most likely case. There are a number or reasons for this outcome. First and foremost, the size of the U.S. forces in Bosnia never exceeded 15,000 troops. The force cap imposed on military planners forced them to substitute military force structure for private contractors. Military planners determined that the mission required 38,000 ground troops; however, once the force cap was imposed, planners assigned military forces to the core military tasks required by the Dayton Accords and used private contractors for logistics support and training assistance. Second, the security environment in Bosnia was only semipermissive, a far different scenario than the U.S. military encountered in the Persian Gulf in 1990. The U.S. and Coalition forces conducted operations in an environment where they had to allocate troops to force protection. The combined Bosniak, Croat, and Serb security forces exceeded 440,000, but they did not provide the security for IFOR or SFOR. The Dayton Accords provided the U.S. and Coalition forces international legitimacy, and the terms of the agreement forced the political parties in Bosnia to comply. Subsequently Bosnia provided little to no support services or force protection support for the U.S. and NATO forces. And the United States and its NATO partners conducted Operation Joint Endeavor as a neutral external force.

CHAPTER FIVE

OPERATION ENDURING FREEDOM

This chapter argues that the events surrounding Operation Enduring Freedom (October 2001–April 2014) support some of the assertions in the literature on supply and demand concerning the use of the private security industry. The operation's main descriptive fact for most observers — that the number of contractors on the battlefield equaled that of U.S. forces — cannot be explained without considering the nature of the intervention, the decisions by senior U.S. leaders to limit the size of U.S. forces in Afghanistan, the scope and duration of the operation, and the nature of the security environment. The results show that Operation Enduring Freedom is another post–cold war example of private security supply-demand behavior.

Operation Enduring Freedom is a most likely case (George and Bennett 2005). The size of the U.S. military and its budget were significantly less than the peak cold war levels at the beginning of Operation Enduring Freedom. Additionally the intervention lasted for over fourteen years. Aside from its military commitments to NATO, Korea, Iraq, and the Philippines, the United States faced competing conflicts around the world during the time of the intervention. For all of these reasons, the likelihood was high that the United States would have to rely on significant support from the private security industry.

In fact the use of contractors was so essential to the mission that numerous scholars focus on this case when studying the rise of the private security industry (Carafano 2008; Kinsey 2006). As this chapter demonstrates, however, there are details beyond supply-demand theory that are necessary to understand the U.S. reliance on the private security industry, most notably the political imposition of various force caps on troop size throughout the mission and the security environment in Afghanistan. This case thus demonstrates both the utility of supply-demand theory as well as some of its limitations. As such it offers a challenging test of theory in the form of a most likely case (George and Bennett 2005).

Overview of Events

When the sun rose on the morning of 11 September 2001, few Americans had ever heard of Osama bin Laden. Fewer still could point to Afghanistan on a map. That would all change after nineteen men hijacked four planes and flew two of them into the World Trade Center and one into the Pentagon and one crashed in a field in Pennsylvania. When bin Laden claimed responsibility for the attacks and the deaths of close to three thousand people, President George W. Bush asked for and received unanimous Senate authorization to use all necessary and appropriate force to respond (Tanner 2002).

The United States demanded that the Taliban government in Afghanistan turn over bin Laden, but the nominal leader of the Taliban, Mullah Omar, simply refused (Tanner 2002). On 20 September 2001 Bush told the nation that bin Laden and the Taliban leadership were complicit in the attacks. On 6 October he gave his final ultimatum to Taliban leadership in Kabul (Wright et al. 2010). Faced with an impending attack from the United States the Taliban mullahs countered with a call for a holy war against those who would invade an Islamic country (Tanner 2002). The United States, backed by its NATO partners and supported by the United Nations, began its military intervention in Afghanistan, known as Operation Enduring Freedom.[1]

Operation Enduring Freedom can be divided into three distinct phases: major combat operations to remove the Taliban regime (2001–3); a stability and security phase (2003–9); and a military surge and withdrawal phase (2009–15). The initial phase began on 7 October 2001, with airstrikes targeting Taliban compounds, command and control facilities, and airfields (Tanner 2002). By mid-October about 1,000 U.S. Special Forces and agents from the Central Intelligence Agency were directly supporting the Afghan Northern Alliance ground offensive against the Taliban (Katzman 2014). In northern Afghanistan, the Northern Alliance captured the town of Mazar-e Sharif on 10 November and the town of Kunduz on 24 November, effectively eliminating the Taliban resistance from the northern part of the country (Wright et al. 2010). Wright et al. suggests that the unprecedented combination of Special Forces directing precision-guided airstrikes in support of the Northern Alliance's ground offensive led to the decisive defeat of the Taliban in northern Afghanistan.

Concurrent with the offensive in the north, Special Forces teams linked up with Northern Alliance forces in the city of Bagram, just north of Kabul. Between 19 October and 13 November, Special Forces directed precision-guided airstrikes against Taliban defensive positions in and around Bagram airfield. On 13 November the Taliban defense collapsed, and on 14 November Northern Alliance forces rolled into Kabul, liberating the city from Taliban rule (Wright et al. 2010). Also in late October about 1,300 marines arrived in Kandahar to put pressure on the Taliban; however, the marines saw very little combat (Katzman 2014).

In southern Afghanistan, Special Forces linked up with Hamid Karzai and his anti-Taliban force in mid-November to support offensive operations against the Taliban defending the area. In a little less than three weeks Taliban forces in Kandahar surrendered to Karzai on 7 December, effectively clearing the south of Taliban resistance (Tanner 2002). The sudden collapse of the Taliban came as a surprise after only two months of combat operations (Tanner 2002). The Afghan Northern and Southern Alliance supported by 110 CIA officers and 316 Special Forces troops and precision-guided airstrikes effectively toppled the Taliban rule in Afghanistan (Herspring 2008).

In December 2001 the council of Afghan leaders met in Bonn, Germany, to establish a framework for an Afghan Interim Authority. The Afghan leaders nominated and Karzai accepted the position of chairman of the governing committee of the Afghan Interim Authority on 22 December (Wright et al. 2010). Although the Taliban had been defeated, the fledging Afghan government faced the task of eliminating Al Qaeda from Afghanistan. Thus military operations shifted to Tora Bora and the Shah-i-Kot Valley in the southeast in late December 2001 and March 2002. The battle for Tora Bora failed to capture bin Laden, though it did remove Al Qaeda from its stronghold in eastern Afghanistan (Wright et al. 2010). However, through the months of January and February 2002, remnants of Al Qaeda began assembling south of Khost. In the first weeks of March the largest U.S. ground battle, Operation Anaconda, commenced to destroy the remaining forces of about 800 Al Qaeda in Afghanistan (Tanner 2002; Katzman 2014). Wright et al. (2010) assert that Operation Anaconda was the largest and most successful combat operation of the Coalition campaign in Afghanistan. As a result of the operation the ability of the Taliban and its ally Al Qaeda to conduct military operations in Afghanistan were shattered (Wright et al. 2010). On 1 May 2003 Secretary of Defense Donald Rumsfeld announced an end to major combat operations in Afghanistan (Katzman 2014).

Following the collapse of the Taliban, the United States and its Coalition partners shifted their focus to a security mission to prevent the military and political resurgence of the Taliban, reconstruction operations, and programs to train Afghan security forces (Wright et al. 2010). Bird and Marshall (2011, 251) point out, "The one time in Afghanistan's history when Western state-building schemes had even a glimmer of a chance of making progress was in the period immediately following the overthrow of the Taliban." However, the problem facing foreign powers has never been how to get into Afghanistan but how to govern and control it (Tanner 2002). The stability phase of Operation Enduring Freedom would prove this again.

Stability and security operations dominated the second distinct phase of Operation Enduring Freedom. Wright et al. (2010) conclude that in March 2002 Afghanistan appeared ready to rise from the ashes of Taliban rule. Following the Bonn Conference in December 2001, the United Nations passed Resolution 1386 calling for the establishment of the International Security Assistance Force (ISAF), 4,500 soldiers strong, to assist the Afghan Interim Authority in the maintenance of security in Kabul and the surrounding area (Wright et al. 2010). The ISAF security mission paralleled the U.S. mission to continue operations to kill or capture the residual Taliban and Al Qaeda remaining in Afghanistan and supervised the creation of an Afghan security force. To accomplish this mission the U.S. military established Combined

Joint Task Force 180 with an informal force cap of 7,000 U.S. servicemen. At the time it appeared the White House, the Pentagon, and Central Command strongly wished to minimize the presence of U.S. forces in Afghanistan (Herspring 2008; Wright et al. 2010; Bird and Marshall 2011). Although there was no official guidance on an official cap of forces, the idea of a "light footprint" guided the planning (Herspring 2008).

The stability phase of Operation Enduring Freedom was dominated by three distinct missions: combat operations to eliminate the Taliban and Al Qaeda threats, reconstruction operations, and building and training the Afghan National Army. However, the light footprint of the United States and ISAF resulted in their forces being stretched thin across all three missions. As a result, in 2003 the Taliban reorganized along the Afghan-Pakistan border and began insurgent attacks against U.S., ISAF, and Afghan forces. From a small core of 2,000 fighters in 2003, the Taliban ranks swelled to 17,000 by 2006. Taliban attacks ranged from long-range rocket attacks to well-coordinated ambushes and full-scale assaults on U.S. and ISAF outposts (Bird and Marshall 2011). Taliban violence against U.S., ISAF, and Afghan forces steadily increased between 2003 and 2007. During this period suicide attacks increased from one or two to 140. Attacks from improvised explosive devices increased to 1,297 in 2007, and the direct attacks from small arms to 2,892 the same year (Bird and Marshall 2011). Bird and Marshall conclude that "the near-lethal combination of blind optimism and neglect prevailed between 2002 and 2005 that laid the ground for the Taliban revival of 2006" (150).

In 2006, while U.S. forces focused on security operations in eastern Afghanistan, ISAF expanded its mission to include security and counter-insurgency in the south of Afghanistan. Led by the United Kingdom and supported by Canadian and Dutch forces, ISAF assumed responsibility for Regional Command South. Initially only 3,300 NATO troops were committed to the area of operation (Bird and Marshall 2011). Yet insurgent attacks steady increased throughout the country by 27 percent compared to 2006 levels. In Regional Command South the levels of violence increased by 60 percent during the same period. By 2008 the security situation in Afghanistan continued to spiral. In response Gen. David McKiernan, commander of ISAF, requested 30,000 additional U.S. troops (Bird and Marshall 2011).

By 2008 violence in Afghanistan had increased dramatically, proving to be the deadliest year for U.S. and ISAF forces (Livingston and O'Hanlon 2014). As the number of attacks spiked through 2008, U.S. forces sustained 155 deaths and ISAF lost 292. Afghan security forces fared worse, sustaining well over 1,100 deaths in 2008 alone (Livingston and O'Hanlon 2014). As a result the United States and Great Britain increased their troop commitments, which became known as "the quiet surge." At the same time, several NATO members announced that they would withdraw troops in the near future. Canada planned to pull out all combat forces by 2011, and the Dutch withdrew by the end of 2010. France and other NATO countries were reluctant to support an increase in the number of troops committed to countering the ever increasing violence in Afghanistan (Bird and Marshall 2011). With the election of Barack Obama as president in November 2008, the United States announced a new strategy for Afghanistan, signaling a new phase in Operation Enduring Freedom.

The military surge and withdrawal phase (2009–14) represents the third distinct phase of Operation Enduring Freedom. In March President Obama announced that the core strategic objective was to disrupt, dismantle, and defeat Al Qaeda in Pakistan and Afghanistan. Secretary of Defense Robert Gates (2014) describes a lively debate that raged among the administration, Congress, and the military commanders over the size of the force necessary to accomplish the task. As a result two U.S. commanders were replaced as ISAF commanders, and Gen. David Petraeus assumed command in June 2010 to implement the new U.S. strategy with 30,000 additional U.S. troops. This represented a significant shift from the light footprint that had guided U.S. policy since 2001.

Coinciding with the surge of U.S. and ISAF forces in Afghanistan, violence reached its most historic and deadly peak in September 2010, with over 1,600 insurgent attacks of all types resulting in 465 U.S. deaths (Livingston and O'Hanlon 2014). Although Afghan security forces increased in size to over 260,000, they sustained over 1,500 fatalities in 2010 and over 1,200 fatalities in 2011. Afghan civilians also bore the brunt of the increased violence, with over 2,500 reported deaths in 2010 and close to 3,000 deaths in 2011 as a result of fighting between pro-government forces and armed opposition groups (Livingston and O'Hanlon 2014). In October 2011 the United States marked ten years of war in Afghanistan, the longest war in the country's history.

Beginning in January 2012 the United States and ISAF began reducing the number of troops deployed to Afghanistan with an eye toward transitioning the responsibility for security to the government of Afghanistan. In early 2012 the Afghan National Security Force took the lead responsibility for security in eighteen provinces, which represented over 50 percent of the Afghan civilian population (Sopko 2012). Although violence began to decrease slightly, the security situation remained tenuous at best, with Afghan security forces sustaining 60 percent of the casualties while conducting 80 percent of all operations.

The United States and ISAF began shifting to a security forces assistance role for the 325,000-strong Afghan security force (Sopko 2013). By June 2013 the Afghan security forces had responsibility for thirty-four provincial capitals based on the Lisbon and Chicago NATO summits that announced the official transition of ISAF to its new role of largely security assistance (U.S. Department of Defense 2013). As U.S. and ISAF troop strengths decreased, so did their number of casualties, falling to 160 in 2013 and 19 by early 2014. Afghan security forces sustained well over 300 deaths in 2013.

Although a pervasive insecurity and a resilient insurgency remain in much of Afghanistan, presidential elections were held in April 2014 that marked the first peaceful democratic transition of power in the country's history. The Special Inspector General for Afghanistan Reconstruction characterizes 2014 as a pivotal year for political and military transition in Afghanistan. Still to be decided is the role that the United States and ISAF will take in the future of Afghanistan. The governments of the United States and Afghanistan are still negotiating a bilateral security agreement to serve as the legal framework for the presence of U.S. forces in Afghanistan after 2014 (U.S. Department of Defense 2014). The intent of the agreement is to outline future defense cooperation between the two countries. The future role of the private security industry in Afghanistan is yet to be determined, however.

Private Contractors in Operation Enduring Freedom

In 2008 the Office of the Under Secretary of Defense for Acquisition, Technology and Logistics reported to the U.S. Congress that "contractors are part of the total force, providing an adaptable mix of unique skill sets, local knowledge, and flexibility that a strictly military force cannot cultivate or resource for all scenarios" (U.S. Department of Defense, Assistant Under Secretary for Office of Program Support under CENTCOM July 2008, 1). They pointed out that the Department of Defense relies more heavily on contracted support during the postconflict phases of an operation, particularly when the duration and scale of the operation increase. Between 2001 and 2014 the ratio of U.S. military troops to private contractors in Afghanistan increased from 1:0 to 1:46, illustrating the increased reliance on contractor support as Operation Enduring Freedom shifted from major combat operations to stability operations.

The large scope of Operation Enduring Freedom (i.e., the three distinct missions) required competencies sometimes in short supply within the military ranks (Kidwell 2005). The private security industry stepped in to provide a wide variety of services that included base support, construction, transportation, security, and training local security forces (Schwartz and Swain 2011). Base support, sometimes referred to as theater support of the Logistics Civilian Augmentation Program (LOGCAP), accounted for approximately 12 percent of the contractor workforce. Construction projects for the military or reconstruction accounted for about 9 percent of the contractor workforce. Contractors providing logistics and maintenance made up the largest contingent at 21 percent. Approximately 17 percent of contractors provided security-related services. Private security contractors performed personal security, convoy security, and static security (U.S. Department of Defense, Assistant Under Secretary for Office of Program Support under CENTCOM 2010).

U.S. citizens, third-country nationals, and local or host-nation nationals accounted for the total reported private security industry workforce in Afghanistan. U.S. citizens typically made up about 30 percent of the total contractor workforce, while most contractors were either private citizens from Afghanistan or hired from a third country. However, the ratio is slightly different when looking at private security contractors. U.S. citizens typically accounted for less than 5 percent of the total private security contractors, which is a subset of the total private security industry present in Afghanistan. Host-nation nationals made up the majority of private security contractors at about 80 percent, and third-country nationals accounted for approximately 15 percent. Although these numbers adjust slightly over the seven-year reporting period, the percentages remained fairly consistent (U.S. Department of Defense, Assistant Under Secretary for Office of Program Support under CENTCOM 2008–14). This reflects the policy of "Afghan First" that directed U.S. and NATO forces to hire Afghans first, buy Afghan products, and build Afghan capacity (Schwartz and Swain 2011).

Individual contractors in Afghanistan have been exposed to the ongoing violence as they work alongside their military partners. As the level of violence increased in Afghanistan the number of private contractor deaths also increased. Coinciding with the spike in violence in 2010 over 400 private contractors died, exceeding the number of U.S. troops killed in the same year. As of May 2012 over 1,110 private contractors had been killed in Operation Enduring Freedom (Livingston and O'Hanlon 2014, 13). As Carafano (2008) points out, contractors are targets as well as combat assets.

Size of the Private Security Industry Used in Operation Enduring Freedom

The number of private military contractors in Afghanistan steadily increased as the duration of the operation increased, although the Department of Defense did not begin gathering data on the number of private contractors in Afghanistan (and Iraq) until the second half of 2007 (Schwartz and Swain 2011). Furthermore the U.S. Government Accountability Office warns that due to the questionable reliability of the data, caution should be used when identifying trends or drawing conclusions about the number of contractor personnel (Schwartz and Swain 2011). Likewise the U.S. Defense Department was not the only organization to hire private contractors. The U.S. Department of State and other countries such as Canada and the United Kingdom employed private contractors to support their operations in Afghanistan. In fact the CEO of Blackwater, Erik Prince (2013), points out that he provided private security contractors in Afghanistan as early as 2002.

Prior to 2007 there are very few empirical data on the number of private contractors supporting the military intervention in Afghanistan. However, data are available on the annual contract obligations for Afghanistan (U.S. Congress, House, Commission on Wartime Contracting 2011). Although this is the total amount of U.S. dollars obligated for all contracts, services contracts in which private contractors are hired are a subset. For example, logistics, support services, technical assistance, guard services, and construction are a few of the service code descriptions that fit the type of work that is typically conducted by private contractors. Thus the data can be used as a proxy for the number of private contractors used in Afghanistan to depict a trend over time. In 2002 there were thirty-one contract actions accounting for over $146 million. Contract obligations began to steadily increase to just under $1 billion by the end of 2004, then increased significantly from 2005 to 2010, from $2.2 billion to $13.5 billion (U.S. Congress, House, Commission on Wartime Contracting 2011). This trend in contract obligations correlates with the trend discussed earlier of an increase in private military contractors. By the second quarter of 2011 contract obligations for Operation Enduring Freedom totaled well over $46 billion, which represented 80 percent of the total spending on the intervention in Afghanistan.

The U.S. Department of Defense first reported on the number of contractors supporting Operation Enduring Freedom in the fall of 2007 (U.S. Department of Defense, Assistant Under Secretary for Office of Program Support under CENTCOM 2007). At the time there were a total of 29,473 contractors working in Afghanistan; 3,387 were U.S. citizens, 2,864 were third-country nationals, and 23,222 were host-nation nationals. There were 3,537 private security contractors, of which 5 were U.S. citizens, 15 third-country nationals, and 3,517 host-nation nationals. The ratio of U.S. military personnel to private contractors in 2008 was 1:1.3. However, if the number of other foreign troops is added to the total military personnel, the ratio 1:0.68.

In the summer of 2010 the number of private military contractors in Afghanistan peaked at 107,479, coinciding with the surge in U.S. and NATO forces (U.S. Department of Defense, Assistant Under Secretary for Office of Program Support under CENTCOM 2010). Of this total, 19,103 were U.S. citizens, 14,984 were third-country nationals, and 73,392 were Afghan nationals. Private security contractors accounted for 17,932 of the total private contractors: 152 U.S. citizens, 1,093 third-country nationals, and 16,687 Afghan nationals. By 2012 the ratio of U.S. military personnel to private contractors was 1:1.07.

In January 2014 the number of private military contractors in Afghanistan decreased to 78,136, reflecting the withdrawal of U.S. and NATO forces; 23,763 were U.S. citizens, 25,145 were third-country nationals, and 29,228 were Afghan nationals. Private security contractors totaled 11,332: 1,007 U.S. citizens, 1,414 third-country nationals, and 8,911 Afghan nationals. The decrease in Afghan nationals conducting private security functions is due to the establishment of the Afghan Public Protection Force. By 2014 the ratio of U.S. military personnel to private contractors was 1:1.46, the highest since the beginning of Operation Enduring Freedom.

Bureaucratic Controls on the Private Security Industry in Operation Enduring Freedom

At the beginning of Operation Enduring Freedom, there were few legal constraints barring the use of the private military industry.

The Department of Defense entered Operation Enduring Freedom using the same procedures for contracting that they had used during Operation Joint Endeavor. However, several new laws and regulations governed the activities of private contractors in Afghanistan. According to Elsea (2010, 2), private contractors in Afghanistan operated under three levels of legal authority: (1) the international order of the laws and usages of war, resolutions of the United Nations Security Council, and relevant treaties; (2) U.S. law; and (3) the domestic law of the host nation. The bilateral agreements between the United States and the government of Afghanistan and the international law of armed conflict are relevant to the discussion of the private security industry in Afghanistan in that they inform contractors' legal status.

In 2002 the United States and the transitional government of Afghanistan signed an agreement that provided immunity for U.S. military and Defense Department civilian personnel in Afghanistan from criminal prosecution by Afghan authorities but not for individual private contractors working in Afghanistan. In 2011 the government of Afghanistan (Mohammadi and Ghani 2011, 2) issued Presidential Decree 62, which asserted sovereignty over the regulation of the more than 20,000 private security contractors in the country. Thus by 2014 about 50 percent of the private security workforce had transitioned to the Afghan Public Protection Force (U.S. Department of Defense, Assistant Under Secretary for Office of Program Support under CENTCOM 2014, 2).

In 2006 international humanitarian law did not allow for a category of quasi-combatants, although it is tempting to argue that private security industry employees are somehow combatants (Cameron 2006). Further it is unlikely that many included in the growing numbers of private military companies can be legally regulated by existing international law on mercenaries because of the complex definition of that concept. The majority of private contractors have civilian status under humanitarian law since they do not satisfy the criteria for combatant status (Cameron 2006). Elsea (2010) points out that the Geneva Conventions and other laws of war do not appear to forbid the use of civilian contractors in occupied territory, yet private contractors who intentionally kill or injure civilians are liable for their conduct regardless of their combatant status.

In 2008 the United States and sixteen other countries signed the Montreux Document, which states that the host nation retains its obligations under international humanitarian and human rights law when hiring private military and security companies (Elsea 2010). The contracting host nation is therefore responsible for the actions of its private contractors. The document urges the contracting host nation to evaluate whether its legislation and procurement regulations are adequate to ensure accountability. Indeed the Montreux Document acknowledges that private military and security companies are not bound to respect international law since they are corporate entities, unlike the parties to a conflict and individuals (Elsea 2010).

Even though the laws of the United States allowed the Department of Defense to use private contractors in Afghanistan, it quickly became apparent that with the increased numbers of contractors in theater, more oversight of their activities was required. In his article addressing civilian contractors and military law, Lindemann (2007, 86) states that prior to the 2007 Defense Authorization Act, the U.S. military did not have a legal mechanism for controlling contractor activities; only the contracting company managed, supervised, and gave directions to its employees. The 2007 Defense Authorization Act empowered military commanders to hold private contractors legally responsible for their actions in a combat zone through the existing military laws outlined in the Uniform Code of Military Justice.

The Department of Defense established the Office of the Assistant Deputy Under Secretary for Defense (Program Support) in 2007 to provide centralized policy, management, and oversight for contracts and contractor performance in support of declared wars, contingency operations, and postconflict operations (U.S. Department of Defense, Assistant Under Secretary for Office of Program Support under CENTCOM 2008, 1). Likewise the Department of Defense established myriad policies, organizations, and procedures to account for and manage contractors in Operation Enduring Freedom and Operation Iraqi Freedom. By 2014 the Department of Defense was still improving its oversight of contractors by establishing specific standards for acquiring, training, and tracking contractors in operational theaters. In fact in January 2014 U.S. Northern Command conducted the first operational contracting support exercise focused on contract support integration, contract support, and contract management (U.S. Department of Defense, Assistant Under Secretary for Office of Program Support under CENTCOM 2014, 6).

At the beginning of Operation Enduring Freedom, the laws of the United States clearly allowed for the use of private contractors to support military operations in Afghanistan. This followed the precedent set in Operation Joint Endeavor. However, with the increase in the use of private contractors in Afghanistan and Iraq, the number of regulations significantly increased to control the activities of private contractors. Still the use of the private security industry increased throughout much of Operation Enduring Freedom.

Duration of Operation Enduring Freedom

On 14 September 2001 the U.S. Congress passed a joint resolution authorizing the use of military force, which allowed President George W. Bush to use the armed forces in response to the terrorist attacks on 11 September. On 4

October the first U.S. servicemen arrived at the military airbase in Karshi-Khanabad, Uzbekistan, to be in position to support combat search and rescue for the initial air campaign (Wright et al. 2010). The air campaign that signaled the beginning of combat operations began the night of 7 October 2001. The first U.S. troops, from the 5th Special Forces Group, entered Afghanistan and linked up with Northern Alliance forces to mark the beginning of the ground campaign against the Taliban. This was the beginning of the longest conflict in U.S. history; in October 2014 the United States and many of its Coalition partners had been involved in Operation Enduring Freedom for thirteen years.

It has been suggested that without a clear political objective and the military's penchant for limiting the number of ground forces in Afghanistan, the expected duration of the intervention would be short. Herspring (2005) argues that the Bush administration focused on military operations to defeat the Taliban while wanting to avoid the post-hostilities reconstruction phase, and Bird and Marshall (2011) point out the Bush administration was unwilling to be involved in nation building in Afghanistan and that during a National Security Council meeting on 12 November, Bush asserted that the United States would not stay in Afghanistan and do police work. However, others note that military planners at U.S. Central Command did give serious consideration to a broader intervention with larger conventional forces (Wright et al. 2010). In fact the final plan for Operation Enduring Freedom called for the use of conventional forces to exploit the expected success of the Northern Alliance offensive against the Taliban.

Scope of Operation Enduring Freedom

During the first phase of Operation Enduring Freedom relatively small numbers of U.S. ground troops were committed, and they operated from only a few key bases in the country (e.g., Bagram Airfield, Kandahar, Kabul, and Mazar-i-Sharif). However, as the operation continued, the number of U.S. and Coalition forces increased, and as violence increased and instability persisted, the military strategy shifted to expand the military footprint across Afghanistan, which increased the number of U.S. and Coalition bases of operation.

In the first months of the intervention, the United States committed

316 Special Forces personnel and 110 CIA officers (Herspring 2008). By late summer 2002 the number had risen to 5,200 U.S. military personnel (Belasco 2009). At the start of 2003 the number of U.S. military personnel had increased to 10,400, and by 2008 this number increased steadily to 30,100, driven by the shift in U.S. military strategy as a result of the increased violence and the decision to surge troops. By early 2010 the number of U.S. military personnel passed the threshold of 100,000 and peaked at 107,900 in July 2011 (U.S. Department of Defense, Assistant Under Secretary for Office of Program Support under CENTCOM January 2014). In line with Obama's announced plan to withdraw from Afghanistan, the number of U.S. military personnel steadily decreased to 53,300 by January 2014. The current plan is for the number to continue to decrease through 2014, with the final number remaining in Afghanistan to be negotiated in the bilateral agreement. As of April 2014, NATO plans to leave between 8,000 and 12,000 military personnel to train the Afghan Security Forces (Sopko 2013).

In line with the increased number of military personnel supporting Operation Enduring Freedom, the number of bases used to conduct operations also increased. Initially the United States deployed into Afghanistan from Karshi-Khanabad Airbase in Uzbekistan and from amphibious transport ships in the Indian Ocean. Once in Afghanistan, the U.S. military primarily operated out of four major bases in the north, central, and southern part of the country. As the number of U.S., Coalition, and Afghan security forces increased, the number of bases also increased, to a peak of 812 across Afghanistan. With troop decreases the number of bases used by the United States and its Coalition partners decreased to 349 by January 2012, and by November 2013 the number was 59 (U.S. Department of Defense 2013).

As noted earlier, U.S. military commanders initially wanted to maintain a small footprint in Afghanistan (2001–2), and they were largely successful in the first two years of the intervention. However, with the introduction of the counterinsurgency campaign in 2003, U.S. and ISAF troop levels steadily increased, along with the number of bases across Afghanistan, requiring additional logistics and basic life support wherever the bases were located. This meant senior political leaders and military commanders had to make difficult decisions about where to focus manpower and to determine the domestic implications of placing large numbers of troops in harm's way (Wright et al. 2010). Thus it is not surprising that the U.S. military began to substitute private contractors for military personnel as the scope of Operation Enduring Freedom expanded.

Other Conflicts or Deployments during Operation Enduring Freedom

On 10 September 2001 the United States had troop commitments in Bosnia, Kosovo, some NATO countries, and Korea and forward-deployed troops in support of allies in Japan. Of the total active military force of 1.3 million, over 250,000 were stationed outside the continental United States. This represented 15.1 percent of the total forces available for contingency military operations. Over 5,700 troops were in Bosnia supporting Operation Joint Endeavor; more than 36,000 troops were stationed in Korea; 40,000 troops were forward-deployed to Okinawa; and over 90,000 military personnel were deployed in support of NATO allies in Europe (U.S. Department of Defense, Defense Manpower Data Center 1954–2012).

As early as 19 September the Bush administration began reviewing plans for an invasion of Iraq (Herspring 2008). Early planning suggested that a U.S. invasion of Iraq would require up to 500,000 troops, similar to the number used in Operation Desert Shield. Yet as military planning continued through 2002, Secretary Rumsfeld required his military commanders to reduce the troop level to below 300,000 (Herspring 2008). Thus under normal military deployment policies, the demand for active duty soldiers for both Operation Enduring Freedom and Operation Iraqi Freedom exceeded the supply, especially for the U.S. Army (Bonds et al. 2010).

By the fall of 2005 the total number of U.S. troops deployed outside of the continental United States exceeded 385,000. This represented 27 percent of the total U.S. military available for other operations. Although the United States continued to maintain military forces forward-deployed in Japan, Korea, and Europe, the troop strengths in each locale were reduced as the number of forces increased in Afghanistan and Iraq. Likewise troop strengths continued to decline in Bosnia and Kosovo. U.S. military commitments would only continue to increase through 2008 and 2009, with the surge of troops to Iraq and Afghanistan placing further demands on the U.S. military.

The U.S. Army provided 75 percent of the ground troops to Operations Enduring Freedom and Iraqi Freedom (Bonds et al. 2010). In order to generate more deployable soldiers, the U.S. military, and the army in particular, increased total size (sometimes referred to as end strength), moved soldiers from Korea and Europe, and decreased the size of the generating force (Bonds et al. 2010). Still the demand for ground forces far exceeded the available supply that the U.S. Department of Defense could generate, even with the activation of National Guard and reserve forces, without significantly increasing the size of the military. As demand for services grew, decision makers in the United States began to substitute private military contractors for military troops in Afghanistan.

The Size of the U.S. Military during Operation Enduring Freedom

On 11 September 2001 the number of U.S. active military stood at 1,385,116. Of this total, the U.S. Army and U.S. Marine Corps made up the available ground force for combat operations in Afghanistan, totaling 480,801 and 172,934, respectively (U.S. Department of Defense, Defense Manpower Data Center 1954–2012). Additionally the U.S. Defense Department employed 671,735 civilians who supported a wide range of functions for the active military. From the end of the cold war to the start of Operation Enduring Freedom the U.S. military saw a 33 percent reduction in its active duty force.

Over the course of Operation Enduring Freedom, the U.S. Defense Department steadily increased both the army and marine corps end strength (Cordesman 2006). Between 2002 and 2010 the army active-duty end strength increased from 487,000 to slightly more than 566,000 soldiers (U.S. Department of Defense, Defense Manpower Data Center 1954–2012). These included nearly 16,000 army reserve soldiers on Title 10 active guard and reserve status as of December 2008 (Bonds et al. 2010). Likewise the U.S. Marine Corps increased in strength to 202,441 by 2010 before decreasing to 192,350 in 2013.

By 2008 approximately 373,000 soldiers in the army had served in Operation Enduring Freedom or Iraqi Freedom. Over 121,000 troops deployed for one year, 173,000 troops for two years, and 79,000 troops for three years or longer (Bonds et al. 2010). The army provided the bulk of U.S. troops to both operations: over 1 million troop years as of December 2008. These deployments represented 52 percent of the total troop deployments within the area of operations and over 75 percent of the deployments on the ground in Iraq, Kuwait, and Afghanistan in 2008 (Bonds et al. 2010).

In 2002 the total active U.S. military was 1,411,634 personnel. Of this number, 660,275 were U.S. Army and U.S. Marine Corps ground troops. This represents a 30 percent decrease in the size of the U.S. military, from a high of 2,130,299 in 1989. As a result the U.S. military increased its use of private military contractors during Operation Enduring Freedom to fill shortfalls in logistics and security. However, by 2010 the total active force increased to 1,430,985 personnel; the U.S. Army increased to 566,045, and the U.S. Marine Corps increased to 202,441. However, there was no concomitant decrease in the use of private contractors.

In 2014, with the U.S. intervention in Iraq complete, the number of U.S. forces deployed to Afghanistan decreasing, and facing budgetary constraints from Congress, the Defense Department began to reduce the size of the U.S. military. At the end of February 2014 the number of military forces on active duty stood at 1,368,137, the lowest since the end of World War II. The active strength of the U.S. Army was 521,685, and the active strength of the U.S. Marine Corps was 192,350.

Military Outlays during Operation Enduring Freedom

From 1996 to 2001 U.S. military spending increased by almost $39 billion (U.S. Office of Management and Budget 2014). The national budget at the start of Operation Enduring Freedom allocated over $304 billion for national defense, 15.6 percent of the total budget or 2.9 percent of GDP. With the start of Operation Enduring Freedom and the impending invasion of Iraq, U.S. defense spending would skyrocket until 2011, when a moderate decrease began.

In 2011 U.S. defense spending peaked at just over $705 billion, 18.8 percent of the national budget or 4.6 percent of GDP (U.S. Office of Management and Budget 2014). The trend reversed after 2012 as operations in Iraq ended and the number of troops deployed in support of Operation Enduring Freedom decreased. It is estimated that by the end of 2014 military spending will have decreased by almost $75 billion.

According to a Center for Strategic and International Studies (Berteau et al. 2011) report, between 2001 and 2010 the U.S. Department of Defense more than doubled its spending on contracts, mainly for products and services. Dollars spent on services contracts accounted for 40 to 42 percent of total Defense Department contract spending. Of the three categories of defense spending, service contracts grew at the fastest rate, 6.1 percent per year over the course of twenty-one years. The trend is the same for Operation Enduring Freedom, when services contracts accounted for over 40 percent of the dollars spent in Afghanistan.

Thus as the duration of the intervention in Afghanistan (and Iraq) increased, the defense budget also increased. Likewise the number of private contractors supporting the Defense Department increased significantly. As the budget peaked, then began to decrease, the number of private contractors also began to decrease. Defense spending for Operation Enduring Freedom is a significant departure from the expected outcome of the supply-demand hypothesis, suggesting that defense spending may not have less of an impact on the choice to substitute the private security industry for military force, as the literature suggests.

Choices Other Than the Private Security Industry

Most of the official U.S. government reports on private contracting acknowledge that the Defense Department relies extensively on private contractors in supporting military operations in Afghanistan (e.g., Commission on Wartime Contracting, Congressional Budget Office, and Congressional Research Service). The U.S. Congress, House, Commission on Wartime Contracting (2009, 2011) noted that the United States would not have been able to conduct large-scale or sustained contingency operations without heavy contractor support. Likewise both the Congressional Research Service (Schwartz and Swain 2011) and the Congressional Budget Office (Orszag 2008) observe that contractors played a critical role in supporting military operations in Afghanistan (and Iraq). It seems as if the U.S. military did not attempt to use any other means as a substitute for military forces.

However, the U.S. military sought out and found both internal and external means to keep the U.S. footprint in Afghanistan as small as possible and minimize the overall increase in the size of the military. These measures included the increase in the Defense Department civilian workforce, activation of the National Guard and reserve, the use of allies and Coalition partners, and the increase in the size of the Afghan Security Forces.

In 2001, 641,763 civilians were employed by the U.S. Defense Department. This number steadily increased as the duration of the intervention in Afghanistan (and Iraq) continued: by 2010 the number jumped to 740,489, then reached its peak of 758,489 in 2012 (U.S. Department of Defense 2013). Of these, a small number were deployed to Afghanistan in support of military operations. In 2008, the year the Defense Department began compiling a database, 274 U.S. government civilians were in Afghanistan (Livingston and O'Hanlon 2014). By 2011 this number had increased tenfold, to 1,176.

In addition to increasing the size of its civilian workforce, the Defense Department relied heavily on the National Guard and reserves to support military operations in Afghanistan. Six days after the attacks of 9/11, President Bush signed a directive making all elements of the U.S. ready reserve available for up to two years of active duty (Wright et al. 2010). Since that time slightly more than 895,000 National Guard and reserve members from the army, navy, air force, and Coast Guard have been activated to serve in support of Operation Enduring Freedom, Operation Iraqi Freedom, or Operation Noble Eagle (U.S. Department of Defense 2014).

On 13 September 2001 NATO invoked Article 5 of its Charter, in support of U.S. military efforts in Afghanistan (Wright et al. 2010). Since that time a total of forty-nine NATO members or other Coalition partners have provided significant support to Operation Enduring Freedom, with the United Kingdom, Germany, Italy, France, Poland, Romania, Australia, Turkey, and Spain each contributing more than 1,000 troops (Livingston and O'Hanlon 2014). As early as February 2002 approximately 5,000 troops from nations other than the United States were deployed in Afghanistan. As the duration of the intervention continued and the security situation eroded, the number of allied and Coalition partners increased, peaking at over 42,000 by the summer of 2011.

The establishment of an Afghan security force began in earnest in the summer of 2003 with the resurgence of the Taliban and the increase in violence across Afghanistan. Wright et al. (2010) point out that for most counterinsurgencies to succeed, they require credible host-nation police, paramilitary, and military forces. In the summer of 2003 the United States and its Coalition partners began to train the Afghan National Army (ANA). The first 6,000 ANA members were ready by the end of the summer. Following the establishment of the ANA, training began in 2004 for an Afghan police force under the Afghan Ministry of Interior Forces.

From 2003 through 2009 the size of the Afghan security force increased from 6,000 to just over 195,000; it increased again from 2009 to 2013, reaching a peak of 352,000. This included close to 200,000 Afghan security forces working for the Ministry of Defense and 150,000 police working for the Ministry of Interior. Although the United States and its Coalition partners reduced the size of their military presence in Afghanistan after 2011 by close to 60 percent, the size of the Afghan security forces increased by almost 60,000 during that same time.

As the demand grew for increased military forces in Afghanistan, U.S. decision makers did have choices other than the private security industry; they chose to activate the National Guard and reserves, increase the overall size of the military, rely on allies and Coalition partners, and build an Afghan security force. The U.S. military acted as the sole purchaser of security in the marketplace, as the theory of monopsony suggests.

Private Security Supply-Demand Behavior: An Assessment

The theory of supply and demand predicts that given a situation where the demand for a service increases, in this case support services and security services, the military should choose to contract for private military support services to fill shortfalls in capability. In the case of Operation Enduring Freedom, private security supply-demand behavior is evident.

An analysis of supply-demand behavior must start with an examination of the initial conditions prior to Operation Enduring Freedom. The previous chapter highlighted the reduction in the size of the U.S. military to a sixty-year low, at just over 1.3 million active duty personnel. This force consisted of approximately 651,000 land forces, which would make up the bulk of the available military personnel deployed to Afghanistan. However, more than 250,000 military personnel were forward-deployed in support of alliances or committed to ongoing operations around the world. Yet given the pre-intervention assumptions and self-imposed constraints on the size of the force planned for the commitment to Afghanistan, there seemed to be sufficient forces available to commit to an intervention in Afghanistan.

The early success of the Afghan Northern Alliance against the Taliban was accomplished by only a small number of U.S. military personnel (i.e., far less than the anticipated deployment of 50,000 to 60,000; Herspring 2005). This early success reinforced the U.S. military's self-imposed limitation on the size of the force deployed to Afghanistan. As a result, when initial combat operations ended with the removal of the Taliban, the number of U.S. troops committed to the posthostility and reconstruction phase remained under 30,000 for the first seven years of the intervention. In addition to the U.S. forces committed to Operation Enduring Freedom, NATO and Coalition partners initially contributed between 5,000 and 30,000 troops during the same period, and the size of the Afghan Security Forces steadily grew to almost 173,000 by 2008. The self-imposed constraint on the size of the U.S. force committed to Afghanistan created a demand for private contractors; thus the U.S. military filled the capability shortfall with over 68,000 private contractors by the end of 2008.

Yet by 2008 the 230,000-strong combined security force was unable to stem the increasing tide of violence that spread across Afghanistan as the Taliban challenged the new government. By the summer of 2008 insurgent attacks increased to over 300 per week, and over 300 U.S. military personnel were killed by the end of that year. Afghan Security Forces and Coalition forces also sustained an increasing number of casualties as the duration of the conflict increased. In early 2009 the fledging Obama administration announced a new strategy for Afghanistan, with the goal of halting the spiral of violence that rocked the country. This required an increase in the number of U.S. troops deployed, with the largest increase among combat troops. However, the demand for ground troops far exceeded the supply available for both Afghanistan and Iraq. With the 2003 invasion of Iraq the number of U.S. troops committed to Operation Iraqi Freedom exceeded 130,000. The number of U.S. troops deployed to Iraq increased through 2008, to over 157,000. With the surge in Iraq, close to 30 percent of the available ground forces were deployed outside the continental United States by the end of 2008.

Increases in the size of the U.S. military, increases in the size of the Afghan Security Forces, and increases in the size of the Coalition forces committed to Operation Enduring Freedom offset some of this demand. Yet the U.S. military was unable to provide sufficient security, logistics, maintenance, and theater-level base support for the increased number of combat troops deployed. As a substitute the U.S. military employed private military contractors to fill the shortfall necessary to successfully implement the new strategy.

The U.S. military employed private contractors in Afghanistan as early as 2002; however, the number of contractors remained below 4,000 per year until 2009. Once the surge of U.S. and Coalition forces began, the number of private military and security contractors increased significantly through 2012, reaching a peak of 107,479. U.S. military spending on service contracts in Operation Enduring Freedom reflects the increased reliance on private contractors as a substitute for military personnel. The total number of private contractors used in Afghanistan is significant because it is equivalent to a 20 percent increase in the overall size of the U.S. Army at the time. Likewise the number of private contractors in Afghanistan in 2012 was three times more than the total number of Coalition forces supporting ISAF.

After 2012 the U.S. strategy for Afghanistan called for a deliberate reduction of military forces and a transition of responsibility for security to the government of Afghanistan. By early 2014 the number of U.S. troops in Afghanistan fell below pre-surge levels to just over 50,000; in turn the number of private contractors decreased to a little over 78,000. Once again U.S. strategy created a self-imposed demand for private contractors to fill the gap in capabilities that the U.S. military was unable to fill.

Summary and Analysis

Supply-demand behavior is evident during the intervention in Afghanistan. Indeed the U.S. military acted as a monopsonist in the early years of the intervention by deliberately limiting the size of U.S. security forces it committed. As the security environment became less permissive and the scope of the intervention increased dramatically by 2009, the demand for U.S. land forces far exceeded the available supply. After 2012, following the Obama administration's new strategy, the U.S. military once again acted as a monopsonist by deliberately reducing the number of U.S. forces committed to the intervention.

The case study provides several alternative explanations. First, when there is a force cap placed on the size of the military force, there is an increase in the use of private contractors. There is evidence to suggest that in 2001 the U.S. military footprint in Afghanistan remained small. In fact the number of U.S. troops did not exceed 40,000 until the summer of 2009, almost eight years into the intervention. When military leaders realized that there were insufficient forces to contain the increase in violence across Afghanistan they chose to substitute military forces for private military companies.

Second, when the host nation does support the intervention, there is an increase in the use of private security. During the early years of Operation Enduring Freedom, the U.S. military did not have host-nation support from the Afghan government, so the U.S. military relied on private military companies instead.

Third, when the security environment is nonpermissive there is an increase in private security. During Operation Enduring Freedom, the U.S. and Coalition partners operated in a nonpermissive security environment while conducting counterinsurgency and reconstruction operations. This required the United States and its Coalition partners to allocate much of their military force to force protection, and the U.S. military significantly increased its use of private military companies and private security companies.

According to Wright et al. (2010), all wars are improvisations, and from the beginning Operation Enduring Freedom was heavily shaped by improvisation. Although the U.S. military enjoyed success early in the campaign to remove the Taliban from power, creating a stable Afghanistan remains elusive. Bird and Marshall (2011) suggest that every conceivable approach, in a variety of combinations, has been attempted. One of the many improvisations has been the heavy reliance on private contractors to support military operations.

From 2012 onward the number of contractors in Afghanistan far outnumbered U.S. forces. Indeed private contractors have played a critical role in Afghanistan and provided significant operational benefits to the U.S. military. They were able to deploy fast, adapt quickly to the changing security environment, and served as a force multiplier to combat forces. As Schwartz (2011) points out, the Department of Defense and Department of State would be unable to execute their missions in Afghanistan (and Iraq) without support of private security contractors.

CHAPTER SIX

OPERATION IRAQI FREEDOM

This chapter provides a cross-comparison case study utilizing the events of Operation Iraqi Freedom, the U.S. military operation in Iraq from March 2003 to December 2011. The details of Iraqi Freedom support some of the assertions in the literature on the use of the private security industry. The intervention in Iraq has proven influential for examining the role of the private security industry in operations as well as the theory of supply and demand to understand their increased use. The most descriptive fact concerning the operation in Iraq is that the number of contractors on the battlefield exceeded the number of U.S. forces. The contractor count cannot be explained without considering the nature of the intervention, the decisions by senior U.S. leaders to limit the size of U.S. forces in Iraq, and the scope and duration of the operation. Again the results tend to corroborate the theory of a post–cold war example of private security supply-demand behavior.

Operation Iraqi Freedom is a most likely case as defined by George and Bennett (2005) because it meets the criterion of contractor presence. In a most likely case, because the independent variable strongly predicts a particular outcome, the outcome must occur or the theory is suspect (George and Bennett 2005). Biddle (2004) points out that a most likely case is one where extreme values put a theory on its strongest possible ground of occurring. He suggests that if the theory is going to be supported (i.e., shown to be true) it should be supported in a most likely case. Biddle argues that for such cases, a valid theory should fail very rarely; if we nevertheless observe failure, this surprising result warrants a greater loss of confidence in the theory than would a single disconfirmatory observation under less ideal conditions. Most cases usually fall somewhere between being most and least likely for particular theories (George and Bennett 2005). Therefore the strength of a theory depends to a considerable extent on the difficulty of the test that the theory has passed or failed (King et al. 1994; Gerring 2001).

As this chapter demonstrates, the size and budget of the U.S. military for Operation Iraqi Freedom were significantly less than the peak cold war levels. The intervention lasted over eight years, during which the United States faced competing conflicts around the world. For all of these reasons, the likelihood that the United States would have to utilize significant support from the private security industry was high. In fact the use of contractors was so essential to the mission that numerous scholars focus on this case when studying the rise of the private security industry.

Overview of Events

The complex and conflictive U.S. relationship with Iraq emerged from the 1979 revolution in Iran, which threatened to destabilize the vital oil-producing Southwest Asia region (Metz 2010a). In September 1980 Saddam Hussein decided to invade Iran, hoping to capitalize on Iran's badly weakened military due to its recent revolution (Allawi 2007). After some initial gains, the war turned against Iraq, and the Reagan administration offered economic and military assistance. In 1988 Iran and Iraq signed a cease-fire. However, U.S.-Iraqi relations flipped dramatically after Saddam invaded Kuwait in 1990 (Metz 2010a).

Following Operation Desert Storm, the United States made deliberate preparations for operations against Iraq focused primarily on defense in the event of a second invasion of Kuwait and conducted air operations to maintain the northern and southern no-fly zones within Iraq. The U.S. military presence in the region served as a deterrent "trip wire" and confirmed our continuing commitment to the Kuwaiti people (Fontenot et al. 2005). After almost two decades of conflict, by 2003 Iraq's economy was less than 1 percent of that of the United States (Stiglitz and Bilmes 2008).

Yet in the face of UN sanctions and diplomatic isolation, Saddam remained firmly in control.

The U.S. Congress passed HR 4655, the Iraq Liberation Act, in October 1998, which made support for Saddam's opponents official U.S. policy. It called for assistance to Iraqi opposition organizations and for the United States to push the UN to create a war crimes tribunal to prosecute Saddam and other senior Iraqi officials (Metz 2010a). But with the election of George W. Bush in 2000 and the subsequent attacks on 11 September 2001 a dramatic shift occurred in U.S. strategy toward Iraq (Metz 2010a; Herspring 2008). Secretary of Defense Donald Rumsfeld and several civilian leaders in the Pentagon favored using military force to get rid of Saddam (Herspring 2005). Allawi (2007) maintains that in official Washington, the ignorance of what was going on inside Iraq before the war was monumental.

Operation Iraqi Freedom grew out of the realization that Saddam would never comply with the 1991 settlement, that the threat Iraq posed globally was growing, and that containment and limited force would neither compel compliance nor inspire the Iraqi military to overthrow the dictator (Metz 2010a). Three primary and interlocking fear-based explanations were used to justify the invasion and occupation of Iraq: Saddam and his Ba'athist regime possessed weapons of mass destruction (WMDs); Saddam would sell the WMDs to terrorist networks; and the Iraqi government had ties to Al Qaeda (Tyner 2006). President Bush's strategy for dealing with Iraq aimed to exhaust diplomatic alternatives and seek UN approval to use armed force in conjunction with allies; however, he would act unilaterally and without explicit UN approval if necessary (Metz 2010a).

The former chairman of the Joint Chiefs of Staff, Gen. Richard Myers, pointed out that in late 2001 the plan for Iraq was badly outdated, being based on the 1991 invasion plan, and did not reflect degraded Iraqi military strength or expanded U.S. technological improvements since Desert Storm (Myers and McConnell 2009). When Gen. Tommy Franks, commander of U.S. Central Command (CENTCOM), briefed Secretary Rumsfeld on the military strategy for Iraq, two objectives emerged: regime change and the removal of WMDs (Myers and McConnell 2009; Herspring 2008). However the military campaign developed by CENTCOM transcended removing

Saddam and the Ba'athists from power (Fontenot et al. 2005); the strategic goals included establishing a stable, secure, prosperous, peaceful, and democratic Iraqi nation that was a fully functioning member of the community of nations.

The objectives for Operation Iraqi Freedom left many scholars arguing whether, under the pretext of a global war on terrorism, the Bush administration had embarked on a massive attempt to remake the political space of the Middle East (Tyner 2006). Operation Iraqi Freedom was "an unusual situation: The United States had very rarely chosen to attack. We had almost always responded to attack. Preparing for preemptive war was a new experience for our force" (Myers and McConnell 2009, 229; Battistella 2006, 2). This may be why that some describe the operation as "the mysterious war" (Keegan 2007).

Operation Iraqi Freedom consisted of four phases: planning and preparation (Phase 1), posturing Coalition forces to conduct sustained combat operations (Phase 2), conventional air and ground operations (Phase 3), and post-hostilities operations (Phase 4). "One key planning assumption was that it was possible to safely conduct lightning-fast, near simultaneous air and ground operations once the *kinetic* phase began. The emphasis on lightning-fast would mean fewer military and civilian casualties, less danger of region instability, mass starvation, refugees, and sabotage of oil fields" (Meyer and McConnell 2009, 219). Scholars questioned how the U.S. military would handle the postconflict stability and reconstruction phase (Myers and McConnell 2009).

The Authorization for Use of Military Force against Iraq resolution of 2002 passed in both houses of Congress on 10 October with the support of a strong majority of both parties in both houses (U.S. Congress, House 2002; Herspring 2008).[1] Bush signed the bill into law on 16 October (Myers and McConnell 2009). On 8 November the United Nations Security Council passed Resolution 1441 by unanimous vote with no abstentions; it declared that Iraq "has been and remains in material breach of its obligations under relevant resolutions," demanded that Saddam provide "immediate, unimpeded, unconditional, and unrestricted access" to weapons inspectors, and warned Iraq that "it [would] face serious consequences as a result of its continued violations of its obligations" (Sifer and Cerf 2003; Myers and McConnell 2009, quoting Metz 2010a, 37).

In early February 2003 Secretary of State Colin Powell briefed the UN Security Council about the grave threat posed by an Iraq that had developed and stockpiled WMDs, continued to defy UN resolutions, and was in league with Al Qaeda (Herspring 2008; Sifer and Cerf 2003; Wright and Reese 2008). On 1 March Turkey's Grand National Assembly rejected the U.S. request to use Turkey's land corridors as an invasion route to Iraq (Wright and Reese 2008).

By mid-March 2003 CENTCOM had sufficient combat power to begin ground offensive operations. Bush made the decision to launch Operation Iraqi Freedom on 16 March and issued an ultimatum with a forty-eight-hour deadline (Fontenot et al. 2005; Herspring 2008). On 20 March Coalition troops breached the berm along the border between Kuwait and Iraq to secure the Rumaila oil fields and to set the conditions for their march up-country (Fontenot et al. 2005, 86). Over the next few days Coalition aircraft averaged between 1,500 and 2,000 air combat sorties a day in support of Operation Iraqi Freedom; the U.S. Air Force launched 100 air-cruise missiles, and Coalition warships launched 500 cruise missiles; and Coalition air forces attacked senior Iraqi leadership, air defense systems, surface-to-surface missiles, and artillery batteries to reduce the threat to Coalition air and ground forces in Kuwait (Fontenot et al. 2005).

When the war began the military campaign itself was less dramatic than expected (Myers and McConnell 2009). Coalition ground forces encountered little initial resistance as they moved into Iraq. In the west Special Operations Forces had entered the country from advanced bases in Jordan and Saudi Arabia and, along with airpower, quickly took control of vast sections of desert, which the Iraqis would have needed had they intended to launch Scud missiles against their neighbors (Myers and McConnell 2009).

After Turkey denied the United States a ground route from the north into Iraq, military planners decided to conduct an airborne operation. On the night of 26 March, six days after the ground war began, fifteen giant C-17 Globemasters dropped almost 1,000 paratroopers of the army's 173rd Airborne Brigade from Vicenza, Italy, on the short, muddy Bashur airstrip in northern

Iraq. The airborne brigade linked up with Special Operations Forces already working with Iraqi Kurd Peshmerga guerrillas (Myers and McConnell 2009). The airborne operation succeeded in preventing the Iraqi divisions in the north from repositioning against the main U.S. ground attack in the south.

The U.S. Army V Corps advanced north toward Baghdad, west of the Euphrates River, while the U.S. Marine Corps I Marine Expeditionary Force advanced north toward Baghdad, east of the Euphrates River. The British Army 1st Armored Division conducted amphibious and ground operations toward Basra in southern Iraq and successfully secured the oil infrastructure (Fontenot et al. 2005). By 5 April lead combat elements of the V (U.S.) Corps had seized the international airport on the outskirts of Baghdad (Fontenot et al. 2005). For the next four days U.S. combat forces struck at the center of Baghdad, forcing the collapse of Iraqi defenses around the city (Herspring 2008).

Although the collapse of the Iraqi Army was swift, it was not without significant resistance to Coalition forces.[2] On 20 March Iraq responded with the first of seventeen theater ballistic missile attacks against troop concentrations in Kuwait (Fontenot et al. 2005). To defend Iraq, Iraqi military commanders fielded seventeen regular army divisions and six Republican Guard divisions. In Baghdad the Special Republican Guard, a force of approximately 15,000 soldiers, had the specific task of defending key sites, while a host of paramilitary and militia forces, including the infamous Fedayeen Saddam and Ba'ath Party militia, defended key cities throughout Iraq (Fontenot et al. 2005).

The Iraqi paramilitary organizations prepared to fight as irregulars rather than as standing conventional forces. The Iraqi regime used many of these paramilitary organizations in the south, in Basra (2,000 fighters), Najaf (12,000 to 14,000 fighters), and Karbala (2,000 to 3,000 fighters); however, Coalition military planners had not anticipated or accounted for these paramilitary fighters (Fontenot et al. 2005). Their tenacious resistance and will to fight foretold the violence that was yet to come. As Myers and McConnell (2009, 242) point out, Phase 4 (post-hostility) proved to be more difficult than the major combat phase: "Though many of us in Washington knew that the future of post-Saddam Iraq was uncertain and risky, we did not expect it to be as violent and challenging as it turned out to be."

On 9 April the major combat operations (Phase 3) of Operation Iraqi Freedom ended, and the disheartened and defeated Republican Guard and Special Republican Guard soldiers and officers returned to their homes, defeated (Myers and McConnell 2009; Fontenot et al. 2005). Fontenot et al. argue that even more astounding than the rapid collapse of resistance was that Baghdad remained standing. Most of the infrastructure — utilities, water, power, and sewage — remained in the condition left by the failed Ba'athist regime. However, others warned that many falsely perceived the U.S. forces' swift and stunning victory over Saddam as the end of hostilities (Wright and Reese 2008).

On 1 May 2003 Bush reinforced this feeling when, standing aboard the USS *Abraham Lincoln* under a large banner proclaiming "Mission Accomplished," he congratulated soldiers, sailors, airmen, and marines for their success in Operation Iraqi Freedom (Wright and Reese 2008; Herspring 2008). On 9 May he appointed L. Paul Bremer as presidential envoy to Iraq with full authority over all U.S. government personnel, activities, and funds there (Bremer and McConnell 2006). Bremer arrived in Baghdad on 12 May to assume leadership of the Coalition Provisional Authority (Herspring 2008).[3] His chain of command ran through Rumsfeld and straight to the president (Bremer and McConnell 2006).

When Bremer arrived in Iraq he found that a "chaotic power vacuum prevailed" (Bremer and McConnell 2006, 9). Wright and Reese (2008) point out that few if any in the White House, the Department of Defense, or the U.S. Army foresaw the impending struggle to create a new Iraq in place of the Saddam regime as the greatest challenge of Operation Iraqi Freedom. The Pentagon assumed that most of the Iraqi Army of 715,000 men, 400,000 of whom were Shiite conscripts, would surrender en masse and that units would remain intact, so the soldiers could be employed on ambitious reconstruction projects that paid a steady living wage (Bremer and McConnell 2006). However, the Iraqi Army had ceased to exist (Bremer and McConnell 2006; Herspring 2008).

There were other signs that the country was now lacking a power structure: the institutions held together by Saddam's reign had collapsed along with his regime, furthering Iraq's descent into chaos; long-suppressed political, religious, and ethnic conflicts bubbled violently to the surface; and some Iraqis, sensing an absence of authority in their country, saw an opportunity to pursue their own goals and objectives, some of them violent (Wright and Reese 2008; Allawi 2007). Bremer and McConnell (2006, 37) write, "At the end of World War II, the United States and the other Allies had clearly defeated the countries we had occupied. The entire nations of Germany and Japan had been mobilized to fight long, relentless wars. They had lost and surrendered." In Iraq, however, the United States defeated a hated regime, not a country.

By the end of May 2003 approximately 160,000 Coalition troops had spread out across Iraq to begin postconflict efforts (Wright and Reese 2008). The security situation in several areas had become grave because "the speed of the war had left us with little time to plan for the ensuing social upheaval, while decades of chronic mismanagement had left Iraq's economy devastated" (Bremer and McConnell 2006, 37). In the meantime General Franks told his subordinate leaders during a 16 April visit to Baghdad to be prepared to conduct an abbreviated period of stability operations and then to redeploy the majority of their forces out of Iraq by September 2003 (Wright and Reese 2008; Delong and Lukeman 2007). Franks recommended that reinforcements still stateside would not be needed to stabilize Iraq (Wright and Reese 2008; Herspring 2008). This proved to be a grave error, as violence in Iraq soon escalated.

On 16 May Bremer issued CPA Order No. 1 — De-Ba'athification of Iraqi Society; this order removed from public life the individuals who had held one of the four top ranks in the Ba'ath Party (Wright and Reese 2008; Herspring 2008). On 23 May he issued CPA Order No. 2 — Dissolution of Entities, which disbanded all of Saddam's military and intelligence institutions (Bremer and McConnell 2006; DeLong and Lukeman 2007). It has been argued that "not only did the decree turn 400,000 former soldiers against the U.S.-led coalition, if one considers the average size of an Iraqi household; the decision directly affected the lives of 2.4 million people — roughly 10 percent of Iraq's population" (Tyner 2006, 79). Bremer admits that the order was not perfect; the CIA warned that as a result of CPA Order No. 1, by nightfall on 16 May up to 50,000 Ba'athists would be driven underground (Bremer and McConnell 2006; Herspring 2008).

Many Coalition military figures believed at the time that these important CPA decisions created a pool of disaffected and unemployed Sunni Arabs from which a growing insurgency could later recruit (Wright and Reese 2008). The Ba'ath Party boasted that it had over 2 million members.[4] Many people had initially joined the party because it was the only way to get a government job (Bremer and McConnell 2006), but as a result of Order No. 1, they were out of work. By midsummer 2003 even many senior Iraqi leaders observed that the security vacuum set up by Order No. 2 had resulted in lawlessness and street crime that had never been experienced before (Herspring 2008). They pointed out that people needed more protection, and Bremer admitted, "The message to most Iraqis is that the Coalition can't provide them the most basic government service: security. We have become the worst of all things—an ineffective occupier" (Bremer and McConnell 2006, 358).

On 19 August a massive truck bomb was driven into the UN compound in Baghdad and detonated. The suicide bomber took the lives of twenty-two people, including Chief UN Envoy Sergio Vieira de Mello (Wright and Reese 2008). By November the Coalition had recorded approximately one thousand insurgent attacks throughout Iraq. Yet despite the increased violence, Rumsfeld insisted that the policy for improving security was on track (Herspring 2008). Although Coalition forces captured Saddam on 13 December, violence continued to rise, and other countries in the international community reconsidered sending troops to aid reconstruction because of the questionable security conditions (Wright and Reese 2008).

Violence in Iraq continued to increase through the remainder of 2003 and into 2004 (Allawi 2007). The insurgency in Baghdad and in the Sunni Triangle was intensifying as the terrorists and insurgents saw Iraq moving to democracy. On 8 June UN Security Council Resolution 1546 recognized the Iraqi interim government (Bremer and McConnell 2006). However, on 16 July Gen. John Abizaid, the new commander of CENTCOM, acknowledged in a press conference that he believed Coalition forces faced a "classical guerrilla-type campaign" (Wright and Reese 2008; Herspring 2008). Until then none of the Coalition's senior commanders had offered overt recognition that an insurgency appeared to be forming in Iraq (Wright and Reese 2008).

Based on prewar assumptions by the Bush administration, an insurgency in postconflict Iraq was unexpected. Bremer acknowledges, "We planned for the wrong contingency" (Bremer and McConnell 2006, 26). The administration assumed that the Iraqi bureaucracy and security forces—both military and police—would return to work once they had new leadership untainted by association with Saddam; however, U.S. policymakers did not understand how fragile and precarious Iraq was after decades of pathological rule (Metz 2010b). According to Bremer and McConnell (2006), the insurgents proved that they were better organized and more difficult to penetrate than expected.

On 30 January 2005 Iraq held its first major democratic elections and millions of Iraqis voted for the first time: voter turnout was approximately 60 percent of eligible voters, although a large majority of Sunni Arabs boycotted the elections. Wright and Reese (2008) highlight the astonishing percentage considering the very real dangers facing voters. From 2004 to 2006 the Iraq conflict changed from a predominantly anti-American insurgency to one dominated by a sectarian war stoked by outside extremists, and by 2006 the insurgents had seized the strategic initiative and changed the nature of the conflict (Metz 2010b).

In 2007 the essential nature of the conflict changed, thus requiring a strategic shift that allowed the United States and the Iraqi government to recapture the initiative (Metz 2010b). The most important contextual component framing this strategic shift was the decaying security situation in Iraq itself. The internal violence had become endemic and paralyzing, and large parts of the country had minimal or no government control (Metz 2010b). Thus the Bush administration made the decision to increase the number of troops in Iraq, commonly called "the surge."

Full implementation of the revised strategy began just as Gen. David Petraeus replaced Gen. George W. Casey Jr. as the overall U.S. military commander in Iraq. As part of the strategy Petraeus and U.S. Ambassador Ryan Crocker developed cease-fires with key Iraqi individuals and organizations. Moreover they capitalized on growing rifts within the insurgency, particularly between Al Qaeda and Sunni Arab tribal leaders. U.S. forces secured the approaches to and "belts" around Baghdad and established a permanent presence in neighborhoods in conflict. As a result security in Baghdad and other violent areas improved dramatically. By the end of the summer of 2007, overall violence, particularly sectarian attacks, was in decline (Metz 2010b).

The security situation in Iraq continued to improve between 2007 and 2009, and the newly elected president, Barack Obama, called for a withdrawal of all American troops by December 2011.[5] This announcement was in line with the previously agreed upon 2009 U.S.-Iraq Security Agreement, which called for the complete withdrawal of U.S. forces. In 2009 the overall levels of violence were 90 percent lower than they were at the height of the sectarian conflict of 2006–7. However, continuing violence has confirmed what some experts questioned at the time about whether stability would continue after all U.S. forces departed at the end of 2011 (Katzman 2011).

On 12 January 2011 Kuwait's prime minister visited Iraq, and a month later the Iraqi prime minister visited Kuwait. These key exchanges took place after the UN Security Council passed three resolutions (1956, 1957, and 1958) on December 15, 2010. The resolutions had the net effect of lifting most of the Saddam-era sanctions on Iraq, although the U.N.-run reparations payments process remains intact (which deducts 5 percent from Iraq's total oil revenues). On 1 January 2012 the State Department transitioned to the lead U.S. agency in Iraq, formally ending the U.S. combat mission there. Between January 2012 and the fall of 2014, the State Department, using security contractors, were able to secure its personnel in Iraq without the presence of U.S. combat forces. However, with the increased level of violence in Iraq, U.S. combat forces have once again returned.

Private Contractors in Operation Iraqi Freedom

The invasion and subsequent occupation of Iraq reveals the confluence of many transnational practices regarding the use of the private security industry. Two practices in particular stand out: the use and movement of private security contractors (e.g., warriors) and the deployment of private contract labor (e.g., workers): "Combined, the transnational movement of warriors and workers demonstrates the business of war and why occupied Iraq signifies a neoliberal, privatized and ultimately de-humanized space" (Tyner 2006, 69). Contractors played a substantial role in supporting U.S. military, reconstruction, and diplomatic operations in Iraq, accounting for a significant portion of the manpower and spending for those activities (Orszag 2008).

Contractors provided a wide range of products and services in Iraq. Most contract obligations were for logistics support, construction, petroleum products, or food. The Congressional Budget Office estimated that as of early 2008 at least 190,000 contractor personnel, including subcontractors, were working on U.S.-funded contracts in the Iraq theater of operations. About 20 percent (38,700) of all contractor personnel working in Iraq were U.S. citizens; roughly 40 percent (70,500) were local nationals, defined as citizens of the country in which they are working, or third-country nationals (81,000), who are neither U.S. citizens nor local nationals (Orszag 2008).

The U.S. Department of Defense employed by far the most contractors in Iraq. For example, in 2004 over 24,000 contractors provided services to U.S. Army forces in Operations Iraqi Freedom and Enduring Freedom under LOGCAP, which for the first sixteen months of Iraqi Freedom had an overall budget that exceeded $5.2 billion (Wright and Reese 2008). Those 24,000 LOGCAP employees freed up critical military manpower for other duties and reduced the number of combat service support soldiers needed for support operations (Wright and Reese 2008). In 2003–4 alone over $750 million was spent on private security for about 6,000 private security contractors (Ricks 2006).

The U.S. Department of State also employed a significant number of contractors in Iraq, many of which were armed security contractors. As of late 2007 about 40 percent of the approximately 6,700 contractor personnel working for the State Department in Iraq were providing armed security (Orszag 2008). Once State assumed the lead role in Iraq, the estimated number of security contractors working for the department increased to approximately 5,500, with some 1,500 providing personal security for diplomatic movements and an additional 4,000 providing perimeter security (Schwartz 2011).

The U.S. government is just one of many entities—including foreign governments, international organizations, and private industry—that employed private security contractors in Afghanistan and Iraq; as of 2011 there were 100 private security companies registered and licensed with the Iraq Ministry of Interior: 72 Iraqi companies and 28 foreign non-U.S. companies (Schwartz

2011). Schwartz points out that third-country nationals are generally cheaper than U.S. Coalition contractors, and local nationals are generally the least expensive to hire, in part because there are no large overhead costs related to transportation, housing, and sustenance. These PSCs employ more than 30,000 armed employees working for a variety of government and private sector clients.

Contractors in Iraq have been exposed to the ongoing violence as they work alongside the military. It has been estimated that 560 to 1,000 contractors had been killed and more than 12,000 wounded between 2003 and 2011 (O'Hanlon and Livingston 2011; Stiglitz and Bilmes 2008). The best documented were the four American contractors who worked for the Blackwater security company who were killed on 31 March 2004 by insurgents in Fallujah (Wright and Reese 2008). Wright and Reese note that in November 2003, the U.S. Army Corps of Engineers and Kellogg, Brown, and Root (KBR) suspended oil industry work in northern Iraq after a KBR engineer was killed. Washington Group International, a large engineering firm, halted work just north of Baghdad after two subcontracted workers were killed. By mid-December 2003, eighteen contractors had been killed in Iraq, and contractor deaths from attacks temporarily halted at least two reconstruction projects. As a result many private firms spent as much as 15 percent of contract costs on either obtaining security providers or purchasing needed equipment for security purposes or both. Many reconstruction projects were canceled outright due to the poor security.

The literature heralds private contractors for performing their roles with great skill and often with bravery on the complex and dangerous noncontiguous battlefield in Iraq (Wright and Reese 2008). For example, Vinnell Corporation provided planners, operations officers, unit trainers, and translators to support the creation of the Iraqi National Army (Wright and Reese 2008; Dobbins et al. 2009). The U.S. Army Corps of Engineers awarded contracts to five civilian firms to collect, sort, and destroy huge stockpiles of unexploded ordnance (estimated to total some 400,000 tons). Some 2,600 contractors destroyed over 450,000 tons of munitions between 2003 and 2006 (Wright and Reese 2008).

In addition armed private security contractors working for the Department of State from 1 January to 18 September 2007 conducted 3,073 missions in which American diplomats or visitors were escorted outside of the secured Green Zone in Baghdad. Of those missions, there were seventy-seven incidents involving PSC personnel using weapons. Over thirty Blackwater employees were killed while performing their security duties; however, no American diplomat or visitor was killed or seriously injured while being escorted by Blackwater (Elsea et al. 2008).

In the final months of Operation Iraqi Freedom, the Department of Defense reported that approximately 64,253 contractors worked in Iraq from January to April 2011 (U.S. Department of Defense, Assistant Under Secretary for Office of Program Support under CENTCOM April 2011). Of these, 18,393 were U.S. citizens, 36,523 were third-country nationals, and 9,337 were Iraq nationals. The main categories of contracts in Iraq and the percentages of contractors working on them are as follows: base support (38,966, 60.6 percent), security (10,448, 16.3 percent), translator or interpreter (4,099, 6.4 percent), logistics or maintenance (324, 0.5 percent), construction (858, 1.3 percent), transportation (1,229, 1.9 percent), communication support (495, 0.8 percent), training (599, 0.9 percent), and other (7,235, 11.2 percent).

According to a Defense Department report, as of mid-2011 the military-contractor ratio in Iraq was 1:1.25. The overall number of contractors decreased as more bases were closed and the size of the U.S. military in Iraq was reduced. However, as the military transitioned with the Department of State, approximately 17,000 to 22,000 contractors to remained after 31 December 2011 to support the Office of Security Cooperation-Iraq (U.S. Department of Defense, Assistant Under Secretary for Office of Program Support under CENTCOM April 2011). However, by January 2014 the total number of contractors working in Iraq decreased to 3,234 (U.S. Department of Defense, Assistant Under Secretary for Office of Program Support under CENTCOM January 2014).

Schooner and Swan (2010) assert that contractors have long and proudly served the United States alongside the military and are making the ultimate sacrifice. They point out that in Iraq more than 1,487 contractors have died since 2003; more than 44,000 have been injured, of which more than 16,000 were seriously wounded. In 2003 contractor deaths represented only 4 percent of all fatalities in Iraq and Afghanistan, but from 2004 to 2007 that number rose to 27 percent, and from 2008 to the second quarter of 2010 contractor fatalities accounted for 40 percent of the combined death toll. In the first two quarters of 2010 alone contractor deaths represented more than half, 53 percent, of all fatalities. Schooner and Swan conclude that this point bears emphasis: since January 2010 more contractors than U.S. military soldiers have died in Iraq and Afghanistan.

Size of the Private Security Industry used in Operation Iraqi Freedom

Between 2003 and 2011 there was a 1:1 ratio of U.S. military troops to private contractors in Iraq. In 2007 the Defense Department began maintaining an official count of PMCs in Iraq. At the height of the surge, there were 162,428 (U.S. Department of Defense, Assistant Under Secretary for Office of Program Support under CENTCOM 2008). Over 26,000 were U.S. citizens, over 62,000 were third-country nations, and over 70,000 were Iraqi nationals. Of this number over 7,704 were private security contractors. The private contractors worked in construction, base support, security, transportation, communication support, and as translators.

At the height of the surge, in 2008, the Defense Department spent over $387 billion on procurement contracts (U.S. Congress, House, Commission on Wartime Contracting 2011). Total Defense procurement represents 65 percent of the total Defense Department outlays. Close to $150 billion was spent on service contracts, representing 38 percent of the total Defense procurement purchases. Service contracts are used to purchase services from private military and security contractors and therefore can be used as a gauge for examining the increasing demand for the private military industry; that is, if the number of contracts goes up, then demand has risen.

Bureaucratic Controls on the Private Security Industry in Operation Iraqi Freedom

At the beginning of Operation Iraqi Freedom, there were few legal constraints barring the use of the private military industry.

The Department of Defense entered Operation Iraqi Freedom using the same procedures for contracting that they had used during Operation Enduring

Freedom. However, several new laws and regulations governed the activities of private contractors in Iraq. Specifically contractors in Iraq operated under three levels of legal authority: the international order of the laws and usages of war and resolutions of the United Nations Security Council; U.S. law; and Iraqi law, including orders of the CPA that had not been superseded (Elsea et al. 2008).

The private security industry in Operation Iraqi Freedom was regulated and their actions adjudicated by the U.S. Defense Department. All U.S. contractor personnel and other U.S. civilian employees in Iraq were subject to prosecution in U.S. courts under the Military Extraterritorial Jurisdiction Act of 2000, the Uniform Code of Military Justice, and the Special Maritime and Territorial Jurisdiction of the United States (Elsea et al. 2008, 20). The Department of Justice is responsible for prosecuting crimes in this category. Elsea et al. point out that the Iraqi judicial system did not have jurisdiction to prosecute contractors without the permission of the relevant member country of the multinational forces in Iraq.

In October 2006 the Department of Defense established the Office of the Assistant Deputy Under Secretary of Defense (Program Support) under the undersecretary of defense for acquisition, technology and logistics to implement the program to track individual contractors working in Iraq and Afghanistan. Section 854 of the FY 2007 National Defense Authorization Act provides centralized policy, management, and oversight to the Department of Defense for contracts and contractor performance in support of declared wars as well as contingency and postconflict operations (U.S. Department of Defense, Under Secretary of Defense for Acquisition, Technology, and Logistics 2008). Thus since 2006 CENTCOM has provided information detailing Defense-funded contractors in the theater of operations in support of U.S. military forces in Iraq on a quarterly basis.

The Defense Department developed the Synchronized Pre-deployment and Operational Tracker (SPOT), a web-based software system, to manage, track, and report the visibility of contractors authorized to accompany U.S. forces overseas (U.S. Department of Defense, Under Secretary of Defense for Acquisition, Technology, and Logistics 2010). In a report to Congress, the undersecretary for acquisition, technology and logistics acknowledged that the main challenges to gaining full accountability of contractors supporting contingency operations was obstacles faced when registering local nationals in the SPOT database. However, the Defense Department recognized that contractors represented a large proportion of the workforce supporting contingency operations and therefore acknowledged that it needed to determine where the joint force was most dependent on contractor support. With that information (i.e., a completed SPOT report) the department could better understand the range and depth of contractor capabilities needed to support the joint force and guide the development of future contingency planning efforts (U.S. Department of Defense, Under Secretary of Defense for Acquisition, Technology, and Logistics 2010). The report concluded that the success of our warfighters is directly affected by the success of the management of our contracting workforce.

On 23 June 2003 the Coalition Provisional Authority issued CPA Order 17, Status of the Coalition, Foreign Liaison Missions, Their Personnel and Contractors (U.S. Department of Defense, Assistant Under Secretary for Office of Program Support under CENTCOM 2008). The order required that contractors operating in Iraq understand and comply with U.S., host-nation, and third-country national laws; treaties and international agreements; U.S. regulations, directives, instructions, and policies; and orders, standard operating procedures, and policies issued by the combatant or operational commanders. Other restrictions on contractors imposed by host-nation regulations included having to register to operate in Iraq; being prohibited from law enforcement activities; being prohibited from joining Coalition and multinational forces in combat operations, except in self-defense; and being subject to all applicable criminal, administrative, commercial, and civil laws and regulations (Elsea et al. 2008).

As the number of private contractors in Iraq increased each year, the U.S. Congress became increasingly concerned with their oversight. Subsequently it directed the Defense Department to improve its supervision and enacted several laws that placed private contractors under the jurisdiction of the Department of Defense to enhance legal controls. Yet unlike what the theory of supply and demand would predict, as the limitations and constraints on the private security industry increased, the number of private contractors supporting Operation Iraqi Freedom did not decrease.

Duration of Operation Iraqi Freedom

Even though combat operations in Iraq began on 17 March 2003, preparations for Operation Iraqi Freedom began on 1 March 1991 — the day after the first Gulf War ended (Fontenot et al. 2005; Ricks 2006). The United States did not begin deploying major combat units to the Gulf region until late 2002, so for the purposes of this study, November 2002 is used as the beginning of Operation Iraqi Freedom. From November 2002 through March 2003 the U.S. military staged military forces in Kuwait in preparation for major combat operations (Myers and McConnell 2009).

President Bush made the decision to launch Operation Iraqi Freedom on 16 March 2003, and the ultimatum was issued to Saddam with a forty-eight-hour deadline. Combat operations began on 19 March (20 March in Iraq), with airstrikes targeting Saddam and his military commanders (Myers and McConnell 2009). Coalition ground forces breached the berm along the Kuwait-Iraq border on 20 March and began their march up-country (Fontenot et al. 2005). Within twenty-one days Iraqi military resistance crumbled and U.S. ground forces occupied Baghdad. On 9 April the major combat phase (Phase 3) of Operation Iraqi Freedom had ended (Myers and McConnell 2009; Keegan 2005).

The post-hostility operation (Phase 4) proved to be more difficult than the major combat phase (Myers and McConnell 2009). For the next eight years the United States and its Coalition partners attempted to stabilize Iraq in order to support the reconstruction efforts and build a new government in the midst of a violent insurgency. On 31 December 2011 Operation Iraqi Freedom ended; all U.S. combat troops departed Iraq, thus turning over security and stability to the sovereign Iraqi government. The military phase lasted nine years and one month. Upon completion of the military operations the U.S. Defense Department transitioned Operation Iraqi Freedom to the Department of State on 1 January 2012.

The Bush administration and senior military planners expected that the duration of the military phase would end in 2003. The expectation at the time was that the Defense Department would hand over responsibility for Iraq to the Coalition Provisional Authority. However, a full-blown insurgency, the level of violence, and the scale of the reconstruction efforts required Defense to maintain responsibility for operations in Iraq for much longer. Therefore the Defense Department required assistance from the private security industry to provide logistics and security over a much longer period of time than expected. The massive reconstruction effort in Iraq, undertaken by the CPA, also required a significant use of private *military* contractors. As a result of the overwhelming level of violence the Defense Department, the State Department, and private military companies were required to increase their use of private *security* contractors to protect their personnel and projects. Thus there was a significant increase in the use of private military contractors and private security contractors in Operation Iraqi Freedom.

Scope of Operation Iraqi Freedom

In March 2003 the Coalition ground forces component had a total of 183,000 soldiers and marines, including 41,000 British troops, 4,000 Australians, a battalion of Spanish soldiers numbering 1,300, and a Polish contingent of Special Operations Forces poised along the Iraqi border (Myers and McConnell 2009). Forty countries provided troops, naval units, or logistical support to Operation Iraqi Freedom (Keegan 2005). In addition over 2,000 Abrams tanks, Stryker fighting vehicles, and Bradley fighting vehicles; 43,000 other vehicles, including more than 18,000 Humvees; more than 700 aircraft; and over 140,000 metric tons of equipment and supplies staged in Kuwait for Operation Iraqi Freedom (Stiglitz and Bilmes 2008). Opposing the Coalition was over 400,000 Iraqi soldiers equipped with thousands of tanks, armored vehicles, and artillery pieces (Keegan 2005).

By the summer of 2004 NATO had contributed 90 troops (from ten countries) in support of the Iraqi Security Forces training mission, and in January 2005 NATO donated 30,000 vehicles and weapons to help equip the new Iraqi Security Forces. In particular Hungary donated 77 T-72 tanks and 36 BMP armored personnel carriers, and Greece provided ships for transporting equipment. Many other countries provided training support: Jordan, the United Arab Emirates, Spain, the United Kingdom, Australia, Poland, Canada, Sweden, Denmark, Austria, Finland, the Czech Republic, Germany, Hungary, Slovenia, Slovakia, Singapore, and Belgium (Wright and Reese 2008).

Iraq covers over 438,000 square kilometers and has more than 3,600 kilometers of borders (U.S. Central Intelligence Agency 2011); this makes Iraq the size of California with a population of more than 30 million people (Bremer and McConnell 2006). The distance from Kuwait to Baghdad is over 350 miles. Iraq is largely landlocked and shares its borders with Saudi Arabia, Jordan, Syria, Turkey, Iran, and Kuwait. The four largest cities are Baghdad, the capital, with a population over 5 million; Mosul, with a population over 1 million; Erbil, with a population over 1 million; and Basra, with a population of 923,000. The Iraqi population is ethnically and politically diverse: Shiites make up 60 percent of the population, Kurds 20 percent, and Sunni Arabs 19 percent (Bremer and McConnell 2006).

When Operation Iraqi Freedom began in March 2003, the tempo of advance maintained by U.S. and Coalition troops from Kuwait to Baghdad was unprecedented, covering a distance of over 350 miles in less than fourteen days of combat (Wright and Reese 2008). The supply lines supporting V (U.S.) Corps extended across a greater distance than the historic Red Ball Express during World War II, and fuel demands exceeded the highest requirement the Red Ball Express had to meet (Fontenot et al. 2005). As the war progressed, the scope and scale of the logistics effort was truly monumental; joint logistics functioned across a span of over 8,000 miles (Fontenot et al. 2005). Wright and Reese suggest that the scope and complexity of planning and monitoring all Coalition military and civilian road movements in a country the size of California should not be underestimated. For example, on an average day, approximately 130 to 140 major logistical convoys were on the roads in Iraq, consisting of roughly 1,800 to 2,200 trucks and around 4,000 personnel.

Beginning in 2003 the United States established over 500 military bases across Iraq (Agence France-Presse 2011). Several were massive compounds that appeared to be designed for long-term U.S. occupation (Stiglitz and Bilmes 2008). The largest were Al-Asad, the main supply base housing about 17,000 troops and contractors in Al Anbar Province, about 120 miles west of Baghdad; Al-Balad, also known as Camp Anaconda, which housed about 22,500 troops and contractors and was the U.S. military's main air transportation and supply hub; Camp Taji, which had the largest shopping center in Iraq; and Al-Talil, a key stopping point in southern Iraq for supply convoys from Kuwait (Stiglitz and Bilmes 2008). The logistics support area at Camp Anaconda became a city in its own right, providing support to 13,000 soldiers in more than 200 buildings surrounded by 13 miles of fences and 49 observation towers for base defense. The base included fuel farms, ammunition bunkers, an airfield, a water treatment plant, and an asphalt plant, among many other fixed facilities (Wright and Reese 2008).

In a report to Congress, Belasco (2011) stated that the cumulative total appropriated from 2001 to 2011 for war operations (including contracting), diplomatic operations, and medical care for Iraq and Afghan war veterans was $1.283 trillion. Of this total 63 percent was allocated for Iraq, 35 percent for Afghanistan, and 2 percent for enhanced security; 0.5 percent was unallocated. Therefore of the $1.283 trillion, $806 billion was allocated for Iraq. Stiglitz and Bilmes (2008, 6) assert that in 2007 the Iraq war cost $400,000 per soldier. In contrast, during World War II the cost per soldier was less than $100,000 in 2007 dollars.

Much of the cost of Operation Iraqi Freedom occurred after 2003, during post-hostility operations. Specifically the reconstruction mission in Iraq was far more ambitious than those in Bosnia and Kosovo (Wright and Reese 2008). The Coalition Provisional Authority confronted the equivalent of both a defeated Germany in 1945 and a failed Soviet Union in 1989. This massive undertaking consumed a great deal more resources and effort than expected (Belasco 2011). Unfortunately many argue that the billions of dollars Americans spent went unrecognized and unappreciated by most Iraqis (Allawi 2007).

The United States and its Coalition partners deployed close to 160,000 troops for Operation Iraqi Freedom. The United States maintained over 130,000 troops in Iraq during 2003 and 2004; by 2008 that number had increased to over 157,000. In 2010 the troop levels began to decrease, and in 2011 they were close to 43,000. When the State Department assumed the lead role in Iraq in 2011, the U.S. military presence was projected to be fewer than 100 troops.

After the conclusion of the combat phase of Operation Iraqi Freedom, U.S. forces occupied bases throughout Iraq, each requiring base support and sustainment. Private military companies provided the logistics support to these base camps. Furthermore the significant level of violence during the insurgency required private security companies to assist in protecting critical infrastructure, reconstruction projects, and diplomats. The massive reconstruction effort undertaken by the CPA also required private contractors to help rebuild Iraq's infrastructure. As a result there was a significant increase in the use of private contractors during the postconflict phase.

Other Conflicts or Deployments during Operation Iraqi Freedom

Scholars have noted that not since World War II have the U.S. armed forces operated in multiple theaters of war while simultaneously conducting security operations and support operations in several other theaters (Fontenot et al. 2005). During Operation Iraqi Freedom the United States also conducted operations in Afghanistan (Operation Enduring Freedom), the Philippines (Operation Enduring Freedom-Philippines), and homeland defense (Operation Noble Eagle). Furthermore the United States maintained its commitments to NATO in Bosnia and Kosovo and maintained its presence in Korea.

On 9 June 2003, 369,000 soldiers were deployed overseas, of which about 140,000 were from the reserve components (Fontenot et al. 2005). These soldiers were serving in 120 countries and conducting missions ranging from combat to deterring adversaries, training the nation's allies, and protecting the nation's vital assets. By 2008 there were over 10,000 soldiers forward-stationed in Korea, Europe, and other overseas locations. Another 27,000 were in military occupational specialties that supported the war efforts (i.e., medical, training, and base support) or other contingency missions (i.e., homeland security, fighting fires, disaster response), but are not located within Iraq or Afghanistan (Bonds et al. 2010).

In addition the army provided 11,000 active-duty soldiers for theater air and missile defense forces and national missile defense and another 4,000 soldiers for a global response force (formerly known as the "division ready brigade"). At the time an average of 3,000 soldiers were unavailable for deployment due to injuries incurred during training. Therefore there were 210,000 soldiers available at any one time to deploy either to Iraq or Afghanistan. The average number of soldiers deployed (to Iraq and Afghanistan) from March 2003 through April 2009 was 117,000. However, the number increased during the surge in Iraq, from September 2005 through April 2009, to 128,000 (Bonds et al. 2010).

In 2002 over 101,000 troops were supporting NATO, with close to 80,000 stationed in Korea, over 3,000 in Bosnia, 2,800 in Kosovo, and slightly over 19,000 in either Afghanistan or the Philippines. This represents 16 percent of the total deployed force and over 20 percent of the available ground forces in the Defense Department. The United States increased its use of private military contractors to fill the shortfalls in personnel to conduct logistics and security during Operation Iraqi Freedom.

Size of the U.S. Military during Operation Iraqi Freedom

At the end of September 2002 the number of U.S. active soldiers was slightly more than 1,400,000. This all-volunteer force included ground combat forces from the U.S. Army and U.S. Marine Corps, totaling 486,542 and 173,733, respectively (U.S. Department of Defense, Defense Manpower Data Center 1954–2012). Additionally the U.S. Defense Department employed 670,166 government civilians, who supported a wide range of functions for the active military. The U.S. military was at its lowest troop size since the end of the cold war.

Over the course of operations in Iraq, the Defense Department sought authority to increase the U.S. Army end strength (Cordesman 2006). Between 2002 and 2008 active-duty end strength increased from 487,000 to 557,000 soldiers, including approximately 541,000 active component soldiers and nearly 16,000 army reserve soldiers on Title 10 active guard and reserve status as of December 2008. From March 2003 through December 2008 the army maintained an average of 117,000 active-duty soldiers in Operations Iraqi Freedom and Enduring Freedom combined. That increased to 128,000 active-duty soldiers between September 2005 and December 2008 (Bonds et al. 2010).

By 2008 approximately 373,000 soldiers in the army had served in Operation Iraqi Freedom or Operation Enduring Freedom. Over 121,000 of these had deployed for one year, 173,000 for two years, and 79,000 for three years or longer. The army provided the bulk of U.S. troops: over 1 million had been sent as of December 2008. These deployments represent 52 percent of the total troop deployments within the area of operations and over 75 percent of the deployments on the ground in Iraq, Kuwait, and Afghanistan in 2008 (Bonds et al. 2010).

In summary the total active U.S. military in 2002 was 1,411,634 personnel. Of this number, 660,275 were U.S. Army and U.S. Marine Corps ground troops. This represents a 50 percent decrease in the size of the military from a high of 2,130,299 in 1989. As a result and in order to sustain operations, the U.S. military increased its use of private military contractors during Operation Iraqi Freedom to fill shortfalls in personnel available to provide logistics and security. Although there were slight increases in the total forces by 2010, this did not decrease the use of private contractors in Operation Iraqi Freedom.

Military Outlays during Operation Iraqi Freedom

By 2003 and the beginning of Operation Iraqi Freedom, the U.S. defense budget had increased from its 1996 low. The government allocated over $404 billion for defense spending (U.S. Office of Management and Budget 2003). This amounted to 3.7 percent of the GDP or 18.7 percent of budget outlays. In a matter of seven years since the intervention in Bosnia, U.S. military spending had increased by over $140 billion per year, a 0.5 percent increase in GDP allocation or a 1 percent increase of total U.S. budget outlays.

In comparison, the U.S. government allocated over $1.4 trillion for human resource spending in 2003 (U.S. Office of Management and Budget 2003), 13.1 percent of GDP or 65.6 percent of total budget outlays. U.S. spending on domestic programs had increased by almost $500 billion between 1995 and 2003, a 1 percent increase in GDP or 4.6 percent of budget outlays.

In turn the U.S. Department of Defense spent over $248 billion on contracts in 2003, increasing to over $379 billion by 2009 (U.S. Department of Defense, Defense Manpower Data Center 1954–2012). This amounted to 63.9 and 59.6 percent (respectively) of the department's total outlays. The spending on service contracts amounted to over $104 billion or 41.9 percent of the total percent of Defense contracts in 2003 and over $160 billion or 42.4 percent of the contracts in 2009. Service contracts differ from product contracts or research and development contracts. Most private military contracts that provide logistics or security support are purchased under service contracts.

Between 1996 and 2003 the United States increased its defense spending by 18.7 percent of total budget outlays. By 2003 total outlays for defense were $404 billion, an increase of $140 billion per year or a 0.5 percent increase in GDP allocations. By 2010 total outlays for defense were over $666 billion. If the use of private contractors increases when defense budgets are reduced, it follows that if outlays for defense increase then the use of private contractors should decrease. However, this did not occur between 2003 and 2010; in fact the use of private contractors increased dramatically.

Choices Other Than the Private Security Industry

Policymakers and military leaders consider many factors when deciding whether to employ private security contractors. For example, increased participation by allies, coalition partners, or the host nation can provide alternatives to the increased use of the private security industry.

The United States and its Coalition partners relied heavily on private military contractors to augment shortfalls in logistics support, assist in training the Iraqi Security Forces, and assist in providing security. After the seizure of Baghdad and the fall of the regime, the security environment in Iraq was nonpermissive. The level of violence exceeded the Coalition's capacity to provide a secure environment for the Iraqi population and the reconstruction effort. In essence the demand for security exceeded the supply of forces able to provide that security.

When Bremer dissolved Saddam's army as well as the security and intelligence services, a security vacuum existed until the establishment of a new Iraqi Security Force (Bremer and McConnell 2006; Allawi 2007). General Myers asserted at the time that the overall objective was simple: to increase the size and competency of the Iraqi forces so they could eventually replace U.S. and Coalition forces (Myers and McConnell 2009). It was believed that this military initiative, in combination with political, economic, and security progress, would lead to a stable Iraq (Myers and McConnell 2009). However, as scholars have pointed out, creating a new Iraqi Security Force proved harder than expected (Metz 2010b; Cordesman 2006). With few effective Iraqi security forces and not enough Americans to secure all of the country around the clock, the insurgency spread and mutated (Metz 2010b; Herspring 2008).

In addition training the Iraqi Security Forces stretched the U.S. Army and Marine Corps to their limits as they provided more than 1,000 officers and noncommissioned officers to that the effort (Myers and McConnell 2009). However, by early 2005 the numbers and capability of the Iraqi Security Forces began to climb, reflecting the vastly increased size of the train-and-equip mission. By January 2005 over 125,000 Iraqi Security Forces were trained and operational; this included the Iraqi Army, Navy, Air Force, National and Local Police, and Border Security Troops (Wright and Reese 2008; Cordesman 2006). With 6,300 trained Iraqi Highway Police, their ability to secure roadways freed up Coalition troops to perform other security missions (Wright and Reese 2008). Likewise with the creation of the Department of Border Enforcement, 32,000 Iraqis were able to secure their borders.

The United States used allies, Coalition partners, and host-nation resources during Operation Iraqi Freedom. Although many countries provided troops and resources, they limited the number of troops on the ground (with the exception of Great Britain; Cordesman 2006). Additionally the United States activated more than 28,000 army National Guard and 13,000 army reserve soldiers, and the U.S. Marine Corps activated over 5,000 reservists. Although Iraqi Security Forces did not significantly participate in the operation until 2006, once their number had increased, the U.S. military began to reduce the number of troops in Iraq. Therefore the use of allies, Coalition partners and reserve and National Guard forces did not result in a decrease of private contractors. However, as the size of the Iraqi Security Forces increased, the number of private contractors decreased.

Private Security Supply-Demand Behavior: An Assessment

In the case of Operation Iraqi Freedom, private security supply-demand behavior is evident.

Chapter 4 provided a detailed review of the downsizing of the U.S. military in the 1990s. Although that reduction placed strains on the U.S. military intervention in Bosnia, the full impact of the downsizing revealed itself during Operation Iraqi Freedom. Specifically the absence of any clear threat encouraged the perception that it was prudent to reduce the armed forces, and strategic ambiguity made it difficult for decision makers and the citizenry to reach a consensus on just what the military requirements should be (Fontenot et al. 2005).

The reduction in the size of the military during the 1990s resulted in enormous pressure on the U.S. military in general, and the army in particular, to man, equip, train, field, and sustain an effective force in a new security environment. These conditions compelled the army to maintain a military force capable of providing for the common defense, but "on the cheap" (Fontenot et al. 2005). The Bush administration concluded that since the military adapted quickly to multinational peacekeeping in Bosnia without extensive preparation, it could adapt equally well to stabilization and counterinsurgency missions in Iraq. Furthermore the military's personnel, training, equipment, and force structure — accompanied by its often-stated reputation as the world's greatest military — led civilian leaders to believe that the overthrow of Saddam would be a simple affair (Metz 2010a).

The Bush administration's prewar assumptions were directly related to the size of the force envisioned for Operation Iraqi Freedom (Herspring 2008). It has been asserted that the administration deliberately did little to prepare for extensive stabilization and reconstruction activities precisely because its political opponents would have used this to derail the intervention (Metz 2010a). Furthermore the Bush administration deliberately downplayed the potential costs and risks of war with Iraq (Herspring 2008). However, Army Chief of Staff Gen. Eric Shinseki testified before Congress in February 2003 that occupation duty in Iraq would require several hundred thousand troops (Myers and McConnell 2009; Herspring 2008).

The historical record demonstrated that to achieve stability in the initial years after military occupation there should be 20 occupying troops for every 1,000 people in the country occupied (Bremer and McConnell 2006; Herspring 2008). With a population of 25 million in Iraq, 500,000 troops on the ground were required to meet this standard (Bremer and McConnell 2006). However, General Franks planned for an invasion force of only 122,000 U.S. troops and 21,000 British troops (Myers and McConnell 2009; Herspring 2008). Likewise most UN peacekeeping missions routinely deployed 1 international police officer for every 10 soldiers; this equates to about 65,000 police needed for Iraq. Therefore the Department of State proposed sending

5,000 armed civilian police to Iraq once the fighting stopped (Dobbins et al. 2009). Yet only 1,500 civilian police were authorized by the White House.

Despite the evidence, senior members of the Bush administration defended their position based on the assumption that in Iraq, the postconflict would present a benign environment. For instance, Deputy Secretary of Defense Paul Wolfowitz argued, "The Iraqi people will greet us as liberators, and . . . they will help us to keep requirements down and we can say with reasonable confidence that the notion of hundreds of thousands of American troops is way off the mark" (Metz 2010a, 17; Herspring 2008, 124). Likewise Secretary Rumsfeld asserted, "The idea that it would take several hundred thousand U.S. forces I think is far from the mark," and Vice President Dick Cheney stated, "I really do believe that we will be greeted as liberators and to suggest that we need several hundred thousand troops there after military operations cease, after the conflict ends, I don't think is accurate. I think that's an overstatement" (Metz 2010a, 17, 18).

However, when policymakers expanded their goals to include regime *replacement* — much harder than regime *removal* — the military should have advised that the force structure was inadequate for that task. The number of forces required to conduct the operation was the single most important variable around which all of the variants of the plan revolved (Fontenot et al. 2005). In spite of this, the force requirement was based on regime removal (Herspring 2008). Therefore the military plan developed for Operation Iraqi Freedom and the number of forces that were allocated for the operation focused only on the defeat of the Iraqi military and the removal of the Saddam regime.

Had military leaders believed that removing Saddam by force would lead to protracted instability and conflict in Iraq, they might have begun preparing for the operation sooner than they did (Metz 2010a). However, some authors posit that even this may have been difficult — perhaps even impossible — under the forceful leadership of Secretary Rumsfeld. In fact Rumsfeld refused to allow military planners to use the Department of State's study on a post-Saddam Iraq conducted between October 2001 and April 2003 (Herspring 2005). Metz (2010a) believes that the secretary was convinced that the military's tendency to assume and prepare for the worst outcome was an impediment to action. Myers and McConnell (2009, 255) argue, "We always understood that there would be a fine line between too many troops and too few. And we were mindful of the strain on overall armed services force levels that sending more troops to Iraq would bring." They explain, "How many would be needed and for how long was hard to judge, and at this point the U.S. government still believed that a significant number of those troops would come from friendly Arab or Muslim nations that had not contributed forces to the major combat operation, but might be willing to help with the stability and reconstruction phase" (250). In hindsight the incompleteness of the plan helped create the conditions for the difficult occupation (Ricks 2006).

In early May 2003 the Bush administration's assumptions seemed to be correct. The security situation was relatively quiet from a military standpoint, and with just over 160,000 Coalition troops in Iraq the overall security situation seemed fairly stable (Myers and McConnell 2009). However, by the time Bremer arrived in Baghdad, he faced a deteriorating security situation (Herspring 2008). Even with over 40,000 Coalition troops in Baghdad, law and order essentially broke down (Delong and Lukeman 2007). Bremer and McConnell (2006, 17) point out that in Baghdad unchecked looting was out of control; therefore establishing law and order was the first priority. There were around 14,000 Iraqi policemen missing from their posts in Baghdad; that is, most of them just disappeared, as did the army (Bremer and McConnell 2006).

The realities in theater were in stark contrast to the prewar assumptions. Even though planners within the U.S. government envisioned the large-scale surrender of Iraqi Army units during the invasion, they assumed that police and justice systems would remain intact (Wright and Reese 2008; Herspring 2008). This would have allowed the Coalition to adopt an advisory role to facilitate bureaucracies that would continue to function in a post-Saddam Iraq. Military plans also called for the rapid handover of responsibility for rebuilding security forces to Iraqi civilians (Wright and Reese 2008). This assumption also proved to be flawed. Many scholars believe the U.S. military fought the battle it wanted to fight, mistakenly believing it would be the only battle it faced (Ricks 2006).

As a result military leaders faced the choice of securing key tactical objectives or establishing law and order. U.S. military planners in Iraq concluded that a force of 300,000 was required to accomplish its mission in light of the security situation (Ricks 2006). In view of that fact, Bremer requested that CENTCOM send more military police to Baghdad to help restore order (Bremer and McConnell 2006; Delong and Lukeman 2007). Concerned over the security situation, Bremer states that he brought up the issue of troops levels to Rumsfeld and Bush. Herspring (2008, 135) credits Bremer for halting the planned withdrawal of U.S. troops from Iraq. Although Bush stated that Secretary Powell was attempting to enlist more troops from friendly countries, there was no increase in troop levels in Iraq until 2007 (Bremer and McConnell 2006).

It was clear by the summer of 2006 that the United States was not on track for the victory described by President Bush (Metz 2010b). Violence continued to increase as Coalition forces fought the postconflict insurgency. Bonds et al. (2010) assert that the demand for active-duty soldiers in Iraq would have exceeded supply under the army's normal deployment policies. Therefore the army took several actions to increase supply: it increased the overall size of the active component; it reassigned soldiers from other missions to the pool of soldiers rotating to Iraq and Afghanistan; and it greatly increased the rate at which soldiers rotated to and from the war (Bonds et al. 2010; Herspring 2008). However, the army retained very limited unutilized capacity to deploy additional active-duty soldiers beyond the current troop levels.

Pressure on the ground forces increased with the increasing violence from the insurgency. Neither the army nor the marine corps was configured for a large-scale, protracted counterinsurgency (Metz 2010b). Metz argues that a decade of defense transformation had created a force optimized for intense, short-duration operations, not stabilization or counterinsurgency. Therefore the Defense Department sought authority to increase army end strength, which did increase from 487,000 in 2002 to 557,000 in December 2008 (Bonds et al. 2010). However, as one retired senior officer pointed out, post–World War II history shows that adding, manning, training, and equipping a new active army brigade would take up to two years (Bicksler et al. 2003).

At the same time, Bush announced a troop increase in Iraq; the main problem was deciding on the size of the increase. Senior military advisors recommended a surge of two army brigade combat teams and two marine battalions, with most of the new forces dedicated to training and advising the Iraqi Security Forces. Bush approved the maximum increase that the Pentagon said it could support—five brigades—and, importantly, using them for population security rather than simply training and advising (Metz 2010b). The result, as mentioned earlier, was a significant reduction in violence by late 2007. This set the conditions for the Obama administration to end combat operations by 2010 and to withdraw all military forces by 2011.

Summary and Analysis

Supply-demand behavior is evident during Operations Iraqi Freedom. Military planners and decision makers began the mission with a force significantly reduced from that used in Operation Desert Storm. The decision to begin Operation Iraqi Freedom with a smaller force resulted in a higher demand for troops during the postconflict phase, when violence increased. The initial demand for an expeditionary logistics force capability was low due to the lower number of troops deployed. However, the demand for logistics increased as military forces spread out across Iraq to establish security.

The decision not to increase the size of the military force in Iraq once the insurgency began resulted in a higher demand for forces to maintain security. Military planners, State Department planners, and contractors conducting reconstruction substituted private security contractors for U.S. military forces to provide security. Likewise military planners substituted private military contractors for military logistics forces for logistics support. Without host-nation support from Iraq, the number of private contractors increased.

The evidence from Operation Iraqi Freedom provides several alternative explanations for the increased reliance on the private security industry. First, a force cap of 160,000 U.S. soldiers required military leaders to reduce the number of combat and logistics forces deployed into theater. When military leaders realized that insufficient forces were available to accomplish all of the critical tasks, they chose to substitute private military companies for combat forces and military logistics support. Second, the U.S. military did not have host-nation support from the Iraqis. As a result the U.S. military relied on private military companies for support. Third, the U.S. and Coalition forces operated in a nonpermissive security environment while conducting counterinsurgency and reconstruction operations, and they allocated a majority of their troops for force protection. As a result the U.S. military significantly increased its use of private military companies and private security companies for support.

Some scholars suggest that forcibly removing Saddam from power was arguably the most momentous act of the Bush administration, its effects profound and far-reaching (Metz 2010a). Furthermore, as Wright and Reese (2008) point out, no army in the world could dream of conducting and sustaining two military campaigns in some of the world's most remote and inhospitable regions, more than ten thousand miles from their home territory. Other scholars claim that the Bush Doctrine fundamentally changed the way the United States would ensure its national security when the Bush administration shifted from a strategy of "shape, respond, prepare" to a new strategy of assure, dissuade, deter forward, and decisively defeat (Fontenot et al. 2005). The new strategy required a fully expeditionary force capable of rapidly imposing America's will on hostile foreign soil and then maintaining a robust presence to ensure the change would be lasting (Fontenot et al. 2005).

Most of the U.S. military was always located in the United States, and most of the forces deployed in Europe, Japan, and Korea were located in garrisons and bases that had been maintained since the end of World War II (Bicksler et al. 2003). In the event of hostilities, U.S. military strategy called for a reinforcement of these forward garrisons. Yet Operation Iraqi Freedom was different. The U.S. military was well trained to defeat Saddam's army and ensure the dictator's regime fell so they could assist with the installation of a new representative government in Iraq (Wright and Reese 2008). However, when Coalition military forces entered Iraq in March 2003 they did not come prepared to rebuild the country they hoped to liberate. Some scholars argue that no U.S. military leader entered Iraq in 2003 expecting to train, equip, or advise the entire body of security forces in a new Iraq on a multiyear basis, and do so in the midst of an intense insurgency (Wright and Reese 2008; Delong and Lukeman 2007).

Military force allocated to Operation Iraqi Freedom achieved its objective of defeating the Iraqi military and deposing Saddam (Ricks 2006; Delong and Lukeman 2007). However, the scope and duration of the postconflict reconstruction phase exceeded the capabilities of the Coalition forces. With few alternatives, it is understandable that the Bush administration and military leaders turned to the private contracting industry to provide security and logistic support. The U.S. military just was not large enough to rebuild a nation the size of California while securing a population of over 30 million people.

Operation Iraqi Freedom is a most likely case for examining private security supply-demand behavior. The empirical results meet two demanding tests. As in Operations Joint Endeavor and Enduring Freedom, the ratio of contractors to U.S. soldiers was 1:1. Given the scale of Operation Iraqi Freedom, with 160,000 U.S. troops eventually deployed, this is remarkable. As in the previous cases, there are a number of overlapping reasons for the extensive use of private military support and private security services in Operation Iraqi Freedom. The force cap imposed on military planners forced them to employ private contractors as they determined that the mission required more ground troops than they were allotted. Once the force cap was imposed, planners assigned military forces to the core tasks of defeating the Iraqi Army, then the insurgency. They used private contractors for logistics support, training assistance, reconstruction, and security. Second, the security environment in Iraq was nonpermissive. The U.S. and Coalition forces conducted operations in an environment where they did not have adequate troops for force protection. The Iraqi Security Forces dissolved in 2003 and were not capable of providing security until 2006. Third, there was no host nation. The U.S. and Coalition forces conducted a regime change and established a new Iraqi government. As a result the United States and its NATO partners conducted Operation Iraqi Freedom as an external hostile force without the support of a host nation.

CHAPTER SEVEN

CROSS-CASE ANALYSIS AND FINDINGS

The present research utilized a cross-comparison test method to analyze the events of four historical cases. The cross-comparison method asks a series of standardized questions in order to identify commonalities or differences in the events which would therefore demonstrate support for the proposed hypotheses. This chapter reviews the findings to determine if they support the hypotheses. Alternative explanations for the outcomes are reviewed and tentative conclusions offered.

Findings from the Case Studies

The theory of supply and demand would assert a general increase in the use of private military contractors as a result of increased demand. During Operations Desert Shield and Desert Storm, the U.S. military hired approximately 10,000 private contractors to provide logistics and transportation. The majority were third-country nationals living in Saudi Arabia or citizens of Saudi Arabia, and there is no evidence that any were employees of a private military firm. During Operation Joint Endeavor, the U.S. military and the U.S. Department of State hired over 14,000 private military contractors to provide logistics, construction, and training in Bosnia. The United States relied primarily on private military companies during Operation Joint Endeavor. During Operation Enduring Freedom, the U.S. military hired just over 107,000 private military and private security contractors at the peak of the surge in 2010 to provide logistics, construction, and security in Afghanistan. The private companies hired U.S. civilians, third-country nationals, and Afghan nationals as contractors. The United States relied primarily on private military companies and private security companies during Operation Enduring Freedom. During Operation Iraqi Freedom, the U.S. military and U.S. Department of State hired on average 130,000 to 160,000 private military and private security contractors to provide logistics, construction, and security in Iraq. The private companies hired U.S. civilians, third-country nationals, and Iraqi nationals as contractors. The United States relied primarily on private military companies and private security companies during Operation Iraqi Freedom. Thus between 1990 and 2014 the United States increased its use of private contractors to support military operations across the four interventions.

The amount of military outlays or amount spent on national defense can serve as an indicator of the amount available to spend for a national army. In 1990 the United States spent over $299 billion for defense, which represented 23.1 percent of the national budget. In 1995 it spent over $272 billion for defense, 17.1 percent of the national budget. In 2003 the amount was over $404 billion for defense, which was 18 percent of the national budget. However, by 2010 the United States spent over $693 billion for defense, which represented 19.3 percent of the national budget. The U.S. defense budget peaked in 2011, at just over $705 billion, 18.8 percent of the national budget. After 2012 the U.S. defense budget began to decrease slowly until 2014. Thus between 1990 and 2014 U.S. defense spending decreased until 1998, then increased steadily until 2011 and began a slow decrease until 2014.

The increasing or decreasing size of the military is a useful indicator of the need for the private security industry. In 1990 the total U.S. active military force was 2,046,144 personnel; of this number the ground force consisted of 732,403 army personnel and 196,652 marine corps personnel (929,055 total). The Defense Department employed 1,034,152 civilians. By 1995 the total U.S. active military force had decreased to 1,518,224 personnel, with ground forces consisting of 508,559 army and 174,639 marine corps personnel (683,198 total). In addition the Defense Department employed 820,189 civilians.

In 2002 the total U.S. active military forces was reduced even further, to

1,411,634 personnel; ground forces consisted of 486,542 army and 173,733 marine corps personnel (660,275 total). The Defense Department also employed 670,166 civilians. The total U.S. active military force remained constant at about 1,430,985 personnel until 2010; ground forces consisted of 566,045 army and 202,441 marine corps personnel (768,486 total). The Defense Department employed 772,601 civilians. By 2014 the size of the U.S. military had decreased to 1,368,137 personnel; ground forces consisted of 521,685 army and 192,350 marine corps personnel. From 1990 to 2002 the U.S. active military force decreased by 37 percent; from 2002 to 2010 the size increased by 2 percent. From 1990 to 2002 the size of the Defense Department civilian workforce decreased by 56 percent; from 2002 to 2014 the size increased by 14 percent.

The number of other conflicts or commitments U.S. forces were dedicated to during an intervention is an indicator of the availability of military forces for the intervention. In 1990 the U.S. military had over 291,000 troops committed to NATO and over 87,000 stationed in Korea. Of the total active force, 609,422 troops were stationed outside of the continental United States, which represented 30 percent of the total force.

In 1995 over 109,000 U.S. military troops were supporting NATO, over 75,000 troops were stationed in Korea, and 1,600 troops were still in Haiti supporting Operation Uphold Democracy. Of the total force, 238,064 troops were stationed outside of the continental United States. This represented 15 percent of the total deployed force.

By 2002 over 101,000 U.S. military troops were supporting NATO; close to 80,000 were stationed in Korea; just over 3,000 were in Bosnia; 2,800 were in Kosovo; and slightly over 19,000 were in either Afghanistan or the Philippines. Of the total force, 16 percent, 230,484 troops, were stationed outside of the continental United States.

Troop commitments continued to increase, and by 2010 there were 105,900 U.S. military troops in Afghanistan, 96,200 in Iraq, and 297,286 in the Philippines, Kosovo, NATO, and Korea; thus 499,386 military personnel (35 percent) were deployed or stationed outside of the continental United States. From 1990 to 2002 the size of the U.S. military forces deployed outside of the United States decreased from 30 percent of the total to 16 percent. After the start of Operation Iraqi Freedom, the size of the U.S. military force deployed outside of the United States increased to 35 percent.

An examination of the duration of the conflicts can be used to determine if trade-offs were made for the use of military force versus the private security industry; that is, as the conflict continues, the theory of supply and demand would posit that there is an increased reliance on the private security industry.

Operations Desert Shield and Desert Storm: 17 months.
Operation Joint Endeavor: 108 months.
Operation Enduring Freedom by October 2014: 156 months.
Operation Iraqi Freedom: 109 months.

Likewise an examination into the scope or scale of each conflict will also reveal likely trade-offs for the use of military forces versus the private security industry. Supply-demand theory would posit that as the scope increases, the likelihood of relying on the private security industry also increases. Scope and scale can be measured by the number of military forces committed to a conflict, the size of the conflict area, or the number of military bases used. For the purposes of this research, the number of U.S. military forces is used. The United States initially (August 1990) deployed 250,000 troops for Operation Desert Shield; in November 1990 250,000 additional troops were deployed to conduct Operation Desert Storm. For Operation Joint Endeavor, the United States deployed 16,200 troops. In the second year of the operation the United States reduced the size of the military force to 8,300. For Operation Enduring Freedom, the United States deployed approximately 5,200 troops to Afghanistan by the end of 2002. The number of troops steadily increased to a peak of 107,900 by 2011. By the end of 2014 the number of troops deployed to Afghanistan will have decreased to below 10,000 as Operation Enduring Freedom comes to an end. The United States deployed 160,000 troops for the initial stage of Operation Iraqi Freedom. That number decreased to 130,000 in late 2003, then increased to 157,000 by 2008 to support the counterinsurgency efforts. By 2010 the number of troops in Iraq decreased to 93,000, with a further decrease to 43,000 in 2011. All combat troops were withdrawn by the end of 2012.

The laws, regulations, and controls in place during an intervention shed some light on the permissiveness of use of the private security industry. Specifically more bureaucratic controls would likely limit the use of the private security industry. In 1990 U.S. Army regulations governed the use of private contractors on the battlefield. The regulation encouraged the U.S. Army to contract for host-nation support as a substitute for military forces. In 1995 the Defense Department formalized the use of the Logistics Civil Augmentation Program, which allowed the use of private military companies to provide support to the U.S. military. The Department of State regulated private military companies working in a foreign country using the Arms Control Act and the International Traffic in Arms Regulation. In 2003 congressional oversight on the use of private contractors began to increase. As the number of private contractors increased — particularly private security contractors — Congress passed several laws that formalized the legal controls over contractors supporting the U.S. military and the Department of State.

Hypotheses

Hypothesis 1: The theory of supply and demand posits that when military outlays decrease, there should be an increase in the use of the private security industry. As can be seen in table 2 there were no decreases in military outlays during Operations Desert Shield and Desert Storm, yet the U.S. military still required the use of host-nation private contractors. In 1995 there was a decrease in military outlays, but the U.S. military used private military companies in Bosnia. In 2001 there began an increase in military outlays, and the U.S. military used private military and private security companies in Afghanistan. By 2003 there was a significant increase in military outlays (which continued through 2011), and the U.S. military increased its use of private military and security companies in Iraq. In 2012 military outlays began to decrease through 2014, and the U.S. military continued to use private military and private security companies in Afghanistan. The evidence provides a mixed outcome that suggests the hypothesis is not supported.

It may be that military spending has to be relatively high to sustain a post-conflict stabilization operation the size of that in Afghanistan and Iraq. The

Table 2. Summary of Findings from the Case Studies

	Operations Desert Shield and Desert Storm	Operation Joint Endeavor	Operation Enduring Freedom	Operation Iraqi Freedom
Use of PMC/PSC	Host-nation contracts: ~10,000	PMC: ~14,000	PMC: ~89,000 PSC: ~18,000	PMC: ~150,000 PSC: ~10,000
When military outlays decrease, there is an increase in the use of private security.	No decrease in military outlays; host-nation contracts	Decrease in military outlays; use of PMC	Increase in military outlays; use of PMC and PSC	Increase in military outlays; use of PMC and PSC
When the size of a national military decreases, there is an increase in the use of private military security.	No decrease in the size of the national military; host-nation contracts	Decrease in the size of the national military; use of PMC	Decrease in the size of the military (2001); modest increase in the size of the military (2006); decrease in the size of the military (2014); use of PMC and PSC	Decrease in the size of the military (2003); modest increase in the size of the military (2006); use of PMC and PSC
When the number of military disputes, military engagements, and militarized conflicts increases, there is an increase in the use of private security internationally.	Supported NATO and Korea, Desert Storm the only conflict; host-nation contracts	Supported NATO and Korea, Joint Endeavor the only conflict; use of PMC	Supported NATO, Korea, Bosnia, Kosovo, Operation Iraqi Freedom, Operation Enduring Freedom; use of PMC and PSC	Supported NATO, Korea, Bosnia, Kosovo, Operation Enduring Freedom, and Operation Iraqi Freedom; use of PMC and PSC
When the duration of a military conflict increases, there is an increase in the use of private security.	Duration of intervention: ~13 months; host-nation contracts	Duration of intervention: ~9 years; use of PMC	Duration of intervention: ~13 years; use of PMC and PSC	Duration of intervention: ~9 years; use of PMC and PSC

When there is a decrease in bureaucratic controls and regulations, there is an increase in the use of private security.	Minimal bureaucratic controls; host-nation contracts	Minimal bureaucratic controls; use of PMC	Minimal to moderate bureaucratic controls; use of PMC and PSC	Minimal to moderate bureaucratic controls; use of PMC and PSC
When there is a force cap placed on the size of the military force, there is an increase in the use of private security.	Initial force cap: 250,000; final force cap: 500,000; host-nation contracts	Initial force cap: 15,000; subsequent force cap: 6,900; use of PMC	Initial force cap: 15,000; subsequent force cap: ~108,000; use of PMC and PSC	Initial force cap: ~130,000; subsequent force cap: ~160,000; use of PMC and PSC
When the security environment is nonpermissive, there is an increase in private security.	Permissive (in Saudi Arabia); host-nation contracts	Semipermissive; use of PMC	Nonpermissive; use of PMC and PSC	Nonpermissive; use of PMC and PSC

moderate increase after 2002 was therefore not sufficient because overall levels of spending were too low to sustain the operation, regardless of the slight increase in spending. In other words, there may be a threshold of total military spending that is needed to support a mission like Iraq and Afghanistan, and even though military spending rose after 2002, it did not approach this threshold until about 2012. The difference is between the degree of change in military spending and the level of spending. This means that change may be in the appropriate direction, but it may not have reached a sufficient level.

Hypothesis 2: The theory of supply and demand asserts that when the size of a national military decreases, there should be an increase in the use of private military security. As table 2 shows, during Operations Desert Shield and Desert Storm there was no decrease in the size of the military; however, the U.S. military still required the use of host-nation support contractors. By

1995 the size of the total force had decreased and private military contractors were used extensively during Operation Joint Endeavor. There was a further decrease in military end strength by 2001 and the United States increased its use of private military and security companies in Operations Enduring Freedom and Iraqi Freedom. Though the size of the force began to increase by 2008, the U.S. military continued to increase its use of private military and security companies in Afghanistan and Iraq. While the size of the military began to steadily decrease between 2012 and 2014, the U.S. military continued to increase its use of the private security industry in Afghanistan. The evidence provides a mixed outcome that suggests the hypothesis is supported in three of the four cases.

Hypothesis 3: The theory of supply and demand states that when the number of military disputes, engagements, and conflicts increases, there should be an increase in the use of the private security industry internationally. As table 2 shows, in 1990, 30 percent of the total U.S. military force was deployed outside the continental United States, and the U.S. military required the use of host-nation private contractors during Operations Desert Shield and Desert Storm. In 1995, 15 percent of the total U.S. military force was deployed outside the continental United States, and the U.S. military utilized private military companies in Operation Joint Endeavor. By 2001, 13 percent of the total U.S. military force was deployed outside the continental United States, and the U.S. military increased its use of private military and security companies for Operation Enduring Freedom. In 2003, 16 percent of the total U.S. military force was deployed outside the continental United States, and the U.S. military increased its use of private military and security companies for Operation Iraqi Freedom. Between 2004 and 2012, 37 percent of the total U.S. military force was deployed outside the continental United States, and the U.S. military continued to increase its use of private military and security companies in support of Operation Iraqi Freedom. The evidence suggests that the hypothesis is supported in all four cases.

Hypothesis 4: The theory of supply and demand posits that when the duration of a military conflict increases, there is a likely increase in the use of the private security industry. Operations Desert Shield and Desert Storm lasted 17 months, and the U.S. military required the use of approximately

10,000 host-nation private contractors for support functions. Operation Joint Endeavor lasted 108 months, and the U.S. military used approximately 14,000 private military contractors. Operation Enduring Freedom lasted 156 months, and the U.S. military increased its use of private military and security companies in Afghanistan. To date approximately 108,000 private contractors have been used during Operation Enduring Freedom. Operation Iraqi Freedom continued for 109 months, and during this time the U.S. military used approximately 150,000 private military and security contractors. The evidence suggests the hypothesis is supported.

Hypothesis 5: According to the theory of supply and demand, when there is a decrease in bureaucratic controls and regulations, there should be an increase in the utilization of the private security industry. In 1990 U.S. Army regulations encouraged contracting for host-nation support as a substitute for military forces, and the U.S. military required the use of host-nation private contractors for Operations Desert Shield and Desert Storm. In 1995 the Defense Department formalized the use of LOGCAP and the Department of State began regulating private military companies working in foreign countries. Even with greater controls the U.S. military used private military companies during Operation Joint Endeavor. In 2001 the U.S. military entered Operation Enduring Freedom under the same bureaucratic controls emplaced during Operation Joint Endeavor. In 2003 congressional oversight on the use of private contractors began to increase, but the U.S. military still increased its use of private military and security companies in Iraq. Bureaucratic controls and regulations increased from 1990 through 2014, at the same time the U.S. military increased its use of the private security industry. The evidence suggests the hypothesis is supported in all four cases. It may be that the initial bureaucratic controls to legalize the use of the private security industry were insufficient to ensure efficient operations, so additional regulations were implemented to improve efficiency, verify business procedures, and enforce compliance of standard operating procedures.

Alternative Explanations

Events and conditions within the four case studies provide evidence of several alternative explanations for the use of private military and security contractors.

First, according to the theory of supply and demand, when decision makers place a force cap on the size of the military during an intervention, there should be an increase in the use of private security. For example, in 1990 the initial force cap of 250,000 U.S. soldiers required military leaders to choose between deploying combat forces or logistics forces into theater for Operations Desert Shield and Desert Storm. When they chose to deploy combat soldiers first, military leaders substituted military logistics support for private host-nation support. In 1995 a force cap of 15,000 U.S. soldiers required military leaders to choose between deploying combat or logistics forces into theater for Operation Joint Endeavor. When they chose to deploy combat soldiers, private military companies were substituted for military logistics support. In 2001 military planners self-imposed a force cap or "light footprint" limiting the initial deployment of troops to well below 10,000 for Operation Enduring Freedom. In 2011 President Obama increased the cap to 108,000 troops deployed to Afghanistan. During Operation Iraqi Freedom (2003) a force cap of 160,000 U.S. soldiers in theater required military leaders to reduce the number of combat and logistics forces. When they realized that insufficient forces were available to accomplish all of the critical tasks, they substituted combat forces and military logistics support for private military companies. The evidence from all four cases suggests that this alternative hypothesis is supported.

Second, the theory of supply and demand states that when a host nation does not provide logistic support or security services during an intervention, there is a likely increase in the use of the private security industry. During Operations Desert Shield and Desert Storm, King Fahd provided significant financial support, transportation, food, housing, equipment, and labor. During Operation Joint Endeavor, the U.S. military did not have host-nation support from the Bosnian Serbs, the Bosnian Croats, or the Bosniaks. As a result the U.S. military relied on private military companies for support. During Operation Enduring Freedom, the U.S. military did not have host-nation support from the Afghans and so relied on private military companies and private security companies for support. During Operation Iraqi Freedom, the U.S. military did not have host-nation support from the Iraqis and so relied on private military companies and private security companies for support.

The evidence from all four cases suggests that this alternative hypothesis is supported.

Third, the theory of supply and demand posits that when the security environment in the target state is nonpermissive, there should be an increase in the use of the private security industry. During Operations Desert Shield and Desert Storm the U.S. and Coalition forces operated in a permissive security environment while preparing for combat operations. As a result they did not have to allocate troops for force protection; the 110,000-man Saudi security forces provided the security. During Operation Joint Endeavor the U.S. and NATO forces operated in a semipermissive security environment while conducting peace enforcement operations, and the U.S. and Coalition forces allocated a portion of their troops for force protection. As a result the U.S. military relied on private military companies for support. During Operation Enduring Freedom the U.S. and Coalition forces operated in a nonpermissive security environment while conducting counterinsurgency and reconstruction operations and allocated a majority of their troops for force protection. As a result the U.S. military significantly increased its use of private military companies and private security companies for support. During Operation Iraqi Freedom the U.S. and Coalition forces operated in a nonpermissive security environment while conducting counterinsurgency and reconstruction operations and allocated a majority of their troops for force protection. As a result the U.S. military significantly increased its use of private military companies and private security companies for support. The evidence from all four cases suggests that this alternative hypothesis is supported.

Summary and Tentative Conclusion

The evidence from the case studies suggests that only two of the five hypotheses under review demonstrate unambiguously significant results: the duration of the military conflict and decreased bureaucratic controls are significant indicators of an increased use of private military contractors. The remaining hypotheses are supported by, at best, with mixed results.

Three of the alternative hypotheses are supported by empirical evidence: when there is a cap on the size of the military force, when there is no host

Table 3. Summary of Hypotheses Findings

	Operations Desert Shield and Desert Storm	Operation Joint Endeavor	Operation Enduring Freedom	Operation Iraqi Freedom	Hypotheses Outcome
Use of PMC/PSC	Host-nation contracts: ~10,000	PMC: ~14,000	PMC: ~89,000 PSC: ~18,000	PMC: ~150,000 PSC: ~10,000	
When military outlays decrease, there is an increase in the use of private security.	Not applicable	Supported	Mixed outcome	Mixed outcome	Not supported
When the size of a national military decreases, there is an increase in the use of private military security.	Not applicable	Supported	Supported initially; not supported after 2006	Supported initially; not supported after 2006	Not supported
When the number of military disputes, military engagements, and militarized conflicts increases, there is an increase in the use of private security internationally.	Not supported	Not supported	Supported	Supported	Not supported
When the duration of a military conflict increases, there is an increase in the use of private security.	Supported	Supported	Supported	Supported	Supported
When there is a decrease in bureaucratic controls and regulations, there is an increase in the use of private security.	Supported	Supported	Supported	Supported	Supported
When there is a cap on the size of the military force, there is an increase in the use of private security.	Supported	Supported	Supported	Supported	Supported

When there is no host nation supporting the intervention, there is an increase in the use of private security.	Supported	Supported	Supported	Supported	Supported
When the security environment is nonpermissive, there is an increase in private security.	Supported	Supported	Supported	Supported	Supported

nation supporting the intervention, and when the security environment is nonpermissive there is an increase in the use of private security. These additional independent variables will be included in the quantitative analysis to determine their statistical significance.

It may be that decreases in military spending, decreases in the size of the military, increased conflict, and increased bureaucratic controls are necessary conditions for the increased use of private military contractors. However, these explanations may not be sufficient to fully understand when the United States is more likely to use private contractors during military interventions. Table 3 summarizes the findings from the alternative explanations.

CHAPTER EIGHT

QUANTITATIVE ANALYSIS OF THE PRIVATE SECURITY INDUSTRY

Statistical methods enjoy a number of advantages, including a stronger claim to external validity and a more systematic treatment of chance and happenstance than case method can provide. Statistical approaches thus result in a broad picture of the relationships between multiple explanatory variables and help to evaluate their explanatory power. More important, findings can be replicated. However, statistical analysis suffers from some important drawbacks. For the purpose of this study, the most important is data availability. The dependent variable relies on the number of private contractors used during a military intervention, and there is no complete data set available covering the time period under investigation.

This chapter is organized into three sections. The first provides the research data sets; the second discusses the statistical results; and the third summarizes and assesses the implications of the findings.

Research Design and Methods

This study uses interrupted time-series analysis of private contractors for the United States from 1950 to 2010. Data availability issues have restricted this research to the United States. The timeframe was selected for three reasons. First, U.S. government statistical data sets are readily available and provide the majority of the data to test the hypotheses. Second, the year 1950 provides a useful starting point to test them. In 1942 Undersecretary of War Robert

Patterson militarized the U.S. war effort, effectively ending the use of private contractors until after 1945. Third, the choice of 1950 to 2010 allows sufficient time to measure supply-demand behavior as it relates to the use of private contractors beyond what is in the extant literature.

Operational Definitions

This research analyzes the reasons the United States uses private contractors during conflicts. The dependent variable is the use of private contractors by the U.S. military. The independent variables are the internal and external conditions facing decision makers when they choose to use private contractors as a substitute for military force.

DEPENDENT VARIABLE

As outlined in the literature, private contractors are used as a substitute for functions that a military force can accomplish. As Avant (2005), Singer (2003), and Kidwell (2005) point out, determining the number of private military companies used by the United States is a difficult endeavor. The operational definition of private contractors is an interval variable that measures the following: any private contractor or private contracting firm that provides logistic support, consulting services, technical services, or security functions as a substitute for a military force. Thus the dependent variable, *contractors*, is the number of private contractors used by the U.S. military in a conflict by year.

There is no single data set available prior to 2008. As a way of addressing this shortcoming, this research uses a newly created data set drawn from several sources. The first comes from the Office of the Deputy Assistant Secretary of Defense, Quarterly Contractor Census Report (U.S. Department of Defense, Assistant Under Secretary for Office of Program Support under CENTCOM 2008–14). Beginning in 2008 the Department of Defense started collecting information on contractors in Iraq and Afghanistan to satisfy the requirements outlined in Section 854 of the 2007 National Defense Authorization Act. The quarterly reports contain data on the number of private contractors supporting the U.S. military in Iraq and Afghanistan.

The second source of data on private contractors comes from a report by the Department of Defense, Office of General Counsel, on overseas jurisdiction (Cook 1997). This report provides data on how many private contractors supported the U.S. military during the 1990s. The report gives the number of contractors supporting military operations in Saudi Arabia, Somalia, Rwanda, Haiti, Bosnia, and Croatia. The data from this report are cross-referenced with several primary and secondary sources. Where there is a discrepancy, the lower number is used to prevent inflation of the data results.

The third source of data on private contractors is from Isenberg (2009), who provides data on the use of contractors in Korea and Vietnam. The data are the total contractors used during the conflict and are not categorized by year; thus it is hard to determine if and when there is an increase or decrease in the use of private contractors over the duration of the conflict.

From these sources only the reported use of private contractors is added to the data set. Diligent effort went into ensuring that the number of contractors used by the United States was not inflated. Where possible, more than one source was used to validate the number of contractors in a conflict.

INDEPENDENT VARIABLES

Five independent variables are used to examine internal and external conditions that U.S. decision makers face when they choose to use private contractors as a substitute for military force: military outlays, the size of the national military, the number of military disputes, the duration of the intervention, and decline in bureaucratic controls. Each variable is operationalized by using available data.

The first independent variable is the size of the Department of Defense Budget, *DoD Budget*. The U.S. defense budget acts as a measure of institutional constraint on the U.S. military. It can be measured in three different ways: the total dollar amount allocated for defense spending, the budget as a percentage of gross national product, or the budget as a percentage of U.S. budget outlays. This study operationalizes the U.S. defense budget as the total dollar amount allocated for defense spending. Data are from the historical budget data compiled by the U.S. Office of Management and Budget 1950–2012).

The second independent variable is the total number of U.S. military personnel, *DoD Personnel*. The total number of U.S. military personnel also acts as a measure of institutional constraints on the U.S. military and policymakers considering the employment of military force. The operational definition is the size of the U.S. military as the total number personnel on active military duty in a given year. The data are from the U.S. Department of Defense, Defense Manpower Data Center (1954–2012).

The third independent variable is the number of conflicts where the United States is involved, *DoD Conflicts*. In addition to the U.S. budget and number of forces available, the number of conflicts in which the United States is involved acts as a measure of institutional constraint. The operational definition is the total number of U.S. forces deployed outside the continental United States. This includes the number of U.S. forces deployed in a conflict and the number committed to regional alliances and strategic partnerships. The total number of U.S. forces deployed represents forces that are not readily available to U.S. policymakers when making decisions about force employment. The data are from the U.S. Department of Defense, Defense Manpower Data Center (1954–2012).

The fourth independent variable is *Duration*, operationalized as the absolute number of days during a year that the United States was involved in a conflict. Each year the conflict continues, the number of days becomes additive. Data for the duration of a conflict come from the U.S. Department of Defense, Defense Manpower Data Center (1954–2012) based on the years the department had military forces deployed in a conflict area. U.S. conflicts are categorized into five global regions; the Middle East, Eastern Europe, Asia, Africa, with the Western Hemisphere as the base category.

The fifth independent variable is bureaucratic controls. Two indicators are used to measure decisions by U.S. policymakers to use private contractors. The first, *71 executive decision*, is the decision in 1971 to encourage the use of host-nation contractors to augment military forces in conflict. The 1971 decision followed the Nixon administration's announcement that it would reduce the military force in Vietnam (Sorely 1999). The second, *92 executive decision*, is the decision in 1992 to implement the Logistics Civil Augmentation Program, which formalized the substitution of military force for private contractors. These decisions are operationalized using interrupted time-series variables to analyze how these discrete decisions impacted the level and trend of contractor use.

CONTROL VARIABLES

Two control variables are used to examine external conditions that U.S. decision makers face when they choose to use private contractors as a substitute for military force. The control variables used in the statistical analysis capture both the host-nation support of the intervention and the security environment in the target state.

Three proxies are used to capture host-nation conditions: the number of U.S. troops that are killed in action due to hostile fire, *DoD KIA*; the number of U.S. troops that are wounded in action due to hostile fire, *DoD WIA*; and the level of mass unrest in a conflict, *Mass Unrest*.

Data on the number of U.S. military personnel killed or wounded are from the U.S. Department of Defense, Defense Manpower Data Center (1954–2012). Following Goldberg (2010), a casualty is defined as any soldier who is lost to his or her organization or unit. The Defense Department classifies casualties as "hostile" if they are sustained as the direct result of combat between U.S. forces and opposing forces, or going to or returning from a combat mission. Killed in action (*KIA*) are those soldiers who die immediately on the battlefield; wounded in action (*WIA*) are those who survive their injuries beyond initial hospitalization. Goldberg points out that casualty rates in Operation Iraqi Freedom have been considerably lower than during the Vietnam conflict, and a greater proportion of troops wounded in Iraq survive their wounds. The survival rate in Iraq was 90.4 percent, while the survival rate in Vietnam was 86.5 percent. Goldberg notes that the increased survival rate in Iraq is due to factors such as advanced body armor, the innovative use of forward aid stations located closer to the combat units, and advances in aeromedical evacuation. Goldberg cites Linda Bilmes's casualty data, pointing out that in Iraq the ratio of wounded to killed was 16:1, while in Vietnam and Korea the ratio was 3:1, and during World War I and World War II the ratio was 2:1.

Mass Unrest is defined as a state of dissatisfaction, disturbance, and agitation, typically involving public demonstrations or disorder. Data on mass unrest come from the Armed Conflict Dataset published by the Uppsala

Conflict Data Program (2012) at the Peace Research Institute in Oslo, specifically the measure of intensity level (state-based). The intensity variable denotes what level of fighting a state-based conflict or dyad reaches in each specific calendar year. The variable has two categories: *minor* means at least 25 but fewer than 1,000 battle-related deaths in one calendar year; *war* means at least 1,000 battle-related deaths in one calendar year. The variable *minor* is used as a proxy to measure mass unrest.

Time-Series Cross-Sectional Analysis

This study relies on a methodology now common in political science, time-series cross-sectional (TSCS) design. Time-series studies allow intensive investigation of long-term trends of one variable. Cross-sectional studies examine multiple variables at one point in time. TSCS looks at multiple points in time with more variables; the data consist of comparable time-series data observed on a variety of units (Beck 2006). The advantage of TSCS is that it allows researchers to look for changes over time and complicated relationships between variables (Beck 2001). Typically the observations are annual, and there is no upper limit on the number of observations. The time-series properties of the data are examined using a time-series method, which means that the researcher can plot the data against time to examine them for trends (Beck 2006).

Interrupted Time-Series Model

In addition to TSCS, this study uses the interrupted time-series design of Lewis-Beck (1986) to investigate the impact of one of the independent variables, *bureaucratic decisions*. Glass et al. (1975) argue that one of the most promising quasi-experimental designs is the interrupted time-series experiment. Glass (1997) explains that the aim of the design is to estimate the trend in the dependent variable prior to the intervention; estimate the trend after the intervention; test for changes in the dependent variable pre- and postintervention; and test for changes in the slope of the trend pre- and postintervention. Lewis-Beck describes the development of a satisfactory statistical model of decision effects as a "decision experiment." He argues that decisions ought to be consciously evaluated as social "treatments" with statistically analyzable effects.

Following Lewis-Beck (1986), the following linear regression models of the interrupted time-series are used in this study:

MODEL 1

$Ln(Contractors\ t) = \beta_0 + \beta_1\ Trend + \beta_2\ 71DecisionLevel + \beta_3\ 71DecisionTrend + \beta_4 DoD\ KIA + \beta_5 Mass\ Unrest + \beta_6 Duration\ Middle\ East + \beta_7 Duration\ East\ Europe + \beta_8 Duration\ Asia + \beta_9 Duration\ Africa + \beta_{10} DoD\ Budget + \beta_{11} DoD\ Personnel + \beta_{12} DoD\ Overseas + e_t$

MODEL 2

$Ln(Contractors\ t) = \beta_0 + \beta_1\ Trend + \beta_2\ 92DecisionLevel + \beta_3\ 92DecisionTrend + \beta_4 DoD\ KIA + \beta_5 Mass\ Unrest + \beta_6 Duration\ Middle\ East + \beta_7 Duration\ East\ Europe + \beta_8 Duration\ Asia + \beta_9 Duration\ Africa + \beta_{10} DoD\ Budget + \beta_{11} DoD\ Personnel + \beta_{12} DoD\ Overseas + e_t$

MODEL 3

$Ln(Contractors\ t) = \beta_0 + \beta_1\ Trend + \beta_2\ 71DecisionLevel + \beta_3\ 71DecisionTrend + \beta_4\ 92DecisionLevel + \beta_5\ 92DecisionTrend + \beta_6 DoD\ KIA + \beta_7 Mass\ Unrest + \beta_8 Duration\ Middle\ East + \beta_9 Duration\ East\ Europe + \beta_{10} Duration\ Asia + \beta_{11} Duration\ Africa + \beta_{12} DoD\ Budget + \beta_{13} DoD\ Personnel + \beta_{14} DoD\ Overseas + e_t$

Where $Ln(Contractors)$ = yearly observations on use of private contractors; β_1 Trend = a counter for years from 1 to N, the number of observations; β_2 71DecisionLevel = a dichotomous variable scored 0 for observations before the decision and 1 for observations after the decision; β_3 71DecisionTrend = a counter for years scored 0 for observations before the decision and 1, 2, 3, . . . for observations after the decision; β_4 92DecisionLevel = a dichotomous variable scored 0 for observations before the decision and 1 for observations after the decision; β_5 92DecisionTrend = a counter for years scored 0 for observations before the decision and 1, 2, 3, . . . for observations after the decision. β_0, β_1, β_2, β_3, β_4, β_5 = the parameters to be estimated; and e_t = error (Lewis-Beck 1986, 1132).

β_0 is the baseline level of the outcome or the value at time zero; β_1 Trend is the slope prior to the intervention or the change over time before the intervention was implemented; β_2 71DecisionLevel and β_4 92DecisionLevel are the changes in level immediately after the intervention or the changes in the outcome measure from the last time point before the intervention of the first time point after the intervention; β_3 71DecisionTrend and β_5 92DecisionTrend are the changes in the slope form pre- to postintervention or the differences in the slope of the time period before the intervention and the slope of the time period after the intervention. Figure 2 provides a graphical depiction of interrupted time series.

Descriptive Statistics

Table 4 provides the mean, standard deviation, and the range for each of the variables used in this study. All the variables have 61 observations. The dependent variable *contractor* has 61 observations, with a minimum score of 0 and maximum of 243735. In terms of frequency of the use of *contractor*, there were 33 years where the United States used private contractors in conflict. The mean, which is the average or the common measure of tendency, is 39334.64.

The independent variable *time trend* has 61 observations, with a minimum score of 1 and a maximum of 61. The variable had a mean score of 30.98. The independent variable *71 executive decision level* has 61 observations, with a minimum score of 0 and a maximum of 1. The variable had a mean score of .6557. The independent variable *71 executive decision trend* has 61 observations, with a minimum score of 1 and a maximum of 40. The variable had a mean score of 13.44. The independent variable *92 executive decision level* has 61 observations, with a minimum score of 0 and a maximum of 1. The variable had a mean score of .3114. The independent variable *92 executive decision trend* has 61 observations, with a minimum score of 0 and maximum of 19. The variable had a mean score of 3.114. The independent variable *DoD KIA* has 61 observations, with a minimum score of 0 and maximum of 16592. The variable had a mean score of 1594.57. The independent variable *Mass Unrest* had 61 observations, with a minimum score of 0 and maximum of 2. The variable had a mean score of .9672. The independent variable *Middle East* had 61 observations, with a minimum score of 0 and maximum of 2855. The variable

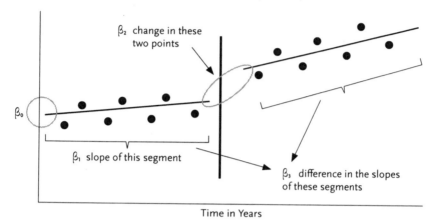

$$Y_t = \beta_0 + \beta_1 T + \beta_2 D + \beta_3 P + e_t$$

T = time from the start of the observation
D = a dummy variable for pre- or postintervention
P = time since the intervention
e_t = the random variation at time t not explained by the model

β_2 change in these two points

β_0

β_1 slope of this segment

β_3 difference in the slopes of these segments

Time in Years

Fig. 2. Interrupted time-series. Source: Perrin 2006.

had a mean score of 217.78. The independent variable *Eastern Europe* had 61 observations, with a minimum score of 0 and maximum of 5140. The variable had a mean score of 610.90. The independent variable *Asia* had 61 observations, with a minimum score of 0 and maximum of 3650. The variable had a mean score of 392.62. The independent variable *Africa* had 61 observations, with a minimum score of 0 and maximum of 940. The variable had a mean score of 22.37. The variable *Western Hemisphere* had 61 observations, with a minimum score of 0 and maximum of 455. The variable had a mean score of 9.91.

The control variable *DoD Budget* had 61 observations, with a minimum score of 13724 and a maximum score of 693586. The variable had a mean score of 202698.8. The control variable *DoD Personnel* had 61 observations, with a minimum score of 1379551 and a maximum score of 3555067. The variable had a mean score of 2157701. The control variable *DoD Overseas* had 61 observations, with a minimum score of 227258 and a maximum score of 1228638. The variable had a mean score of 578773.4.

Table 4. Descriptive Statistics

Variables	Obs.	Mean	Std. Dev.	Min.	Max.
Contractors	61	39334.64	66597.05	0	243735
Time Trend	61	30.98	17.76	1	61
71 Executive Decision Level	61	0.6557	0.479	0	1
71 Executive Decision Trend	61	13.44	13.61	0	40
92 Executive Decision Level	61	0.3114	0.4669	0	1
92 Executive Decision Trend	61	3.114	5.5949	0	19
DoD KIA	61	1594.57	3759.04	0	16592
Mass Unrest	61	0.9672	0.9481	0	2
Duration Middle East	61	217.78	617.76	0	2855
Duration East Europe	61	610.9	1369.07	0	5140
Duration Asia	61	392.62	863.91	0	3650
Duration Africa	61	22.37	129.74	0	940
Duration Western Hemisphere	61	9.91	59.29	0	455
DoD Budget	61	202698.8	171953.2	137240	693586
DoD Personnel	61	2157701	640687.8	1379551	3555067
DoD Conflicts	61	578773.4	289525	227258	1228638

Statistical Analysis

A brief discussion of some methodological issues is warranted before analyzing the statistical results. The first is the issue of multicollinearity. An assessment of the influence of multicollinearity is performed by estimating the variance inflation factor (VIF). When employing standard regression, it is desirable to have explanatory variables that are highly correlated to a response variable. However, to obtain reliable estimates, it is not desirable for explanatory variables to be correlated with each other. Thus the greater the multicollinearity, the greater the standard errors. When high multicollinearity is present, confidence intervals for coefficients tend to be very wide and t-statistics tend to be very small. Coefficients will have to be larger in order to be statistically significant; that is, it will be harder to reject the null hypothesis when multicollinearity is present. Multicollinearity is a concern when estimates average above 1 and the VIF model is above 10. The VIF score of the models suggests that multicollinearity is an issue in the estimates of the three models under review.[1]

The variables exhibiting a high correlation are *Time Trend, 71 executive decision level, 71 executive decision trend, 92 executive decision level,* and *92 executive decision trend.* Multicollinearity is par for the course when a model consists of two or more interrupted time-series variables. Where you have multiple regressions you almost always have multicollinearity, especially in time-series data where dummy variables are used. Multicollinearity does not bias parameter estimates, but it inflates their variance, making them inefficient or untrustworthy. However, if the goal is simply to predict Y from a set of X variables, then multicollinearity is not a problem. The predictions will still be accurate, and the overall R2 (or adjusted R2) quantifies how well the model predicts the Y values. One approach is to run a couple of different models and compare their degree of multicollinearity with that of the original model.

The second methodological issue is serial correlation. Autocorrelation is a violation of the assumption that the errors are uncorrelated and independent, meaning that the size and direction of one error term has no bearing on the size and direction of another. Autocorrelation is usually associated with time-series data since by definition, as time-series data is ordered in time. Since the past is the best predictor of the future, what occurs in time t is the best predictor of what will occur in time $t+1$. Usually the observations are not independent, which means that an observation from one year is probably not too far off the observation of the previous year. For the error term, this means that differences between the predicted and actual (error) in one time period is probably related (positively) to the error in the next. As a consequence the ordinary least squares (OLS) estimators are no longer efficient, the estimated variances of OLS estimators are biased, and the estimated R^2 will not be a reliable estimate of the true R^2. The statistical test used to detect serial correlation is the Durbin-Watson d test (Gujarati 2003).

The results of the Durbin-Watson d test (Gujarati 2003) on Model 3 fall into the zone of indecision. The Durbin-Watson d test is structured so that there is an acceptance region and a rejection region. In between is a zone of indecision where it is recommended that the null hypotheses, no autocorrelation, neither be accepted or rejected. Therefore autocorrelation may be a problem in Model 3. As a result Model 4 is developed using the Prais-Winsten transformation for the first observation (Gujarati 2003).

The first model represents the first test of the hypotheses under investigation. Model 1 includes the dependent variable, *contractors*; the independent variables *DoD Budget, DoD Personnel, DoD Overseas*, duration of the conflict using four independent variables covering four geographic regions *Middle East, East Europe, Asia*, and *Africa*; an interrupted time-series test of the independent variable *71 executive decision*; and test of the control variable intensity *DoD KIA* and *Mass Unrest*.

MODEL 1

$$\text{Ln(Contractors t)} = \beta_0 + \beta_1 \text{ Trend} + \beta_2 \text{ 71DecisionLevel} + \beta_3 \text{ 71DecisionTrend} + \beta_4 \text{DoD KIA} + \beta_5 \text{Mass Unrest} + \beta_6 \text{Duration Middle East} + \beta_7 \text{Duration East Europe} + \beta_8 \text{Duration Asia} + \beta_9 \text{Duration Africa} + \beta_{10} \text{DoD Budget} + \beta_{11} \text{DoD Personnel} + \beta_{12} \text{DoD Overseas} + e_t$$

The variable representing defense budgets, *DoD Budget*, is statistically significant at the $p<.01$ level. The coefficient for the *DoD Budget* variable is -4.92, which suggests that for every decrease of $100 million there is a corresponding increase of approximately 495 private contractors, holding other variables constant. Neither of the variables representing defense personnel, *DoD Personnel*, nor the variable *DoD Overseas* is statistically significant.

The variable representing duration, *Middle East*, is statistically significant at the $p<.05$ level. The coefficient for the *Middle East* variable is -.001, which suggests that when conflicts in the Middle East are reduced by 300 days, there is a corresponding decrease in private contractors by about 3, holding all other variables constant. The variables representing duration in *East Europe, Asia*, and *Africa* are statistically insignificant.

The variable representing *Time Trend* is statistically significant at the $p<.05$ level. The coefficient of the *Time Trend* variable is .270, which suggests that for every year before 1971 there was a .27 percent increase in the use of private contractors, holding other variables constant. *71 executive decision level* is statistically significant at the $p<.01$ level. The coefficient of the *71 executive decision level* is -4.06, which suggests that the level of contractor use decreased by about 4 percent immediately after the decision, holding

Table 5. Statistical Results

	Model 1	Model 2	Model 3	Model 4
Intercept	45.68**	-9.16	-11.07	13.28
	(2.08)	(-0.45)	(-0.39)	(0.38)
DoD Budget	-4.92**	-3.69**	-5.90**	-6.35**
	(-1.84)	(-1.97)	(-1.90)	(-2.21)
DoD Personnel	-1.04	-1.42*	-1.12	-1.33*
	(-0.95)	(-1.53)	(-1.09)	(-1.29)
DoD Overseas	1.49	4.95***	5.90**	5.29**
	(0.56)	(2.62)	(2.04)	(1.81)
DURATION				
Middle East	-.001**	-.001	-.0008	-.0005
	(-1.91)	(-0.82)	(-0.66)	(-0.44)
East Europe	-.0003	-.0004	-.0004	-.0004
	(-1.13)	(-1.22)	(-1.11)	(-1.08)
Asia	.0007	-.0004	-.00004	-.00004
	(1.20)	(-0.92)	(-0.07)	(-0.07)
Africa	-.001	-.004**	-.003*	-.003*
	(-0.48)	(-1.67)	(-1.60)	(-1.56)
BUREAUCRATIC CONTROLS				
Time Trend	.270**	.267**	.288**	.298**
	(1.91)	(2.02)	(2.10)	(2.18)
71 Exec Dec (Level)	-4.06***		.011	-.275
	(-2.69)		(0.01)	(-0.14)
71 Exec Dec (Trend)	.344**		.152	.245
	(1.94)		(0.78)	(1.16)
92 Exec Dec (Level)		7.21***	7.02***	6.21**
		(3.56)	(2.83)	(2.42)
92 Exec Dec (Trend)		.081	-.013	-.109
		(0.32)	(-0.04)	(-0.36)
INTENSITY				
DoD KIA	.551***	.709***	.685***	.740***
	(3.52)	(4.95)	(4.48)	(4.65)
Mass Unrest	1.75***	1.64***	1.38**	1.40**
	(2.65)	(2.89)	(2.08)	(2.12)
Obs	61	61	61	61
R2	.866	.887	.889	.891
Adj R2	.833	.859	.855	.857

Notes: *, **, and *** indicate statistical significance at the p<.10, p<.05, and p<.01 level
(1.296<.10, 1.671<.05, and 2.390<.01), respectively. One-tailed test.
Standard errors are in the parentheses below the estimates.

other variables constant. *71 executive decision trend* is statistically significant at the p<.05 level. The coefficient of *71 executive decision trend* is .344, which suggests that the rate of change after the decision increased by .34 percent every year, holding other variables constant (see figure 3).

DoD KIA is statistically significant at the p<.01 level. The coefficient for this intensity variable is .551, which suggests that as the intensity of a conflict increases by 1,000 military casualties there is an increase of approximately 550 private contractors, holding other variables constant. The variable representing intensity *Mass Unrest* is also statistically significant at the p<.01 level. The coefficient for the intensity variable is 1.75, which suggests that as the intensity of the conflict increases for every 1,000 civilian casualties there is an increase of approximately 1,750 private contractors, holding other variables constant.

The second model represents the second test of the hypotheses under investigation. Model 2 includes the dependent variable, *contractors*; the independent variables *DoD Budget, DoD Personnel, DoD Overseas*, the duration of the conflict using four independent variables covering four geographic regions *Middle East, East Europe, Asia*, and *Africa*; an interrupted time-series test of the independent variable *92 executive decision*; and a test of the intensity of the conflict using two independent variables, *DoD KIA* and *Mass Unrest*.

MODEL 2

$$\text{Ln(Contractors t)} = \beta_0 + \beta_1 \text{ Trend} + \beta_2 \text{ 92DecisionLevel} + \beta_3 \text{ 92DecisionTrend} + \beta_4\text{DoD KIA} + \beta_5\text{Mass Unrest} + \beta_6\text{Duration Middle East} + \beta_7\text{Duration East Europe} + \beta_8\text{Duration Asia} + \beta_9\text{Duration Africa} + \beta_{10}\text{DoD Budget} + \beta_{11}\text{DoD Personnel} + \beta_{12}\text{DoD Overseas} + e_t$$

DoD Budget is statistically significant at the p<.05 level. The coefficient for the *DoD Budget* variable is -3.69, which suggests that for every decrease of $100 million there is a corresponding increase of about 370 private contractors, holding other variables constant. *DoD Personnel* is statistically significant at the p<.10 level. The coefficient for the *DoD Personnel* variable is -1.42, which suggests that for every 1,000 decrease in DoD personnel there is a corresponding increase of approximately 1,400 private contractors, holding other variables constant. *DoD Overseas* is statistically significant at the p<.01

level. The coefficient for the conflict variable is 4.95, which suggests that for every 1,000 Defense Department personnel committed overseas, there is a corresponding increase of approximately 4,900 private contractors, holding other variables constant.

The variables representing duration in the *Middle East, East Europe*, and, *Asia* are not statistically significant. The variable representing duration in *Africa* is, however, statistically significant at the p<.10 level. The coefficient for *Africa* is -.004, which suggests that in Africa, for every 1,000 days' decrease in the duration of the conflict, there is a corresponding decrease of approximately 4 private contractors, holding other variables constant.

Moving to the interrupted time-series variables, *Time Trend* is statistically significant at the p<.05 level. The coefficient of the *Time Trend* variable is .267, which suggests that for every year before the 1992 decision there was a 26 percent increase in the use of private contractors, holding other variables constant. *92 executive decision level* is statistically significant at the p<.01 level. The coefficient of the *92 executive decision level* is 7.21, which suggests that the level of contractor use increased by approximately 72 percent after the 1992 decision, holding other variables constant. *92 executive decision trend* is not statistically significant. The coefficient of the *92 executive decision trend* is 0.81 (see figure 4).

DoD KIA is statistically significant at the p<.01 level. The coefficient for the intensity variable is .709, which suggests that as the intensity of a conflict increases by 1,000 military casualties there is an increase of approximately 700 private contractors, holding other variables constant. *Mass Unrest* is also statistically significant at the p<.01 level. The coefficient for the intensity variable is 1.64, which suggests that as the intensity of the conflict increases, for every 1,000 civilian casualties there is an increase of approximately 1,640 private contractors, holding other variables constant.

The third model represents the third test of the hypotheses under investigation. Model 3 includes the dependent variable, *contractors*; the independent variables *DoD Budget, DoD Personnel, DoD Overseas*, the duration of the conflict using four independent variables covering four geographic regions *Middle East, East Europe, Asia*, and *Africa*; an interrupted time-series test of the independent variables *71 executive decision* and *92 executive decision*;

and a test of the intensity of the conflict using two independent variables, *DoD KIA* and *Mass Unrest*.

MODEL 3

$$\text{Ln(Contractors t)} = \beta_0 + \beta_1 \text{ Trend} + \beta_2 \text{ 71DecisionLevel} + \beta_3 \text{ 71Decision-}$$
$$\text{sionTrend} + \beta_4 \text{ 92DecisionLevel} + \beta_5 \text{ 92DecisionTrend} + \beta_6 \text{DoD KIA}$$
$$+ \beta_7 \text{Mass Unrest} + \beta_8 \text{Duration Middle East} + \beta_9 \text{Duration East Europe}$$
$$+ \beta_{10} \text{Duration Asia} + \beta_{11} \text{Duration Africa} + \beta_{12} \text{DoD Budget} + \beta_{13} \text{DoD}$$
$$\text{Personnel} + \beta_{14} \text{DoD Overseas} + e_t$$

Again *DoD Budget* is statistically significant at the $p<.05$ level. The coefficient for the *DoD Budget* variable is -5.90, which suggests that for every decrease of \$100 million there is a corresponding increase of approximately 590 private contractors, holding other variables constant. While *DoD Personnel* is not statistically significant, *DoD Overseas* is statistically significant at the $p<.05$ level. The coefficient for the conflict variable is 5.90, which suggests that for every 1,000 Defense Department personnel committed overseas, there is a corresponding increase of approximately 5,900 private contractors, holding other variables constant.

Once again the variable representing duration in the *Middle East, East Europe*, and *Asia* is not statistically significant. The variable representing duration in *Africa* is statistically significant at the $p<.10$ level. The coefficient for *Africa* is -.003, which suggests that for every 1,000 days decrease in the duration of the conflict, there is a corresponding decrease of approximately 3 private contractors, holding other variables constant.

Time Trend is statistically significant at the $p<.05$ level with a coefficient of .288. This suggests that for every year before the 1971 decision there was approximately a 28 percent increase in the use of private contractors, holding other variables constant. *71 executive decision level* and *71 executive decision trend* are not statistically significant.

92 executive decision level is statistically significant at the $p<.01$ level, with a coefficient of 7.02, which suggests that the level of contractor use increased by approximately 70 percent after the 1992 decision, holding other variables constant. *92 executive decision trend* is not statistically significant (see figure 5).

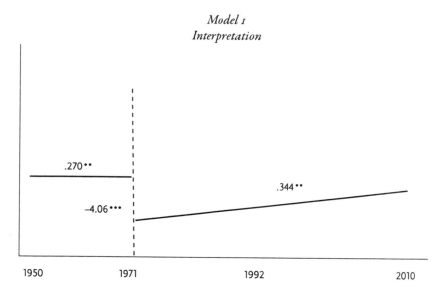

Fig. 3. Time-series analysis of the 1971 executive decision.

DoD KIA is statistically significant at the p<.01 level. The coefficient for the intensity variable is .685, which suggests that as the intensity of a conflict increases by 1,000 military casualties there is an increase of approximately 680 private contractors, holding other variables constant. *Mass Unrest* is statistically significant at the p<.05 level, with a coefficient of 1.38, which suggests that as the intensity of the conflict increases, for every 1,000 civilian casualties there is an increase of approximately 1,380 private contractors, holding other variables constant.

The fourth model represents the fourth test of the hypotheses under investigation. Model 4 is developed from Model 3 using the Prais-Winsten transformation for the first observation. Like Model 3, Model 4 includes the dependent variable, *contractors*; the independent variables *DoD Budget, DoD Personnel, DoD Overseas*, the duration of the conflict using four independent variables covering four geographic regions *Middle East, East Europe, Asia*, and *Africa*; an interrupted time-series test of the independent variables *71 executive decision* and *92 executive decision*; and a test of the intensity of the conflict using two independent variables, *DoD KIA* and *Mass Unrest*.

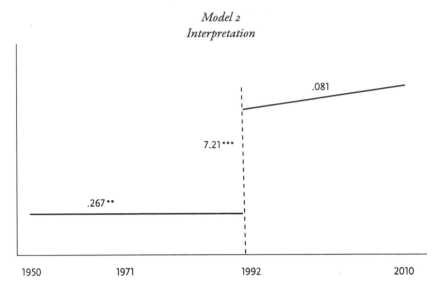

Fig. 4. Time-series analysis of the 1992 executive decision.

MODEL 4 (USING PRAIS-WINSTEN TRANSFORMATION)

Ln(Contractors t)= β_0 + β_1 Trend + β_2 71DecisionLevel + β_3 71DecisionTrend + β_4 92DecisionLevel + β_5 92DecisionTrend + β_6DoD KIA + β_7Mass Unrest + β_8Duration Middle East + β_9Duration East Europe + β_{10}Duration Asia + β_{11}Duration Africa + β_{12}DoD Budget + β_{13}DoD Personnel + β_{14}DoD Overseas + e_t

DoD Budget is statistically significant at the p<.05 level. The coefficient for the *DoD Budget* variable is -6.35, which suggests that for every decrease of $100 million there is a corresponding increase of approximately 640 private contractors, holding other variables constant. *DoD Personnel* is statistically significant at the p<.10 level. The coefficient for the *DoD Personnel* variable is -1.33, which suggests that for every 1,000 decrease in Defense Department personnel there is a corresponding increase of approximately 1,300 private contractors, holding other variables constant. *DoD Overseas* is statistically significant at the p<.05 level. The coefficient for the conflict variable is 5.29, which suggests that for every 1,000 Defense Department personnel committed

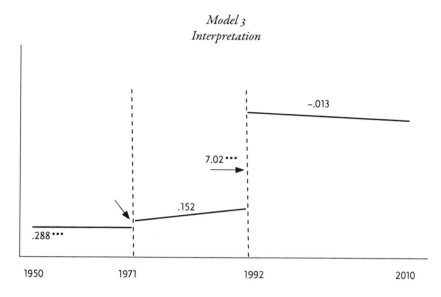

Fig. 5. Time-series analysis of the 1971 and 1992 executive decisions.

overseas, there is a corresponding increase of approximately 5,300 private contractors, holding other variables constant.

Middle East, East Europe, and *Asia* are again not statistically significant. The variable representing duration in *Africa* is statistically significant at the p<.10 level. The coefficient for *Africa* is -.003, which suggests that for every 1,000 days decrease in the duration of the conflict, there is a corresponding decrease of approximately 3 private contractors, holding other variables constant.

Time Trend is statistically significant at the p<.05 level. The coefficient of the *Time Trend* variable is .298, which suggests that for every year before the 1971 decision there was approximately a 29 percent increase in the use of private contractors, holding other variables constant. *71 executive decision level* and *71 executive decision trend* are not statistically significant.

92 executive decision level is statistically significant at the p<.05 level. The coefficient of the *92 executive decision level* is 6.21, which suggests that the level of contractor use increased by approximately 60 percent after the 1992 decision, holding other variables constant. *92 executive decision trend* is not statistically significant.

DoD KIA is statistically significant at the p<.01 level. The coefficient for the intensity variable is .740, which suggests that as the intensity of a conflict increases, by 1,000 military casualties there is an increase of approximately 740 private contractors, holding other variables constant. *Mass Unrest* is also statistically significant at the p<.05 level. The coefficient for the intensity variable is 1.40, which suggests that as the intensity of the conflict increases, for every 1,000 civilian casualties there is an increase of approximately 1,400 private contractors, holding other variables constant.

Discussion of Findings

In general the results of the statistical tests demonstrate the basic working of supply and demand theory. When the Defense Department budget decreases, there is a statistically significant increase in the use of private contractors. Likewise when the number of Defense personnel decreases, there is a statistically significant increase in the use of private contractors. Furthermore when the number of conflicts or engagements in which Defense personnel are involved rises, there is a statistically significant increase in the use of private contractors. The direction of the causal effect of Defense budget, Defense personnel, and Defense personnel involved in conflicts is consistent with the extant literature and supports the hypotheses in this study. This may help explain the underlying conditions that led to the demand for the use of private contractors. In essence reductions in military budgets result in an increased demand for private contractors. In like manner decreases in the size of national militaries result in an increased demand for private contractors. Finally as the numbers of U.S. troops are committed to conflicts or engagements around the world increase, the results are an increased demand for private contractors to augment the military.

On the other hand, as the duration of a conflict increases, there is not a statistically significant increase in the number of private contractors used by the United States. Although the U.S. interventions in Eastern Europe (Bosnia and Kosovo) and the Middle East (Iraq and Afghanistan) lasted more than a year, it appears that the duration of the conflict is not correlated with an increased use of private contractors.

When there is a decrease in the executive bureaucratic controls and

Table 6. Summary of Findings

	Supply and demand behavior
When military outlays decrease, there is an increase in the use of private security.	Significant
When the size of a national military decreases, there is an increase in the use of private military security.	Significant
When the number of a military disputes, military engagements, and militarized conflicts increases, there is an increase in the use of private security internationally.	Significant
When the duration of a military conflict increases, there is an increase in the use of private security.	Not significant
When there is a decrease in bureaucratic controls and regulations, there is an increase in the use of private security.	Significant
When the security environment is nonpermissive, there is an increase in private security.	Significant

regulations, there is an increase in the use of private contractors by the U.S. military. In 1971 the Defense Department established a policy encouraging the use of host-nation private contractors to support military forces deployed outside the United States. In 1992 the department went further and established the Logistics Civil Augmentation Program to ensure the availability of private contractors in the event that a host nation could not or would not provide support. This may help explain the steady rise of the private security industry beginning in the 1990s. The direction of the causal effect of the executive decisions to use private contractors supports the hypotheses in this study.

As the intensity of a conflict increases in the target state, the reliance on private contractors tends to increase. This is evident in conflicts where the security environment is particularly intense and there are insufficient U.S. forces or host-nation security forces to conduct combat operations and protect the population. The intensity of the conflict can be measured by the level of U.S. casualties (killed or wounded) and the level of casualties in the host nation (mass unrest). This may help explain the significant rise of private security contractors in Iraq and Afghanistan. The direction of the causal effect of the intensity of a conflict in the target nation supports the hypotheses in this study. In essence, as the demand for security increases, there is a corresponding increase in the supply of private contractors.

This chapter focused on a statistical analysis to provide additional information on which factors are important to the increased use of private contractors by the United States. The statistical findings lend support to the hypotheses on the increased use of private contractors and provide a broad picture of the relationships among multiple explanatory variables. More important, the findings of the statistical analysis can now be replicated in future research. The results of the findings should dispel the notion that the private contracting industry mysteriously appeared at the end of the cold war. Indeed the increased use of private contractors by the United States demonstrates normal behavior predicted by the theory of supply and demand.

CONCLUSION

The theory of supply and demand was used to frame the cross-comparison of four historical case studies and a series of standardized questions that sought to examine the increased reliance on the private security industry in U.S. foreign policy in the past two decades. Specifically this research sought to demonstrate that the use of private security contractors by the United States is not a new phenomenon; that the recent increased use of private security as an instrument of military policy or foreign policy may in fact be a consequence of deliberate policy decisions of successive presidential administrations; and that the security environment in the target state of an intervention is a factor that results in an increase of private security contractors. The goal of this analysis was to move beyond most of the extant literature that describes the phenomenon and develop a theory that helps explains why there has been a rapid growth in the reliance on the private security industry.

The theory of supply and demand would posit that when political leaders choose to reduce their nation's military force structure, they may face conflicts beyond their anticipated scope and duration. Such decision makers are left with no choice but to legalize and legitimize the use of PMCs, resulting in the increased use of PMCs as a deliberate tool of foreign policy. Using the supply and demand theory as the theoretical approach, this research built upon the three key influences emphasized first by Singer (2003) and then by others: the decreasing supply of national troops, decreasing national defense budgets, and rising demand from global conflicts and humanitarian emergencies.

As the previous chapters demonstrate, the basic theory, and thus insights from the descriptive literature, have value; however, they failed to provide an exhaustive explanation of this important phenomenon. The additional elements added to the relatively sparse theory resulted in a more convincing explanation for the increased use of PMCs. In sum this study added precision to our understanding of the causes of the increased use of PMCs.

Findings

This study asserted that the private security industry fills vacuums created when the U.S. government does not have the means or the will to fully provide domestic and international security. To understand the broader context of the private security industry's relationship to mature democracies this study focused initially on five hypotheses, with three additional hypotheses added to this study upon completion of the case studies.

Using a mixed-methods approach, the hypotheses were tested using both a qualitative and a quantitative approach. The qualitative approached relied on cross-comparison test case method, using a series of structured focused questions to compare the outcome of four historical cases where the United States used private contractors. The controlled comparison helped identify the outcome of the dependent variable, private contractors, and provided a historical explanation of the use of private contractors in relation to a set of independent variables. In this instance structured, focused comparison helped to tease out exactly how supply, demand, and other pressures help to stimulate the rise of PMCs.

The quantitative approach relied on a statistical method, using interrupted time-series to examine the use of private contractors by the United States from 1950 to 2010. The quantitative component analyzed a larger time period and increased the generalizability of the findings. It also provided insight on the relative explanatory weight of different causal influences.

The findings of the current research demonstrate that three key influences asserted in the extant literature — the decreasing supply of national troops, decreasing national defense budgets, and the rising demand from global conflicts and humanitarian emergencies—are very important to understanding the rise of the private security industry in the past two decades. Yet as this research shows, the nature of the security environment in the target state and the reduction (or elimination) of bureaucratic controls in the acting state are also important to explaining the increased reliance on the private security industry. Two other variables that were prevalent in the case studies that may be factors in the increased reliance on private contractors are limitations on the number of troops committed to an intervention and the duration of the intervention.

The current research provides an additional explanation for when and why the United States chooses to use the private security industry. In fact it presents a significant improvement in the arguments of Singer (2003) and Avant (2005), who do not empirically examine the theories they advance about the rise of private contractors. Nevertheless a weakness of the current research that should be addressed in future studies is the availability and accuracy of data on the number of private contractors used by the United States, which invariably raise questions about reliability of any findings. Since there was no readily available data set to model the phenomena under investigation, a complete data set had to be constructed. For much of the aggregate data, multiple existing databases on contracting were tapped. However, in doing so there were at times problems associated with determining the accuracy of the data across different sources. In some cases the number of private contractors used ranged widely across existing sources. Of note, after 2007 the accuracy of data improved. Despite tedious attention to reduce coding errors in the data set, it is possible that in a few cases the numbers of private contractors used by the United States are incorrect. Where there were inconsistencies in the literature or the data sets, in most cases the more conservative number was used.

State policymakers may be able to use the results of the present research to inform decisions on military budgeting, structure, or civil-military relations. As the worldwide economic crisis continues, policymakers faced with budget choices will look to reduce their military expenditures and possibly their military force structure. However, if they are faced with foreign policy problems requiring military intervention, it should not be surprising if they substitute national military forces for private security forces. It is likely that more state policymakers will move toward the legalization of private security companies. The trend toward legalization will lead toward further legitimization of the use of private security contractors. The United States has certainly set the example in the past thirty years for other nations to follow.

Future Research

Several areas for future research are evident from this study. First, the continued development and refinement of a database on the number of private contractors used by the United States and other nations is certainly needed. Second, the data set could be refined to identify the typology of private contractors used, for example security, logistics, or consulting. Third, as the field of study advances, improved data collection and available databases that include more cases beyond the United States may provide alternative answers to the examination of the theory of supply and demand for the rationale behind the increased use of the private security industry in this study and improve the robustness of the theory.

NOTES

INTRODUCTION

1. Smith (2008, 183) suggests that the industrial war paradigm is defined by the sequence peace-crisis-war-resolution, which will result in peace again, with war, the military action, being the deciding factor. In the new paradigm there is no predefined sequence but rather a continuous crisscrossing between confrontation and conflict, where peace is not necessarily either the starting or ending point.

2. Smith (2008, 198) points out that since the end of 1945 the development of the industrial-age military held constant the primacy of defense over attack. He asserts that a triangular relationship existed between the people, the army, and the state. The state will mostly favor defense. In addition to the willingness of the people to pay for their defense, in defense there is the simplicity of matching the political objective with the military. Furthermore defense enables the forming and sustaining of political will in a way attack or offense never does. Finally, defense enables a moral advantage, which is appreciated and necessary for the people—who consider it a bonus of the political leadership—and is preferred by the military.

3. The definition in international law as set out in Additional Protocol I to Article 47 of the Geneva Convention (1977) defines a mercenary as one who:

> Is specifically recruited locally or abroad in order to fight in an armed conflict;
> Does, in fact, take direct part in the hostilities;
> Is motivated to take part in the hostilities essentially by the desire for private gain and, in fact, is promised by or on behalf of a party to the conflict, material compensation substantially in excess of that promised or paid to combatants of similar rank and functions in the armed forces of that party;

Is neither a national of a party to the conflict nor a resident of territory controlled by a party to the conflict; and

Has not been sent by a state which is not a party to the conflict on official duty as a member of the armed forces. (quoted in Shearer 1998, 17)

Kinsey (2006, 19) points out that "all criteria must be met consecutively for a prosecution to go ahead under Article 47." To the disappointment of some and the relief of others, most authors agree that the private security industry does not fit the legal definition of a mercenary.

4. The Commission on Wartime Contracting is an independent, bipartisan legislative commission established in Section 841 of the National Defense Authorization Act for Fiscal Year 2008 (Public Law 110-181) to study federal agency contracting for reconstruction, logistical support, and security functions in Iraq and Afghanistan.

1. A THEORETICAL FRAMEWORK

1. Circular A-76 is a federal executive branch policy for managing public-private competitions to perform functions for the federal government. It states that, whenever possible, and to achieve greater efficiency and productivity, the federal government should conduct competitions between public agencies and the private sector to determine who should perform the work.

3. OPERATIONS DESERT SHIELD AND DESERT STORM

1. The converse of a least likely case is a most likely case, which I discuss in chapter 4.

4. OPERATION JOINT ENDEAVOR

1. For a detailed discussion of the conflict, see Zametica 1992.
2. For a detailed discussion of the peace negotiations, see Holbrooke 1999.
3. Reeve (2001, 11) points out that the British Army also found similar financial, equipment, and manpower savings in Bosnia and Croatia by using contractor elements for support. For example, the British awarded a food contract to Bookers Foodservices, which saved £560,000 during the first year of use and a further savings projected at almost £2 million.

5. OPERATION ENDURING FREEDOM

1. On 4 October 2001 NATO formally invoked Article 5 of the 1949 North Atlantic Treaty. The United Nations passed UN Resolution 1368 condemning the attacks on the United States, and UN Resolution 1373 on combating terrorism. The Organization of American States invoked the Inter-American Treaty of Reciprocal Assistance (the Rio Treaty), which is similar to Article 5 of the NATO treaty. On 14 September 2001 Australia invoked the ANZUS Treaty, which pledged Australian and New Zealand

support for the United States. Great Britain, Canada, Australia, France, Japan, and Turkey offered immediate military support for Operation Enduring Freedom. See Wright et al. (2005) for a more detailed discussion of the military coalition.

6. OPERATION IRAQI FREEDOM

1. The Senate passed the resolution with 77 yes votes and 23 no votes. The House of Representatives passed the resolution with 296 yes votes, 133 no votes, and 3 abstentions (U.S. Congress, House 2002).
2. For a detailed discussion of the military plans to defend Iraq, see Woods et al. 2006.
3. For a detailed discussion of the Coalition Provisional Authority, see Dobbins et al. 2009.
4. For a detailed discussion of the Ba'ath Party, see Allawi 2007, chapter 8.
5. For a detailed discussion of the situation in Iraq from 2006 to 2009, see U.S. Congress, House, Special Inspector General for Iraq Reconstruction 2009.

8. QUANTITATIVE ANALYSIS

1. The composite VIF score of model 1 is 23.76, the composite VIF score of model 2 is 17.87, and the composite VIF score of model 3 is 30.06. The results suggest that multicollinearity is a factor in the estimates.

BIBLIOGRAPHY

Adam, Gerhard. 2009. "Economic Theory: Supply and Demand." *Science 2.0*. 10 July. http://www.science20.com/gerhard_adam/blog/economic_theory_%E2%80%93 _supply_and_demand (accessed 25 December 2010).

Agapos, A. M., and Paul R. Dunlap. 1970. "The Theory of Price Determination in Government-Industry Relationships." *Quarterly Journal of Economics* 84, no. 1: 85–99.

Agence France-Presse. 2011. "Only 20 U.S. Bases Left in Iraq: Spokesman." Yahoo.com News. 17 October (accessed October 2011).

Albright, Madeleine. 2003. *Madam Secretary*. New York: Miramax Books.

Allawi, Ali A. 2007. *The Occupation of Iraq: Winning the War, Losing the Peace*. London: Yale University Press.

Avant, Deborah D. 2005. *The Market for Force: The Consequences of Privatizing Security*. Oxford: Oxford University Press, Inc.

Battistella, Dario. 2006. *The Return of State War*. Colchester, UK: European Consortium for Political Research.

Beck, Nathaniel. 2001. "Time-Series–Cross-Section Data: What Have We Learned in the Past Few Years?" *Annual Review of Political Science* 4: 271–93.

———. 2006. "Time Series–Cross Sectional Data: Cross-Sectional Issues." Presentation, University of Texas, Dallas, 10 November.

Beinhocker, Eric D. 2007. *The Origin of Wealth*. Boston: Harvard Business School Press.

Belasco, Amy. 2009. "Troop Levels in the Afghan and Iraq Wars FY 2001–FY 2012: Cost and Other Potential Issues." CRS Report for Congress. Washington DC: Congressional Research Service.

———. 2011. "The Cost of Iraq, Afghanistan, and Other Global War on Terror Operations Since 9/11." CRS Report for Congress. Washington DC: Congressional Research Service.

Bennett, A., and C. Elman. 2006. "Complex Causal Relations and Case Study Methods: The Example of Path Dependence." *Political Analysis* 14: 250–67.

Bennett, Andrew, Joseph Lepgold, and Danny Unger. 1994. "Burden-Sharing in the Persian Gulf War." *International Organization* 48: 39–75. doi:10.1017/S0020818300000813.

Berteau, David, Jochim Hofbauer, Jesse Ellman, Gregory Kiley, and Buy Ben-Ari. 2011. "DOD Workforce Cost Realism Assessment." Washington DC: Center for Strategic and International Studies.

Bicksler, Barbara A., Curtis L. Gilroy, and John T. Warner. 2003. *The All-Volunteer Force Thirty Years of Service.* Washington DC: Brassey's.

Biddle, Stephen. 2004. *Military Power: Explaining Victory and Defeat in Modern Battle.* Princeton NJ: Princeton University Press.

Bird, Tim, and Alex Marshall. 2011. *Afghanistan: How the West Lost Its Way.* New Haven CT: Yale University Press.

Boal, William M., and Michael R. Ransom. 2010. "Monopsony in American Labor Markets." EH.net. http://eh.net/?s=Monopsony+in+American+Labor+Markets (accessed January 2012).

Bonds, Timothy M., Dave Baiocchi, and Laurie L. McDonald. 2010. "Army Deployments to OIF and OEF." Santa Monica CA: RAND.

Bourque, Stephen. 2002. *Jayhawk! The VII Corps in the Persian Gulf War.* CMH Pub 70-73-1. Washington DC: Department of the Army, Center for Military History.

Bourque, Stephen, and John W. Burdan III. 2007. *The Road to Safwan: The 1st Squadron, 4th Cavalry in the 1991 Persian Gulf War.* Denton: University of North Texas Press.

Boyd, Josh. 2000. "Actional Legitimation: No Crisis Necessary." *Journal of Public Relations Research* 12, no. 4. https://www.cerias.purdue.edu/assets/pdf/bibtex_archive/2008-5.pdf (accessed October 2011).

Bremer, L. Paul, III, with Malcolm McConnell. 2006. *My Year in Iraq: The Struggle to Build a Future of Hope.* New York: Simon & Schuster.

Brown, Michael E., Sean M. Lynn-Jones, and Steven E. Miller. 2000. *Rational Choice and Security Studies: Stephen Walt and His Critics.* Cambridge MA: MIT Press.

Bueno de Mesquita, Bruce. 1985. "Toward a Scientific Understanding of International Conflict: A Personal View." *International Studies Quarterly* 29: 121–36.

Burg, Steven L., and Paul S. Shoup. 1999. *The War in Bosnia-Herzegovina.* Armonk NY: M. W. Sharpe.

Cameron, Lindsey. 2006. "Private Military Companies: Their Status under International Law and Its Impact on Their Regulation." *International Review of the Red Cross* 88, no. 863.

Cancian, Mark. 2008. "Contractors: The New Element of Military Force Structure." *Parameters* (Autumn): 61–77.

Carafano, James Jay. 2008. *Private Sector, Public War: Contractors in Combat—Afghanistan, Iraq, and Future Conflicts.* Westport CT: Praeger Security International.

Chatterjee, Pratap. 2004. *Iraq, Inc.: A Profitable Occupation.* New York: Seven Stories Press.

Chesterman, Simon, and Chia Lehnardt. 2007. *From Mercenaries to Market*. Oxford: Oxford University Press.

Chesterman, Simon, Chia Lehnardt, and Angelina Fisher. 2009. *Private Security, Public Order: The Outsourcing of Public Services and Its Limits*. Oxford: Oxford University Press.

Cigar, Norman. 1995. "The Right to Defence: Thoughts on the Bosnian Arms Embargo." Occasional Paper 63. London: Institute for European Defence and Strategic Studies.

Clancy, Tom, and Fred Franks. 1997. *Into the Storm: A Study in Command*. New York: G. P. Putnam's Sons.

Clements, Dennis C., and Margaret A. Young. 2005. "The History of the Army's Logistic Civilian Augmentation Program: An Analysis of Its Oversight from Past to Present." Monterey CA: Naval Post Graduate School.

Conn, Stetson, Rose C. Engelman, and Byron Fairchild. 1997. *Guarding the United States and its Outposts*. Historical Series. Washington DC: Center of Military History, U.S. Army.

Cook, John S. 1997. "Overseas Jurisdiction Advisory Committee, Section 1151, Public Law 104-106." Report to the Secretary of Defense, Attorney General, Congress of the United States, Department of Defense, Office of General Counsel. 18 April. Washington DC.

Cordesman, Anthony H. 1997. *Saudi Arabia: Guarding the Desert Kingdom*. Boulder CO: Westview Press.

———. 2003. *Saudi Arabia Enters the Twenty-First Century: The Military and International Security Dimensions*. Westport CT: Praeger.

———. 2006. *Iraqi Security Forces: A Strategy for Success*. Westport CT: Praeger Security International.

Daggett, Steven. 2010. "Cost of Major U.S. Wars." CRS Report to Congress. 29 June. Washington DC: Congressional Research Service.

Dale, Catherine. 2011. "War in Afghanistan: Strategy, Operations, and Issues for Congress." CRS Report to Congress. 9 March. Washington DC: Congressional Research Service.

Davis, James R. 2000. *Fortune's Warriors*. Vancouver: Douglas & McIntyre.

"Definition of 'Microeconomics.'" N.d. *Economic Times*. http://economictimes.indiatimes.com/definition/microeconomics (accessed May 2014).

DeLong, Michael, and Noah Lukeman. 2007. *A General Speaks Out: The Truth about the Wars in Afghanistan and Iraq*. St Paul MN: Zenith Press.

Dobbins, James, Seth G. Jones, Benjamin Runkle, and Siddharth Mohandas. 2009. *Occupying Iraq: A History of the Coalition Provision Authority*. Arlington VA: RAND, National Security Research Division.

Eckstein, H. 1975. "Case Studies and Theory in Political Science." In *Handbook of Political Science*. Vol. 7: *Political Science: Scope and Theory*, edited by F. I. Greenstein and N. W. Polsby. Reading MA: Addison-Wesley.

"Economics." N.d. Investopedia. http://www.investopedia.com/terms/e/economics.asp (accessed May 2014).

Elsea, Jennifer K. 2010. "Private Security Contractors in Iraq and Afghanistan: Legal Issues." CRS Report to Congress. Washington DC: Congressional Research Service.

Elsea, Jenifer K., Moshe Schwartz, and Kennon H. Nakamura. 2008. "Private Security Contractors in Iraq: Background, Legal Status, and Other Issues." CRS Report to Congress. Washington DC: Congressional Research Service.

Fainaru, Steve. 2008. *Big Boy Rules*. Philadelphia: Da Capo Press.

Flyvbjerg, Bent. 2006. "Five Misunderstandings about Case-Study Research." *Qualitative Inquiry* 12, no. 2.

Fontenot, Gregory, E. J. Degen, and David Tohn. 2005. *On Point: The United States Army in Operation Iraqi Freedom*. Annapolis MD: Naval Institute Press.

Frank, Robert. 1991. *Microeconomics and Behavior*. New York: McGraw Hill.

Gaddis, John Lewis. 2002. *The Landscape of History*. New York: Oxford University Press.

Garth, H. H., and Wright Mills. 1967. *From Max Weber: Essays in Sociology*. Oxford: Oxford University Press.

Gates, Robert. 2014. *Duty: Memoirs of a Secretary at War*. New York: Knopf.

George, Alexander L. 1979. "Case Studies and Theory Development: The Method of Structured, Focused Comparison." In *Diplomacy: New Approaches in History, Theory, and Policy*, edited by Paul Gordon Lauren. New York: Free Press.

George, Alexander L., and Andrew Bennett. 2005. *Case Studies and Theory Development in the Social Sciences*. Cambridge MA: Belfer Center for Science and International Affairs.

Gerring, John. 2001. *Social Science Methodology A Critical Framework*. New York: Cambridge University Press.

Glass, G. V. 1997. "Interrupted Time-Series Quasi-experiments." In *Complementary Methods for Research in Education*, 2nd ed., edited by Richard M. Jaeger. Washington DC: American Educational Research Association.

Glass, Gene V., V. L. Willson, and J. M. Gottman. 1975. *Design and Analysis of Time Series Experiments*. Boulder: Colorado Associated University Press.

Goldberg, Matthew S. 2010. "Death and Injury Rates of U.S. Military Personnel in Iraq." *Military Medicine* 175 (April): 220–26.

Gordon, Michael R., and Bernard E. Trainor. 1995. *The Generals' War*. New York: Little, Brown.

Grasso, Valerie Ann Bailey. 2013. *Circular A-76 and the Moratorium on DoD Competitions: Background and Issues for Congress*. January. Washington DC: Congressional Research Service.

Gujarati, Damodar N. 2003. *Basic Econometrics*. 4th ed. New York: McGraw-Hill.

Herring, George C. 2008. *From Colony to Super Power: U.S. Foreign Relations since 1776*. New York: Oxford University Press.

Herspring, Dale R. 2005. *The Pentagon and the Presidency: Civil Military Relations from FDR to George W. Bush*. Lawrence: University of Kansas Press.

———. 2008. *Rumsfeld's War: The Arrogance of Power*. Lawrence: University of Kansas Press.

Holbrooke, Richard. 1999. *To End a War*. New York: Random House.

Human Security Report Project. 2010. *Human Security Report 2009/2010: The Causes of Peace and the Shrinking Costs of War*. New York: Oxford University Press.

Isenberg, David. 2009. *Shadow Force: Private Security Contractors in Iraq*. Westport CT: Praeger Security International.

Jaffe, Lorna S. 1993. *The Development of the Base Force 1989–1992*. Washington DC: Joint History Office, Office of the Chairman of the Joints Chiefs of Staff.

Johnson, Douglas V., II. 1999. *Warriors in Peace Operations*. Carlisle PA: U.S. Army War College, Strategic Studies Institute.

Jones, James L., Jennifer K. Elsea, and Nina M. Serafino. 2010. *Security in Iraq*. New York: Nova Science.

Kane, Tim. 2006. "Global U.S. Troop Deployment, 1950–2005." Washington DC: Center for Data Analysis, Heritage Foundation.

Katzman, Kenneth. 2011. "Iraq: Politics, Governance, and Human Rights." CRS Report to Congress. Washington DC: Congressional Research Service.

———. 2014. "Afghanistan: Post-Taliban Governance, Security, and U.S. Policy." CRS Report to Congress. Washington DC: Congressional Research Service.

Kaufman, Joyce P. 2002. *NATO and the Former Yugoslavia: Crisis, Conflict, and the Atlantic Alliance*. Oxford: Rowman & Littlefield.

Keegan, John. 2005. *The Iraq War*. New York: First Vintage Books.

Khor, Andre Kah Him. 2009. "Social Contract Theory, Legitimacy Theory and Corporate Social and Environmental Disclosure Policies: Constructing a Theoretical Framework." Unpublished paper, Nottingham University Business School. http://www.nottingham .ac.uk/business/about/research/index.aspx (accessed November 2009).

Kidwell, Deborah C. 2005. *Public War, Private Fight? The United States and Private Military Companies*. Global War on Terrorism Occasional Paper 12. Fort Leavenworth KS: Combat Studies Institute.

Kim, K. H., Susan Farrell, and Ewan Clague. 1971. *The All-Volunteer Army: An Analysis of Demand and Supply*. New York: Praeger.

King, Gary, Robert O. Keohane, and Sidney Verba. 1994. *Designing Social Inquiry: Scientific Inference in Qualitative Research*. Princeton NJ: Princeton University Press.

Kinsey, Christopher. 2006. *Corporate Soldiers and International Security: The Rise of Private Military Companies*. New York: Routledge.

Kirkpatrick, Charles E. 2006. *Ruck It Up: The Post–Cold War Transformation of V Corps, 1990–2001*. Washington DC: Center for Military History, Department of the Army.

Kisangani, Emizet F., and Jeffery Pickering. 2008 "International Military Intervention, 1989–2005." Ann Arbor: Inter-University Consortium for Political and Social Research, Data Collection 21282, University of Michigan.

Klajn, Lajco. 2007. *The Past in Present Times*. Lanham MD: University Press of America.

Krahmann, Elke. 2010. *States, Citizens and the Privatization of Security*. Cambridge, UK: Cambridge University Press.

Kuhn, Thomas S. 1996. *The Structure of Scientific Revolution*. Chicago: University of Chicago Press.

Laurie, Clayton D., and Ronald H. Cole. 1997. *The Role of Federal Military Forces in Domestic Disorders 1877–1945*. Army Historical Series. Washington DC: Center of Military History, U.S. Army.

Lebow, Richard Ned. 2001. "Social Science and History: Ranchers versus Farmers?" In *Bridges and Boundaries: Historians, Political Scientists, and the Study of International Relations*, edited by Colin Elman and Miriam Fendius Elman. Cambridge MA: MIT Press.

Lewis-Beck, Michael S. 1986. "Interrupted Time Series." In *New Tools for Social Scientists: Advances and Applications in Research Methods*, edited by William D. Berry and Michael S. Lewis-Beck. Beverly Hills CA: Sage.

Leyden, Andrew. 1997. *Gulf War Debriefing Book: An After Action Report*. Grants Pass OR: Hellgates Press.

Lindemann, Marc. 2007. "Civilian Contractors under Military Law." *Parameters* (Autumn).

Livingston, Ian S., and Michael O' Hanlon. 2013. *Iraq Index*. July. Washington DC: Brookings Institute.

———. 2014. *Afghanistan Index*. May. Washington DC: Brookings Institute.

Lock, Peter. 1998. "Strategic Analysis, Military Downsizing and Growth in the Security Industry in Sub-Saharan Africa." *Strategic Analysis: A Monthly Journal of the IDSA* 22, no. 9. http://www.ciaonet.org/olj/sa/sa_98lop01.html (accessed August 2012).

Machiavelli, Niccolo. 1952. *The Prince*. Oxford: Oxford University Press.

Mahoney, J., and G. Goertz. 2006. "A Tale of Two Cultures: Contrasting Quantitative and Qualitative Research." *Political Analysis* 14: 227–49.

Mandel, Robert. 2002. *Armies without States: The Privatization of Security*. New York: L. Rienner.

Mankiw, N. Gregory. 2008. *Brief Principles of Macroeconomics*. Mason OH: South-Western Cengage Learning.

Mansfield, Edwin. 1985. *Microeconomics Theory and Application*. New York: Norton.

Metz, Steven. 2001. *The American Army in the Balkans: Strategic Alternatives and Implications*. Carlisle PA: Strategic Studies Institute, U.S. Army War College.

———. 2010a. *Decisionmaking in Operation Iraqi Freedom: Removing Saddam Hussein By Force*. February. Carlisle PA: Strategic Studies Institute, U.S. Army War College.

———. 2010b. *Decisionmaking in Operation Iraqi Freedom: The Strategic Shift of 2007*. May. Carlisle PA: Strategic Studies Institute, U.S. Army War College.

Mohammadi, Bismullah Khan, and Ashraf Gahni. 2011. "The Bridging Strategy for Implementation of Presidential Decree 62 (Dissolution of Private Security Companies) Bridging Period March 22, 2011 to March 20, 2012." March. Government of the Islamic Republic of Afghanistan.

Munden, Ronald, L. 1999. *SFOR Procedural Guide. Book 1: The Planning Process*. Fort Hood TX: Camber Corporation.

Myers, Richard B., with Malcolm McConnell. 2009. *Eyes on the Horizon: Serving on the Front Lines of National Security*. New York: Threshold Editions.

O'Hanlon, Michael E., and Ian Livingston. 2011. "Iraq Index Tracking Variables of Reconstruction and Security in Post-Saddam Iraq." November. Washington DC: Brookings Institution.

"Operation Joint Endeavor." N.d. Global Security. http://www.globalsecurity.org/military /ops/joint_endeavor.htm (accessed June 2014).

Operation Joint Endeavor Fact Sheet, No. 006-B. 1995. BosniaLink. 11 December. http://www .dtic.mil/bosnia/ (accessed May 2012).

"Operation Joint Forge." N.d. Global Security. http://www.globalsecurity.org/military /ops/joint_forge.htm (accessed June 2014).

Orszag, Peter R. 2008. *Contractors' Support of U.S. Operations in Iraq*. Washington DC: Congressional Budget Office.

Ortiz, Carlos. 2010. *Private Armed Forces and Global Security: A Reference Handbook*. Westport CT: Praeger.

Pagonis, William, and Jeffrey L. Cruikshank. 1992. *Moving Mountains*. Boston: Harvard Business School Press.

Parkin, Michael. 1993. *Economics*. 2nd ed. New York: Addison-Wesley.

Pearson, Frederic S., and Robert A. Baumann. 1993 "International Military Intervention, 1946–1988." Ann Arbor: Inter-University Consortium for Political and Social Research, Data Collection 6035, University of Michigan. http://www.icpsr.umich.edu/icpsrweb /ICPSR/studies/6035 (accessed June 2012).

Pelton, Robert Young. 2006. *Licensed to Kill: Hired Guns in the War on Terror*. New York: Crown.

Percy, Sarah. 2007. *Mercenaries: The History of a Norm in International Relations*. Oxford: Oxford University Press.

Perrin, Benjamin. 2006. "Promoting Compliance of Private Security and Military Companies with International Humanitarian Law." *International Review of the Red Cross* 88, no. 862.

Powell, Colin. 1995. *My American Journey*. New York: Random House.

Prince, Erik. 2013. *Civilian Warrior*. New York: Penguin Press.

"Private Military Companies." N.d. PrivateMilitary.org. http://www.privatemilitary.org/ (accessed March 2010).

Rasor, Dina, and Robert Bauman. 2007. *Betraying Our Troops*. New York: Palgrave Macmillan.

Reeve, David W. 2001. "Contractors in British Logistics Support." *Army Logistician* 33, no. 3: 10.

Richmond, Lloyd M. 1995. *Strategy and Force Planning*. Newport RI: Naval War College Press.

Ricks, Thomas E. 2006. *Fiasco: The American Military Adventure in Iraq*. New York: Penguin Press.

Rose, Gideon. 2010. *How Wars End: Why We Always Fight the Last Battle*. New York: Simon & Schuster Paperbacks.

Rosen, Fred. 2005. *Contract Warriors: How Mercenaries Changed History and the War on Terrorism*. New York: Penguin.

Scahill, James. 2007. *Blackwater: The Rise of the World's Most Powerful Mercenary Army*. New York: Nation Books Avalon.

Scales, Robert H. 1994. *Certain Victory: The U.S. Army in the Gulf War*. Fort Leavenworth KS: Command and General Staff College Press.

Schaub, Gary, Jr., and Volker Franke. 2009–10. "Contractors as Military Professionals?" *Parameters* 39, no. 4: 88–104.

Schooner, Steven L., and Collin D. Swan. 2010. "Contractors and the Ultimate Sacrifice." *Service Contractor*. Professional Service Council. Arlington VA.

Schwartz, Moshe. 2011. "The Department of Defense's Use of Private Security Contractors in Afghanistan and Iraq: Background, Analysis, and Options for Congress." CRS Report to Congress. Washington DC: Congressional Research Service.

Schwartz, Moshe, and Joyprada Swain. 2011. "Department of Defense Contractors in Afghanistan and Iraq: Background and Analysis." CRS Report to Congress. 13 May. Washington DC: Congressional Research Service.

Security Statistics. 2010. Human Security Report Project. http://www.hsrgroup.org /our-work/security-stats/Organized-Violence.aspx (accessed 25 December 2010).

Shearer, David. 1998. *Private Armies and Military Intervention*. Adelphi Paper 316. Oxford: Oxford University Press.

Sheehy, Benedict, Jackson Maogoto, and Virginia Newell. 2009. *Legal Control of the Private Military Corporation*. New York: Palgrave Macmillan.

Shrader, Charles R. 1999. *Contractors on the Battlefield*. Landpower Essay Series. Arlington VA: Association of the U.S. Army, Institute for Land Warfare.

Sifer, Micah L., and Christopher Cerf. 2003. *The Iraq War Reader: History, Documents, Opinions*. New York. Simon & Schuster.

Singer, Peter W. 2003. *Corporate Warriors: The Rise of the Privatized Military Industry*. Ithaca NY: Cornell University Press.

Smith, Adam. 1994. *An Inquiry into the Nature and Causes of the Wealth of Nations*. New York: Modern Library.

Smith, Ron. 2009. *Military Economics: The Interaction of Power and Money*. New York: Palgrave Macmillan.

Smith, Rupert. 2008. *The Utility of Force*. New York: First Vintage Books.

Snider, Don M. 1993. *Strategy, Forces and Budgets: Dominant Influences in Executive Decision Making, Post–Cold War, 1989–91*. Carlisle PA: Strategic Studies Institute, U.S. Army War College.

Sopko, John F. 2012. "Quarterly Report to the United States Congress." October 30. Arlington VA: Special Inspector General for Afghanistan Reconstruction.

———. 2013. "Quarterly Report to the United States Congress." October 30. Arlington VA: Special Inspector General for Afghanistan Reconstruction.

———. 2014. "Department of State Assistance to Afghanistan: $4 Billion Obligated between 2002 and 2013." Arlington VA: Special Inspector General for Afghanistan Reconstruction.

Sorely, Lewis. 1999. *A Better War: The Unexamined Victories and Final Tragedy of America's Last Years in Vietnam*. Orlando FL: Harcourt.

Spearin, Christopher. 2005. "Humanitarians and Mercenaries: Partners in Security Governance?" In *New Threats and New Actors in International Security*, edited by Elke Krahmann. New York: Palgrave Macmillan.

Stewart, Richard. 2010. *War in the Persian Gulf: Operations Desert Shield and Desert Storm, August 1990–March 1991*. Washington DC: Center of Military History.

Stiglitz, Joseph E., and Linda J. Bilmes. 2008. *The Three Trillion Dollar War: The True Cost of the Iraq Conflict*. New York: Norton.

Sultan, Khaled Bin. 1995. *Desert Warrior: A Personal View of the Gulf War*. London: Harper Collins.

Swain, Richard M. 1994. *Lucky War: Third Army in Desert Storm*. Fort Leavenworth KS: Command and General Staff College Press.

———. 2003. *Neither War nor Not War: Army Command in Europe during the Time of Peace Operations*. Carlisle PA: Strategic Studies Institute, U.S. Army War College.

Szeliga, Keith. 2007. "Watching Your Step: A Contractor's Guide to Revolving-Door Restrictions." Washington DC: George Washington University Law School.

Tanner, Stephen. 2002. *Afghanistan: A Military History from Alexander the Great to the Fall of the Taliban*. Cambridge MA: Da Capo Press.

Tilling, Matthew V. 2004. "Communication at the Edge: Voluntary Social and Environmental Reporting in the Annual Report of a Legitimacy Threatened Corporation." Paper presented at the Fourth Asia Pacific Interdisciplinary Research in Accounting Conference, Singapore, July.

Thomson, Janice E. 1994. *Mercenaries, Pirates, and Sovereigns*. Princeton NJ: Princeton University Press.

Thompson, William R. 2003. "A Streetcar Named Sarajevo: Catalysts, Multiple Causation Chains, and Rivalry Structures." *International Studies Quarterly* 47: 453–74.

Tickler, Peter. 1987. *The Modern Mercenary: Dog of War, or Soldier of Honour?* London: Patrick Stephens, Thorson Group.

Turvey, Ralph. 1971. *Demand and Supply*. London: George Allen & Unwin.

Tyner, James. 2006. *The Business of War Workers: Warriors and Hostages in Occupied Iraq*. Burlington VT: Ashgate.

Uppsala Conflict Data Program. 2012. Armed Conflict Dataset. Version 4-2012. July. Peace Research Institute, Oslo, Sweden. http://www.pcr.uu.se/research/ucdp/datasets /ucdp_prio_armed_conflict_dataset/ (accessed June 2012).

The U.S. Army in Bosnia and Herzegovina. 2003. Army in Europe Pamphlet 525-100. 7 October. Heidelberg, Germany: Headquarters, U.S. Army, Europe, and Seventh Army, U.S. Army Installation Management, Agency, Europe Region Office.

U.S. Census Bureau. N.d. http://www.census.gov/ (accessed March–April 2008).

U.S. Central Intelligence Agency. 2011. "Iraq." World Fact Book. https://www.cia.gov /library/publications/the-world-factbook/ (accessed January 2012).

U.S. Congress, 106th Congress. 2000. "Military Extraterritorial Jurisdiction Act of 2000." Public Law 106-523, 18 USC, Sect. 3261 67 (2000). https://www.congress.gov/ (accessed 1 October 2007).

U.S. Congress, House. 2002. HJ Res. 114: "Authorization for Use of Military Force against Iraq Resolution of 2002." Govtrack.us. http://www.govtrack.us/congress /bill.xpd?bill=hj107-114 (accessed January 2012).

———. 2004. "Ronald W. Reagan Defense Authorization Act for 2005." Public Law 108-75, Sect. 1206. 28 October.

———. 2012. Special Inspector General for Afghanistan Reconstruction Quarterly Report to the U.S. Congress. 30 January.

———. 2013. Special Inspector General for Afghanistan Reconstruction Quarterly Report to the U.S. Congress. 30 January.

U.S. Congress, House, Commission on Wartime Contracting in Iraq and Afghanistan. 2009. "At What Cost? Contingency Contracting in Iraq and Afghanistan." Interim Report. June. Washington DC.

———. 2010a. "Special Report on Iraq Transition Panning: Better Planning for Defense-to-State Transition in Iraq Needed to Avoid Mistakes and Waste." Special Report 3. 12 July.

———. 2010b. "Transforming Wartime Contracting Controlling Cost, Reducing Risk." Final Report. August.

U.S. Congress, House, Special Inspector General for Iraq Reconstruction. 2009. Quarterly Report and Semiannual Report to the U.S. Congress. 30 July.

U.S. Department of the Army. 1971. *Use and Administration of Locals in Foreign Areas during Hostilities.* DA PAM 690-80. 12 February. Washington DC: U.S. Department of the Army.

———. 1985. Logistics Civil Augmentation Program. Army Regulation 700-137. 16 December. Washington DC: U.S. Department of the Army.

———. 2006. Host Nation Support. Army Regulation 570-9. Washington DC: U.S. Department of the Army.

U.S. Department of Defense. 2008. *Joint Operations.* Field Manual 3-0. Washington DC: U.S. Department of the Army.

———. 2013. Report on Progress toward Security and Stability in Afghanistan. November.

———. 2014. Report on Progress toward Security and Stability in Afghanistan. April.

U.S. Department of Defense, Assistant Under Secretary for Office of Program Support under CENTCOM. 2008–14. Quarterly Contractor Reports. http://www.acq.osd.mil /log/PS/ (accessed July 2014).

U.S. Department of Defense, Defense Manpower Data Center. 1954–2012. Historical Reports. https://www.dmdc.osd.mil/appj/dwp/dwp_reports.jsp (accessed November 2014).

U.S. Department of Defense, Under Secretary of Defense for Acquisition, Technology, and Logistics. 2008. "Department of Defense Program for Planning, Managing, and Accounting for Contractor Services and Contractor Personnel during Contingency Operations." Report to the Congress of the United States. April. http://www.acq .osd.mil/log/PS/p_vault/final_section854_report_Congress_Apr08.pdf (accessed June 2011).

———. 2010. "Department of Defense Program for Contingency Contracting Planning, Oversight, and Visibility." Report to Congress of the United States. November. http://www.acq.osd.mil/log/PS/reports/Final_report_without_transmittal _letters_21Nov2010.pdf (accessed June 2011)

U.S. Department of State. 2008. "Status of Forces Agreement between the United States of American and the Republic of Iraq." 17 November. http://www.state.gov/documents /organization/122074.pdf (accessed March 2012).

U.S. Government Accountability Office. 1998a. "Bosnia: Military Services Providing Needed Capabilities but a Few Challenges Emerge." April. Washington DC: National Security and International Affairs Division.

———.1998b. "Bosnia Peace Operations: Pace of Implementing Dayton Accelerated as International Involvement Increases." June. Washington DC: National Security and International Affairs Division.

———. 1998c. "Bosnia Peace Operations: Mission, Structure, and Transition Strategy of NATO's Stabilization Force." October. Washington DC: National Security and International Affairs Division.

U.S. Office of Management and Budget. 1950–2012. Historical Tables. http://www.white house.gov/omb/budget/historicals (accessed June 2012).

———. 1995. Historical Tables. http://www.whitehouse.gov/omb/budget/historicals (accessed June 2012).

———. 2003. Historical Tables. http://www.whitehouse.gov/omb/budget/historicals (accessed June 2012).

———. 2014. Historical Tables. http://www.whitehouse.gov/omb/budget/historicals (accessed June 2012).

Verkuil, Paul R. 2007. *Outsourcing Sovereignty: Why Privatization of Government Functions Threatens Democracy and What We Can Do about It.* New York: Cambridge University Press.

Watkins, Thayer. 2012. "An Economic Welfare Analysis of Protected Monopsony." Unpublished paper. San Jose State University Department of Economics. http://www.sjsu.edu/faculty/watkins/monopswelf.htm (accessed January 2012).

Weber, Max. 1947. *The Theory of Social and Economic Organization*. New York: Oxford University.

The White House. 2008a. Executive Office of the President of the United States, Office of Management and Budget. http://www.whitehouse.gov/omb (accessed March–April 2008).

———. 2008b. USAspending.gov. http://usaspending.gov/ (accessed March 2008).

Whitson, Anthony K. 2001. "Logistical Contractors on the Peacekeeping (PKO) Battlefield: A Guide for the Operational Commander." Newport RI: Naval War College, Department of the Navy.

Woods, Kevin M., Michael R. Pease, Mark E. Stout, Williamson Murrary, and James Lacy. 2006. *Iraqi Perspectives Project: A View of Operation Iraqi Freedom from Saddam's Senior Leadership*. Norfolk VA: Joint Center for Operational Analysis, U.S. Joint Forces Command.

Woodward, Bob. 1991. *The Commanders*. New York. Simon & Schuster.

Woodward, Susan. 1995. *Balkan Tragedy*. Washington DC: Brookings Institute.

Wright, Donald P., James R. Bird, Steven E. Clay, Peter W. Connors, Scott C. Farquhar, Lynn Chandler Garcia, and Dennis F. Van Wey. 2010. *A Different Kind of War: The United States Army in Operation Enduring Freedom*. Fort Leavenworth KS: Combat Studies Institute Press, U.S. Army Combined Arms Center.

Wright, Donald P., and Timothy R. Reese. 2008. *On Point II: Transition to a New Campaign. The United States Army in Operation Iraqi Freedom May 2003–January 2005*. Fort Leavenworth KS: Combat Studies Institute Press, U.S. Army Combined Arms Center.

Zametica, John. 1992. *The Yugoslav Conflict*. London: International Institute for Strategic Studies.

INDEX

King, Gary, 12, 45, 50

Kinsey, Christopher, 4–7, 10, 18–19, 33–34, 103

Kirkpatrick, Charles E., 82

Korea, 46, 65, 118, 148, 149, 165, 177; contractors in, 175; military commitments to, 50, 67, 78, 92, 102, 117; troops deployed in, 158, 162

Krahmann, Elke, 19, 22, 37, 40, 57

Krajina, 79

Kuwait, 14, 50, 119, 131–32, 137, 144, 150; invasion of, by Iraq, 51–53, 72, 128; liberation of, 70; and Operation Desert Storm, 61–62, 65–66; and Operation Iraqi Freedom, 145–47

law of diminishing return, 24, 25

Lewis-Beck, Michael S., 178, 179

liberal conscience, 4

Liberalism, 19

logistical support, 64, 74, 92, 97; during Operation Iraqi Freedom, 145; PMC provision of, 2, 58; Saudi provision of, 75; U.S. Army shortage of, 98

logisticians, 56, 61, 73

Logistics Civil Augmentation Program (LOGCAP), 58, 82–84, 88, 89, 99, 109, 138, 168

Mandel, Robert, 16

Mansfield, Edwin, 24, 26

market, 10, 18, 19, 22, 24, 25, 29, 30, 33; competition, 23; demand curve of, 26–27; economy, 16; forces, 19

Marshall, Alex, 105, 115, 125

mass unrest, 177, 178, 180, 182, 184–93

McKiernan, David, 106

Medicaid, 33

mercenaries, 4, 16–17, 20, 22, 37, 113

mercenarism, 36

mercenary (concept), 4, 20, 37, 199n3

methodology, 12, 178

Metz, Steven, 79, 97

microeconomics, 23, 24, 30

Middle East, 130, 176, 179, 180, 182, 184–92

military economics, 27

military firms, 3

Military Professional Resource Incorporated (MPRI), 21, 85

military units, multinational, 6, 89, 97, 98, 142, 143, 153

monopsony, 29–30, 32–33, 122

Montreux Document, 113

Muslim-Croat Federation, 80

national budget, 34, 47, 119, 161

National Defense Act (1920), 37

National Defense Authorization Act, 142, 174, 200n4

National Guard, 32, 47, 67–70, 73, 118; in Afghanistan, 121–22; in Bosnia, 95; in Iraq, 152; in Saudi Arabia, 71

national interests, 18

national security, 2, 23, 31–32, 34, 42, 45, 158

National Security Council, 115

NATO, 80–82, 89–90, 95, 98, 100–103, 116–18, 148–49; Article 5 in Charter of, 121; forward defense of, 72, 162, 165; in Operation Enduring Freedom, 106–8, 110–12, 123; in Operation Iraqi Freedom, 145, 159; in Operation Joint Endeavor, 50, 67, 78, 92–93, 145, 170; peacekeeping operations of, 77

need curve, 31

Neutrality Act (1794), 37

new institutionalism, 18

nongovernmental organizations (NGOs), 10–11, 86

160, 163–70; privatization of security related to, 18, 26, 29, 193, 194, 197
"the surge," 136
Swain, Richard M., 51, 54, 61, 63, 67–68, 72–74, 76, 82, 100
Swan, Collin D., 140, 141
Synchronized Pre-deployment and Operational Tracker (SPOT), 142–43
Syria, 146

Taliban, 14, 103, 104, 105, 106, 115, 122–23, 125
Task Force Eagle, 82, 83
Thomson, Janice E., 20, 36
Tickler, Peter, 4
Tito, Josip Broz, 78, 79
Tora Bora, 104–5
Turgot, Jacques, 24
Turkey, 121, 131, 146
Turvey, Ralph, 27

UNITA rebels, 21
unitary actors, 14
United Kingdom, 22, 34, 106, 110, 121, 145
United Nations, 105; High Representative, 82; peacekeepers of, 35, 38, 61, 103; Protection Force, 79; Security Council, 52, 80, 112, 130, 142
U.S. Agency for International Development (USAID), 91
U.S. Army Corps of Engineers, 88, 139
U.S. Census Bureau, 12

U.S. Department of Justice, 86, 91, 142
U.S. embassy in Baghdad, 8
U.S. Marine Corps, 61, 67, 68, 118, 119; as all-volunteer force, 93, 149, 150; divisions of, 96; in Operation Enduring Freedom, 104; in Operation Iraqi Freedom, 132, 133, 145, 152, 156
U.S. Office of Budget and Analysis, 12
USS *Abraham Lincoln*, 133
utilitarianism, 24, 25
Uzbekistan, 115, 116

Vietnam, 12, 64, 65, 88, 98, 175–77
violence, 45; and contractor fatalities, 110, 139; controlling of, 18; escalation of, in Iraq, 134–37, 139, 145, 148, 151, 156–57; global, 20; levels of, in Afghanistan, 106–8, 115–16, 122–23, 125; nonstate, 20; PMCs assisting in ending of, 21; state monopoly over, 22

Wackenhut Security, 6
Warsaw Pact, 93, 97
weapons of mass destruction (WMDs), 129, 131
Weber, Max, 36
Westphalia, Peace of, 20
The Wild Geese (film), 4
World Bank, 86

Yugoslavia, 38, 78–80, 96

CPSIA information can be obtained at www.ICGtesting.com
Printed in the USA
BVOW05s2358040615

403300BV00001B/25/P